A Dictionary of their Origins and Backgrounds

PLACE-NAMES
OF THE
WORLD

ADRIAN ROOM

ANGUS
& ROBERTSON
PUBLISHERS

ANGUS & ROBERTSON PUBLISHERS

Unit 4, Eden Park, 31 Waterloo Road,
North Ryde, NSW, Australia 2113, and
16 Golden Square, London W1R 4BN,
United Kingdom

First published in the United Kingdom by
David & Charles (Holdings) Ltd in 1974
This revised paperback edition first
published in Australia by Angus &
Robertson Publishers and Angus &
Robertson (UK) in 1987

Copyright © Adrian Room 1987

National Library of Australia
Cataloguing-in-publication data
Room, Adrian.
  Place-names of the world.
  Rev ed.
  Bibliography.
  ISBN 0 207 15539 9.
  1. Names, Geographical. 2. Gazetteers.
  I. Title.
910'.3

Typeset in Palatino by
Setrite Typesetters Ltd
Printed in Singapore

CONTENTS

INTRODUCTION

The aim of this book is to give the derivations of over one thousand of the world's place-names. Nearly all the countries of the world and the majority of their capitals are included; a wide range of major natural geographical features (oceans, seas, rivers, lakes, mountains, islands, capes, deserts and the like); all American states and their capitals and all Soviet republics and their capitals; a large number of political and administrative divisions of countries (provinces, territories and so forth), some of which are strictly speaking historical but still widely used, such as the provinces of France; many towns and cities important because of their economic standing or historical associations; a selection of tourist regions and resorts; the chief regions of Antarctica.

As the emphasis of the book is on place-names of the world, and as there already exist a large number of works dealing with English place-names, I have included very few British names, with the exception of those of the constituent countries of the British Isles, the chief islands and island groups around the British Isles, and the three main Channel Islands.

The prime concern of the book is to give the origin of the names and not to deal with the places themselves. Any information of a geographical or historical nature given in the entry for a particular place is included to help elucidate the origin of the name. Put another way, the book is a toponymical rather than an etymological dictionary. Toponymy—place-name study—is, although a relatively new science, one that involves not merely the linguist but equally the geographer and the historian. The name of Dresden, for example, tells the linguist that the derivation is from a Slavonic word meaning 'forest'; the geographer will expect the city to be surrounded by a forest, as indeed it is; and the historian will be interested in the fact that at some stage in the past a Slavonic people was inhabiting what is now German territory. To the toponymist, however, and to the general student of place-names, the name will reflect all three aspects, and from its derivation he can learn that here is a city which was once inhabited by a Slavonic race and which was, and probably still is, close to or surrounded by a forest. In short, a place-name frequently gives a clue, or a whole set of clues, telling us its background and as often as not revealing an unexpected or perhaps unrealised aspect of its past.

This particular example illustrates an important if obvious fact: that a place-name is not a random thing. It is a name given, by a person or persons, even if in a form in which it is not known today, or in a language which no longer exists, to a particular place for a particular reason. What that reason was depends on a number of factors, but chiefly on the historical dating of the naming, the stage of cultural development of the namer or namers, and the social, political, religious or patriotic attitudes or motives of the namer or namers. At an early stage in the development of civilisation, for example, geographical names were given which simply indicated the nature or appearance of the place named, such as the Rocky Mountains or the Red Sea. At a more advanced level, many places were named after their owner, whether a whole tribe, as in the case of France, or an individual, as with the Weddell Sea. Yet another category of names is those that are virtually dedications—to a person, perhaps, to a historic incident, or even to another place of the same name—as is the case with, respectively, Vancouver, Réunion and Venezuela.

Broadly speaking, the simpler a name is, in whatever language, the older the place is likely to be. Thus the Yellow Sea, Madrid, the Volga and the Alps are all ancient names referring to the physical properties of the places—the silt washed down the river, the wood with which the town was originally built, the colour of the river and the rocks on the mountains. On the other hand, many ancient names reflect the names of the tribes or peoples who once lived there, as we have seen in the case of Dresden, and as is also the case with, for example, Bonn, also in Germany, but probably with a name of Celtic origin, and even Russia, with a name that is very likely of Swedish origin (though this is still disputed, not least, understandably enough, by the Russians themselves).

This one factor alone, that tribes were constantly migrating from one part of the world to another, only to intermingle with other tribes or to die out altogether, frequently complicates the toponymist's already complex task of determining the true origin of a name. His work is also made no easier by the fact that languages, like their native speakers, were similarly transferred and transformed and similarly became extinct, with the result that a place-name as we know it today may be quite different in form and pronunciation from its original version, and may very well have changed a number of times as new people, speaking different languages, successively inhabited it. Just one simple example of this is Istanbul, which until quite recently was Constantinople and originally Byzantium—not to mention that at one stage it was also New Rome and, to the Slavs, Tsargrad.

There is, however, a historical era, beginning roughly in the Middle Ages, when—although there are always exceptions—it is possible to see a definite pattern emerge in the bestowing of place-names. Many names, for example, with the element 'bridge' or 'ford' (in any language) are of mediaeval origin, since it was frequently at a particular bridge or ford over a river that a town or settlement would grow up. This was the case with Bruges in Belgium, Pontoise in France, Osnabrück in Germany, Alcántara (from the Arabic) in Spain, Zamość in Poland and Oxford and Woodbridge in England.

A little later, in the 15th and 16th centuries, a whole succession of religious names—mostly saints' names—were given by Spanish and Portuguese missionaries, settlers and explorers. Frequently a place would be named after the saint on whose feast-day it was sighted or founded (this was particularly true of the great Italian-born but Spanish-serving explorer Columbus), thus incidentally helping the historian to determine not only the year but the very day when a place was discovered or settled. Such religious names are especially abundant in Central and South America and the West Indies.

In the following three centuries it was the turn of the French, English and Dutch colonisers to sprinkle their names in newly settled or discovered countries, notably in North America (French and English), Africa (French, English and Dutch) and Australia (English and Dutch). The place-names of North America, and in particular Canada, present a special problem as in many cases they are direct translations of American-Indian names—into French or English, or even into French and then into English—which frequently were originally those of tribes or tribal leaders rather than their territories (on the basis that a particular tribe or Indian chief would own and occupy a particular territory), and of which the original form has rarely been accurately recorded. Many of the place-names of the United States, however, still survive in their Indian form—just over half of America's states have Indian names—but have meanings that, because of corrupted or incorrectly preserved forms, are open to dispute. These names of the 17th, 18th and 19th centuries were not for the most part religious in origin, but, where not translations from native names, were those of important national rulers and leaders and their families, as illustrated by the Orange Free State, Adelaide and the still frequent and ubiquitous Victoria.

Finally, in the 20th century, and providing one more labour for the already Herculean task of the place-name researcher, there has come a kind of full circle in which, as countries that were once colonies achieve independence, still further names appear, many of them paradoxically but understandably ancient (in the native language), such as Ghana and Sri Lanka. This is especially in evidence, of course, in Africa, where a country on achieving independence will not only assume a new name but will rename most of its towns and cities and, in fact, any place that has a 'colonial' name. In a different context, but for similar reasons, one of the countries that in the present century has had what must arguably be the greatest 'place-name turn-over' in the world is the Soviet Union, where since the 1917 Revolution hundreds of places, from the largest of cities to the smallest of streets, have acquired new names—and sometimes with not just one change of name but several successively (see *Pushkin*, for example).

Every place-name is, therefore, at any given moment in time, a sign of its times.

It is perhaps to be expected that European place-names

are better researched than any others. The sociologist may also be interested to discover that they are the most prosaic. Compare, for example, Germany's Cologne (colony), France's Provence (province), Italy's Apennines (peaks) and England's Northampton (town in the north by a meadow) with North America's fresh and colourful Medicine Hat, Alabama and Baton Rouge. Yet some of the best-known European places have names that to this day, and after exhaustive research, have not yielded one conclusive meaning. Even world-famous capitals such as London, Berlin and Moscow have had so many derivations ascribed to them that it would be a major undertaking—and quite impossible in the present book—to quote them all. In a number of cases, too, many places have acquired not merely an uncertain etymology but a completely false one. A common example of this is when a legend or mythical character comes to be assoicated with a place in an attempt to explain an unknown name—a 'folk etymology', in fact—and then subsequently the name is popularly explained as deriving from the legend or mytho-logical figure, instead of vice versa. A familiar instance of this is Rome, supposedly founded by its first king, Romulus, and named after him. But Romulus, like his twin brother Remus, belongs to Roman mythology (he was the son of Mars, the god of war) and not to reality. The same is true of many figures of classical mythology, so that the links be-tween Europa, loved by Zeus, Atlas, who supported the sky, and Athene, patroness of arts and crafts and goddess of wisdom, and Europe, the Atlantic Ocean and Athens are, alas, only links in name. Some of these legends and mythical links are, however, either so well known or so original, both in and beyond Europe, that in a few cases I have felt it valid or interesting to quote them (see, for example, *Warsaw*, *Berne* and *Ararat*).

If well-known place-names cause such difficulty and con-fusion—and 'folk etymology' is only one example of this—it is not surprising that comparatively few of the world's place-names have been really accurately and satisfactorily explained. And even if one toponymist reaches a (to him) conclusive explanation of a name, it is very likely that another, equally 'reliable' authority will give a completely different derivation. (This is to say nothing of the uninten-tional or purely careless mistakes that creep in when one authority is basing his material on that of another.) It is for this reason that the entries in the present book contain with what must seem bewildering frequency the terms 'probably', 'possibly' and 'perhaps' which, I should explain, are not given arbitrarily, but are used to give the following shades of meaning:

> 'probably' means that the information given, although not finally established as correct, is, as far as can be told from the facts available, likely to be the most reliable, and is generally accepted;
> 'possibly' means that the information given is based on incomplete research or conflicting data, but nevertheless is acceptable as a serious attempt at explanation until further facts are available;
> 'perhaps' means that the information given is inconclusive, likely to seem inconsistent when compared to other known facts, and yet worthy of serious consideration in its own right (ie it is not ruled out altogether as impossible).

When working with such seemingly unstable and even unreliable material, I am all too aware that in a book of this kind, which must itself rely heavily on other sources, there is a very real possibility that inaccuracies will have been passed on, as indeed I have found to be the case in the authorities I have consulted. I have not, of course, knowingly or deliberately included inaccurate information, and have in fact gone to considerable pains to ensure, by means of checking and cross-checking in a number of works, that the derivations provided are as reliable as possible, given the data available. In certain cases, however, where different authorities have been at variance with one another over the derivation of a name, or where there has been obviously conflicting evidence, I have used my judgement to give what seems to be the most likely explanation, always aiming to use in controversial instances 'probably' rather than 'possibly' and 'possibly' rather than 'perhaps'. There are, of course, names whose origin cannot even now be guessed at, and I have not hesitated to include these—if only to show that little or nothing *is* known about certain place-names and to illustrate the fact that place-name study is not only a complex and at times frustrating subject but also an infant science which, although now rapidly developing, is not yet really much out of its cradle.

In spite of an increasing tendency for place-names in present-day atlases, encyclopaedias and reference works to be given in their native version or spelling, I have given in almost every case the accepted English variant of a name, so that Zaragoza, Köln, Vlissingen and Livorno are dealt with under Saragossa, Cologne, Flushing and Leghorn. But where a place is known by two equally acceptable names—even if one is now historically inappropriate—I have given both, often with a cross-reference, as with Persia and Iran, Siam and Thailand, Mount Godwin-Austen and K2, Canton and Kwangchow. Similarly, although the majority of place-names dealt with are the modern ones, I have in a few cases included information on the former name or names of a place, either under the modern heading, or in one or two instances, where it seemed historically justifiable, separately: thus a reference to Tsaritsyn appears under the heading for Volgograd, but St Petersburg and Petrograd are dealt with separately from Leningrad, under their own headings. There are also cases where I have thought it interesting or useful to include the native name of a place, or that used by a neighbouring country for it, under its accepted English name, so that under Everest there is an explanation of its Tibetan name of Chomolungma, and under Lake Lucerne a reference to its German name of Vierwaldstättersee.

As explained, the book is highly selective, and for this reason I have not included self-explanatory names such as the Rocky Mountains, the Indian Ocean, the English Channel or Northern Territory, Australia. Here again there are a few exceptions: where the 'obvious' name has a background or a meaning that is perhaps not quite so obvious, as is the case, for example, with the North Sea or the Blue Mountains in Australia, I have included it.

Each name is followed by a brief geographical 'pointer', so that it can be located and so that confusion is avoided between similar names (such as Dominica and the Dominican Republic, Montpelier and Montpellier, Granada and Grenada). The locations as given are deliberately general, and compass bearings, in particular, are approximate, and are given to 'two significant letters' (ie south-east not east-south-east). The descriptions are brief but should be adequate to determine what the place is and where it is. Other names mentioned in descriptions which have their own entries are cross-referenced.

In conclusion, I should like to think that this book, in its admittedly modest scope, may prove of interest not only to professional toponymists but to all who are attracted to the study of place-names and who can appreciate the important part they play in revealing to us the historical, social and linguistic background of the many countries and cultures of the world.

Note: Chinese names appear as headwords in the familiar Wade-Giles spelling, but the Pinyin spelling is also provided, since this is the version that is now internationally accepted for romanised Chinese names.

LANGUAGE GUIDE

The following notes are designed to serve as a guide to some of the ancient languages mentioned in a number of the main entries in the book.

Amharic
The ancient language of Ethiopia (Abyssinia) dating back to the 11th century BC. It exists today as the modern state language of Ethiopia and is spoken by about 6 million people.

Carthaginian
The ancient language of North Africa (in the region with Carthage as its centre) spoken by emigrants from Palestine. It is one of the forerunners of modern Hebrew.

Celtic
The ancient language of the Celts, the people who originally inhabited southern Germany before 1000 BC and who later overran France, Spain, Portugal, northern Italy, the British Isles and Greece. It is represented today by the Gaelic languages of Ireland and Scotland, by Welsh and by Breton.

Etruscan
The ancient language of the Etruscans (Tuscans) who inhabited northern Italy (modern Tuscany) some time before 800 BC.

Gaulish
The ancient Celtic language of Gaul (modern France), which died out about AD 600 with the introduction of Latin.

Germanic

The ancient language of the Germans, a large group of tribes speaking a common Indo-European language who before 100 BC inhabited a territory in central Europe bounded by the lower Rhine, the Vistula, the Danube, and the Baltic and North Seas and southern Scandinavia. Germanic languages today are divided into: 1. East Germanic (Gothic, now extinct); 2. North Germanic or Scandinavian (Icelandic, Norwegian, Danish, Swedish); 3. West Germanic (German, Dutch, Friesian, English).

Gothic

The extinct Germanic language of the Goths, a people who settled on the shores of the Black Sea about AD 200. They disappeared as a nation in the 5th century AD.

Iberian

The ancient language of the Iberians, the pre-Celtic people who, about 1600 BC, inhabited the Spanish peninsula and south-west France.

Illyrian

The ancient language of the Illyrians, who, before 1800 BC, inhabited the coastal region on the Adriatic in what is now north-west Yugoslavia.

Indo-European

The ancient language of the people who about 3000 BC inhabited northern central Europe and western Asia. About 2000 BC their common language began to split into what is now one of the world's largest families of languages, including Hindustani, Sanskrit, Iranian, Slavonic, Germanic, Baltic, Latin, Romance (French, Italian, Spanish, Portuguese, Romanian and others), Celtic, Greek, Albanian and Armenian.

Iranian

The ancient language of the Persians, whose chief modern descendants are Persian, Afghan and Balochi, spoken respectively in Iran (Persia), Afghanistan and Baluchistan by a total of about 30 million people.

Ligurian
The ancient language of the Ligurians, who, before 800 BC, inhabited the coast of the French and Italian rivieras. It survives as a north Italian dialect, spoken along the coast of the Ligurian Sea.

Old High German
A forerunner of modern German spoken in Germany between AD 700 and 1050. It was the language used by Benedictine monks for translating Latin church texts into the vernacular. ('High' because it was spoken chiefly in upper or southern Germany.)

Phoenician
A variant of Cathaginian spoken before 1600 BC by the Phoenicians, a people who inhabited what is now Lebanon but who travelled extensively and set up colonies in Cyprus, North Africa, Malta, Sicily and Spain.

Phrygian
The ancient language of the Phrygians, who inhabited Asia Minor (Anatolia) about 1200 BC.

Sanskrit
An ancient Indo-European language of India dating back to about 1500 BC. All the Indo-Aryan languages (Hindi, Urdu, Sinhalese, etc) are at least partially derived from it, and it has remained in use in India for sacred and literary purposes.

Scandinavian
The former common Germanic language of Scandinavia, now represented by Icelandic, Norwegian, Danish and Swedish.

Slavonic
The former common language of the Slavs, an Indo-European people who appear to have originated in the Carpathians, and who by the 7th century AD occupied the area lying between the Baltic, the Elbe, the Adriatic and the Black Sea. In the 16th century they were driven out of what is now East Germany. Their language is now divided into three groups: 1. eastern Slavonic (Russian, Ukrainian, Byelorussian); 2. southern Slavonic (Bulgarian, Macedonian, Serbo-Croat, Slovene); 3. western Slavonic (Czech, Slovak, Polish, Wendish).

ELEMENTS OF NON-ENGLISH PLACE-NAMES

The following list contains both separate words and parts of words. If the element usually begins a name, it is followed by a hyphen (as ober-); if it usually ends a name, it is preceded by a hyphen (as -leben). Capital letters, as for words and elements beginning a name and German nouns, are not given.

It is hoped that the list will help to explain at least part of the meaning of a number of place-names that are not given in the main part of this book, and that the language will serve as a guide to the geographical whereabouts of the place concerned or as a clue to the nationality of its namer.

-abad	Iranian	town
ain	Arabic	well, spring
al	Arabic	the
alt	German	old
alto	Italian, Spanish, Portuguese	high
am	German	on the
bach	German	stream
bad	German	mineral springs
bahia	Spanish, Portuguese	bay
bajo	Spanish	low
ban	Cambodian, Thai	village
bas(se)	French	low
basso	Italian	low
baum	German	tree
beau	French	beautiful
bel-	Slavonic	white
bel(le)	French	beautiful
-berg	German, Norwegian	mountain
beth	Arabic	house
bianco	Italian	white
bir	Arabic	well
blanc	French	white

blanco	Spanish	white
blank	Germanic	white
bocca	Italian, Portuguese	mouth
boden	German	meadow
bolshoi	Russian	great
-bosch	Dutch	wood
bouche	French	mouth
-bourg	French	fortified town
-brod	Slavonic	ford
-brück	German	bridge
-brunn	German	spring, well
buena	Spanish	good
-burg	German	fortified town
-bus	Slavonic	dwelling place
-by	Scandinavian	town
byel-	Slavonic	white
cabo	Spanish, Portuguese	cape
campo	Italian, Spanish	field, plain
casa	Italian, Spanish, Portuguese	house
castelho	Portuguese	castle
castello	Italian	castle
castillo	Spanish	castle
château	French	castle
chow	Chinese	town of 2nd rank
cima	Italian	peak
città	Italian	town, city
ciudad	Spanish	town, city
col	French	pass, neck
colle	Italian	pass, neck
cordillera	Spanish	mountain range
costa	Italian, Spanish, Portuguese	coast
côte	French	coast; slope, hill
court	French	enclosure
croce	Italian	cross
croix	French	cross
cruz	Spanish	cross
dal	Norwegian, Swedish	valley
-dam	Dutch	dam, embankment
dar	Arabic	house, country
darya	Iranian	sea, river
de	French, Spanish	of
di	Italian	of
-dorf	German	village
-dorp	Dutch	village
el	Arabic	the

-ey	Scandinavian	island
-feld	German	field
fels	German	cliff
felsö	Hungarian	upper
fiume	Italian	river
fu	Chinese	town of 1st rank
-furt	German	ford
-garten	German	garden
-gau	German	province, district
gebel	Arabic	mountain
gora	Slavonic	mountain
-gorod	Slavonic	town
-grad	Slavonic	town
gran	Italian	great
grand(e)	French	great
grande	Spanish, Portuguese	great
gross	German	great
-hafen	German	port, harbour
hai	Chinese	sea, lake
haut(e)	French	high
heim	German	home, dwelling place, village
ho	Chinese	river
hof	German	settlement
holm	Scandinavian	island
horn	German	peak
hsien	Chinese	town of 3rd rank
-ia	Latin	territory (of)
île	French	island
ilha	Portuguese	island
-ingen	German	belonging to
isla	Spanish	island
isle	Old French	island
isola	Italian	island
-istan	Iranian	country
jebel	Arabic	mountain
kap	German	cape
kara	Turkish	black
ker	Breton	village
kiang	Chinese	river
king	Chinese	town
kirch	German	church
kop	Dutch	head, hill
krasno-	Russian	red, beautiful
kum	Turkish	sand
la	French, Spanish, Italian	the

lac	French	lake
lago	Italian, Spanish, Portuguese	lake
lang	German	long
las	Spanish	the
le	French	the
-leben	German	dwelling-place
les	French	the
los	Spanish	the
maly	Slavonic	little
-mark	Indo-European	boundary
matt	German	meadow
meer	German	sea
mer	French	sea
mont	French	mount(ain)
monte	Italian, Spanish	mount(ain)
most	Slavonic	bridge
-mund	German	mouth
nagy	Hungarian	great
nan	Chinese	south
negro	Spanish	black
nero	Italian	black
neu	German	new
neuf, neuve	French	new
nieder	German	lower
nizhny	Russian	lower
noir	French	black
nord	German, French, Norwegian	north
nouveau, nouvelle	French	new
novi, nov(o)-	Slavonic	new
nowa, nowy	Polish	new
nueva, nuevo	Spanish	new
nuovo	Italian	new
ny	Danish, Swedish	new
ober-	German	upper, higher
-oe	Danish, Swedish	island
ostrov	Slavonic	island
oude	Dutch	old
para-	Indian (American)	river
peña	Spanish	rock
petit	French	little
pod-	Slavonic	under, below
-pol(is)	Greek	town
pont	French	bridge
ponte	Italian, Portuguese	bridge

pore (*see* pur)		
porto	Italian, Portuguese	port
pueblo	Spanish	village
puente	Spanish	bridge
puerto	Spanish	port
punta	Italian, Spanish	cape, headland
pur	Sanskrit	town
ras	Arabic	cape, headland
rio	Spanish, Portuguese	river
saki	Japanese	cape, mountain
san	Italian, Spanish	saint
santa, santo	Spanish	saint
são	Portuguese	saint
-see	German	sea, lake
selo	Russian	village
serra	Portuguese	mountain range
sierra	Spanish	mountain range
-sk(y)	Russian	belonging to
sous	French	under
sri	Sanskrit	holy
-stad	Swedish, Dutch	town
-stadt	German	town
-stan	Iranian	country
star	Slavonic	old
-statt	German	settlement, town
-stein	German	stone, castle
sur	French	on
-tal, -thal	German	valley
trans-	Latin	beyond, across
tre-	Breton	village
unter-	German	under, below
val	French, Italian	valley
vár	Hungarian	fort, town
veliky	Slavonic	great
verde	Spanish	green
viejo	Spanish	old
vieux	French	old
vila	Portuguese	town
villa	Spanish	town
ville	French	town
wad(i)	Arabic	river
-wald	German	wood
za-	Slavonic	beyond
-zee	Dutch	sea
zemlya	Russian	land

PLACE-NAMES
OF THE WORLD

Names appearing in *italic* type
in this section of the book
have a separate entry in their own right.

A

Aachen

City in west of West *Germany*, south-west of *Cologne*, near Belgian and Dutch frontiers

From Old High German aha = 'water'; town was originally Roman settlement by mineral springs, with Latin name Aquae Grani = 'waters of Granus'. French name is *Aix-la-Chapelle*.

Aarhus

2nd largest city in *Denmark*, on east coast of *Jutland*

From Danish aa = 'river' (+ 'r') + os = 'mouth'; city is at mouth of small River Molle which flows into *Kattegat*.

Abadan

Seaport in south-west *Iran* near head of Persian Gulf

Said to be named after holy man Abbad ben Al-Hussain in 8th or 9th century, with '—an' added to form place name from personal name.

Abidjan

Capital of *Ivory Coast*, West *Africa*

Name is that of Abidji tribe here.

Abruzzi

Region in southern central *Italy*

Probably from ancient tribal name Aprutium, possibly related to Latin abruptus = 'abrupt, steep', as region is highest and most rugged part of *Apennines*.

Abyssinia

Alternative name for *Ethiopia*

Portuguese version of Arabic habesh = 'mixed', referring to mixed black and white peoples here in early times.

Accra

Capital of *Ghana*, on Gulf of *Guinea*, West *Africa*

Probably from African (Akan) nkran = 'black ant', name given to members of Nigerian tribes who came to settle in region in 16th century.

Addis Ababa
Capital of *Ethiopia*, North-East *Africa*
From Amharic addis = 'new' + abeba = 'flower'. Site for capital was chosen in 1887 by Emperor Menelek II.

Adelaide
Capital of state of South *Australia*
Named in honour of English queen Adelaide, wife of William IV, in whose reign city was founded (1836).

Adélie Land
Antarctic territory between *Wilkes Land* and King George V Land
Named after wife of French explorer J. Dumont d'Urville, who discovered it in 1840.

Aden
Capital of People's Democratic Republic of *Yemen*, in south-west *Arabia*, east of southern entrance to *Red Sea*
From Arabic root = 'saddle', referring to location.

Admiralty Islands
In *Bismarck Archipelago*, north-east of *Papua New Guinea*, South *Pacific*
Discovered by Dutch in 1616 who named them 'The Twenty-One Islands' (there are in fact about 40). Renamed Admiralty Islands in 1767 in honour of British Admiralty. (Not to be confused with *Amirante Islands*.)

Adriatic Sea
Arm of *Mediterranean* between *Italy* and *Balkan* Peninsula
Named after Roman city of Adria, probably in turn derived from Illyrian adur = 'water, sea'. City was once (6th–5th centuries BC) a port but is now 22 km (14 miles) inland.

Aegean Sea
Arm of *Mediterranean* between *Greece* and *Turkey*
Probably from Greek aiges = 'wave', though in legend name is connected with Aegeus, who drowned himself here on hearing, falsely, that his son Theseus was dead.

Afghanistan
Republic in central *Asia*
Said to be from name of legendary forefather of all Afghans
—Afghana + Iranian stan = 'country'.

Africa
Continent crossed by equator
Name perhaps comes from ancient Berber tribe of north
Africa, and may have sense 'cave dwellers'. When Romans
captured Carthage in 2nd century BC they named the province they set up here Africa, after the tribe (territory of
province corresponded to modern *Tunisia*). Name then
gradually spread south to whole continent.

Aix
Name of: 1. Aix-en-Provence, town in south *France*;
2. Aix-la-Chapelle, French name for *Aachen*; 3. Aix-
les-Bains, resort and spa in *Savoy*, south-east *France*
All derived from Latin aquae = 'waters' (ie mineral
springs). Aix-en-Provence was originally Aquae Sextiae,
after Roman proconsul Sextius who founded it in 123 BC;
Aix-la-Chapelle is named after church here in which
Emperor Charlemagne is buried (see also *Aachen*); Aix-les-
Bains = 'waters of the baths'.

Ajaccio
Capital of *Corsica*
From Latin ad jacum = 'by the shore'; city is seaport on
Mediterranean.

Akron
City in *Ohio*, USA
From Greek akron = 'summit'; city is at top of divide be-
tween two rivers. Founded in 1825.

Alabama
Southern state of USA
From Indian (Cree) word adopted by first French settlers:
perhaps alba-aya-mule = 'we clear a way through the
wood', or alibamo = 'we stay here'. Name was that of tribe.

Åland Islands
At entrance to Gulf of *Bothnia, Finland*
From Swedish å = 'water' + 'land'. Finnish name is
Ahvenanmaa.

Alaska
State in extreme north-west of North *America*, belonging to USA
From Aleutian A-la-as-ka (also rendered as Alaelisa, Alaxa)
= 'mainland' (ie as distinct from *Aleutian Islands*). Originally belonged to *Russia* when it was known, in English, as
Russian America. Sold to *America* in 1867 with assumption
that native name = 'great land'.

Albania
Republic in south-east *Europe* on *Adriatic Sea*
Possibly from Arbenia or Arberia, medieval name of
southern part of country, or from Illyrian olba = 'settle-
ment'. Albanian name for country is Shqipëri, from
Albanian shqipe = 'eagle'.

Albany
Capital of *New York* state, USA
Founded by Dutch in 1614 with name Fort Orange (see
Orange Free State); renamed Albany in 1664 in honour of
Duke of York, future English king James II, whose Scottish
title was Duke of Albany (although there is no British place
of this name).

Albert, Lake
In Central *Africa*, between *Zaïre* and *Uganda*
Discovered by English explorer Sir Samuel Baker in 1864
and named after Prince Albert, husband of Queen Victoria.
Native (Bantu) name is Nyasa (see *Nyasaland*). Renamed
Lake Mobutu Sese Seko in 1973.

Alberta
Western province of *Canada*
Territory named in 1882 by Scottish Marquis of Lorne,
Governor General of *Canada*, after his wife Princess Louise
Caroline Alberta (also, no doubt, with complimentary re-
ference to Albert, Prince Consort, husband of Queen Vic-
toria). Constituted a province in 1905.

Albuquerque
City in *New Mexico*, USA
Founded in 1706 and named after Viceroy of New Spain, Duke Alburquerque. Omission of first 'r' may be result of confusion with better-known Alfonso Albuquerque (1453–1515), Portuguese Viceroy of Portuguese Indies from 1508.

Alderney
Most northerly of Channel Islands, close to west coast of *Normandy*, *France*
Roman name was possibly Riduna; later name was Adreni or Alrene; probably from Old Norse word = 'island near the coast'.

Aleutian Islands
Chain extending west of *Alaska*, USA
Named after native inhabitants, Aleuts, with own name of uncertain meaning. Not derived from Russian word lysy = 'bald'.

Alexandria
City and seaport in *Egypt*, on *Mediterranean*
Named after Alexander the Great, who founded it in 331 BC.

Algarve
Province in south *Portugal*
From Arabic al-Gharb = 'the west'; region was situated at western edge of Arabian territory.

Algeciras
Resort and seaport in province of *Cadiz*, *Andalusia*, southern *Spain*
From Arabic al-Jazīrah al-Khaḍrā' = 'the green island'; Arabs from African desert landed here in 711 and were impressed by abundance of green plants.

Algeria
State in North *Africa*
Named after its capital, *Algiers*.

Algiers
Capital of *Algeria*
From Arabic al-Jazā'ir = 'the islands'; city was built on 4 islands, joined to mainland in 1525.

Alicante
Province of south-east *Spain* and its capital
Founded by Phocaeans (from Asia Minor) in 325 BC as Acra-Leuca = 'white summit'. Roman name was Lucentum = 'shining', later rendered by Arabs as al-Akant.

Alice Springs
Town in Northern Territory, *Australia*
Named after wife of Sir Charles Todd, who established a base for a telegraph line here in 1872. Name frequently shortened to The Alice.

Alma-Ata
Capital of republic of *Kazakhstan*, USSR
Founded in 1896 on site of Kazakh settlement of Almaty = 'apple, apple-tree'. City today is centre of fruit-growing region. Until 1921 name was Verny, Russian = 'true, reliable' (in sense of 'stronghold').

Alps
Mountain system of south central *Europe*
Debatably from Celtic alp = 'rock, mountain', though perhaps connected with Latin alba = 'white'.

Alsace
Historic territory in north-east *France*
Of uncertain origin. Once thought to be connected with Indo-European aliso = 'alder'. No proof that name is derived from River Ill. Original meaning lost as early as 7th century, when was called Alsatia.

Altai Mountains
South *Siberia*, USSR
Probably from Turkish alatau = 'speckled mountains' (ie covered with patchy vegetation and having snowy peaks). Or possibly from Turkish and Mongolian altan = 'gold'.

Amazon, River
One of the world's longest rivers, in South *America*
Probably from Indian (Tepiguarani) amazunu, amassunu
= 'big wave', with reference to famous bore (the pororoca)
in lower reaches; name was taken by Spanish explorers of
16th century to be derived from Amazons, female warriors
of Greek legend, since Indian women of the Tepua tribe
fought alongside the men (though Spaniards may have
mistaken long-haired men for women).

America
Great landmass of western hemisphere, divided into
North America, Central America and South America
Discovered by Columbus in 1492, but named in 1507 after
latinised forename of Italian explorer Amerigo Vespucci,
who in 1503 named South America 'The New World'.

Amiens
City of north *France* on River *Somme*, north of *Paris*
Roman name was Ambianum, after Celtic tribe Ambiani,
with name probably = 'water-dwellers' (from Sanskrit
ambu = 'water'). Pre-Roman name was Samarobriva =
'bridge over the Somme', from ancient name of river—
Samara— + Celtic briva = 'bridge'.

Amirante Islands
South-west of *Seychelles*, Indian Ocean
Discovered in 1502 by Portuguese explorer Vasco da Gama
and named in his honour, as leader of the expedition, as
Ilhas do Almirante = 'Admiral's islands'.

Amman
Capital of *Jordan*
From name of ancient Egyptian god Ammon, in sense of
'protected by Ammon'.

Amritsar
City in *Punjab, India*
From Sanskrit amrita saras = 'lake of immortality'; city was
founded around a sacred pool by Sikhs in 16th century.

Amsterdam
Capital of *Netherlands*
Named after River Amstel, on which city stands + 'dam' (ie
'dam on River Amstel').

Anaheim
City south-east of *Los Angeles, California*, USA
From name of nearby River Santa Ana + German heim = 'home'; town was founded by German immigrants.

Anatolia
Alternative name for Asia Minor, ie part of *Turkey* which lies in *Asia*
From Greek anatole = 'sunrise'; region is in eastern *Turkey*.

Anchorage
Largest town in *Alaska*, USA, in south of state
With simple sense of 'harbour, port'. Original name was Knik Anchorage, but 1st word (probably Eskimo = 'fire') was dropped when town was officially established about 1914.

Ancona
City and seaport in east central *Italy*, on *Adriatic*, capital of the *Marches*
Founded in 380 BC by Greeks from *Syracuse*. Name derives from Greek ankon = 'elbow, angle', with reference to coastline on which city is situated.

Andalusia
Historic province in south *Spain*
Named after Vandals, Germanic tribe who set up kingdom here in 5th century AD. Initial 'v' from name Vandalusia was dropped by Arabs, who conquered it in 8th century.

Andaman Islands
In north part of Indian Ocean, south-west of *Burma*
Probably from Malay Pulo Handuman = 'islands of Handuman' (a native god). Unlikely to be derived from handuman = 'monkey'.

Andes
Mountain range in South *America*, running down west coast
Perhaps from Indian or Inca anta = 'copper' (found as a deposit in mountains), or from Indian (Quechua) anti = 'east' (ie in relation to Cusco, ancient capital of Incas).

Andorra
Small state in *Pyrenees*
Very old name, of unexplained origin. Perhaps connected with Basque andurrial = 'heath'.

Andreanof Islands
West group of *Aleutian Islands,* in *Bering Sea*
Named after Russian navigator Andrean Tolstykh, who discovered them in 1761.

Anglesey
Island and county of *Wales, Great Britain*, off north-west coast
Not from Angles ey = 'island of the Angles' but from Old Norse onguls ey = 'island of the strait'. Celtic name was Mon, probably related to Isle of *Man*.

Angola
People's Republic in south-western *Africa*
From Bantu name Ngola, of unknown meaning but possibly a royal title.

Anguilla
One of *Leeward Islands, West Indies*
From Spanish anguila = 'eel'; so named by Columbus in 1493, probably with reference to its long shape.

Anjou
Historic province in west *France*
From the name of its capital, Angers, in turn from Gaulish tribe Andecavi, with their own name of Indo-European origin = 'water-dwellers'.

Ankara
Capital of *Turkey*
In 7th century BC had Phrygian name Ankire, perhaps from Indo-European ank = 'angled, crooked'. Not likely to have connection with 'anchor', and perhaps derives from Phrygian word meaning 'gorge, ravine'. Arabs called it Qal'at as-Salāsil = 'fortress of the chains'.

Annapolis
State capital of *Maryland*, USA
Founded in 1649 as Providence; renamed Annapolis in 1694 after English princess (later queen) Anne + Greek polis = 'town'.

Antananarivo
Formerly *Tananarive*, capital of *Madagascar*
Both names are of same origin. Prefix 'an-' indicates location (ie = 'at').

Antarctic
Icy landmass and continent surrounding South Pole
From Greek anti = 'opposite' + *Arctic*.

Antibes
Port and resort in south *France*, south-west of *Nice*
Arose in 5th century BC as Greek colony with name of Antipolis = 'opposite the town'; town is on opposite (west) side of bay to *Nice*.

Antigua
One of *Leeward Islands, West Indies*
Discovered in 1493 by Columbus and named by him after church of Santa Maria la Antigua in *Seville, Spain*. Name of church = 'Saint Mary the Ancient'. Became independent state (with Barbuda) in 1981.

Antilles
Alternative name—as Greater and Lesser Antilles—of *West Indies*
Map of 1474 shows an island in this part of the ocean named Antilia, from Latin ante = 'before, in front of' + illas = 'islands'. After discovery of *America* name spread to all islands lying 'before' the east coast here.

Antioch
City in south *Turkey*
Founded at end of 4th century BC by Seleucus (general in army of Alexander the Great) who named it after his father Antiochus. Modern (Turkish) name is Antakya.

Antipodes Islands
In *Pacific*, south-east of *New Zealand*
From Greek antipodes = 'with feet opposite'. Islands are almost exactly on opposite side of world to Greenwich, from where meridian (0°) is measured.

Antwerp
City and port in north *Belgium*
More likely to be derived from Germanic anda werpum = 'opposite the alluvium', than from an der werp = 'by the wharf'. City is on River *Scheldt*.

Aosta
Town in north *Italy*, north-west of *Turin*, capital of Valle d'Aosta province
Founded by Romans in 25 BC and named Augusta Praetoria in honour of Emperor Augustus.

Apennines
Mountain chain running down centre of *Italy*
From Celtic pen = 'peak' (same word as for English Pennines).

Appalachian Mountains
Great range of mountains along east coast of North *America*
Named after Indian tribe of Apalachee or Apalachi, whose territory was here. Name was recorded in 1528 (as Apalachen) as that of Indian province.

Apulia
Region in south *Italy*
From Indo-European ap = 'water'; region is low-lying in north and south and borders on *Adriatic*.

Aquitaine
Historic province in south-west *France*
From Latin aqua = 'water'; region is fertile plain bounded on west by Bay of *Biscay* and drained by River *Garonne* and its tributaries.

Arabia
Great peninsula in South-West *Asia*
Named after Arabs, whose name may mean 'nomad', although some have derived it from Assyrian arbob = 'man of high position', since Arabs are 'master race' here.

Arafura Sea
Section of South-West *Pacific*, between *Australia* and *New Guinea*
Perhaps from native (Galela) halefuru = 'uninhabited region', or from Malay alifura = 'heathens, wild ones', or alfuren = 'forest people'. Name was originally that of island inhabitants here, as well as that of territory where they lived.

Aragon
Historic region in north-east *Spain*
From Celtic or pre-Celtic ar = 'to flow'. Name first applied to River Aragon, tributary of River *Ebro*, then to whole kingdom.

Aral Sea
In republic of *Kazakhstan*, USSR
From Mongolian aral = 'island', or Kazakh aral = 'bushes', or perhaps Kirghiz aral-dengis = 'island sea'.

Ararat, Mount
In north-east *Turkey*, near frontier with *Armenia*
Name probably connected with ancient people and country of Urartu (9th–6th centuries BC). Legend links name with story of Armenian king, Ara the Handsome, said to have spurned the love of the Babylonian princess Shamiram (Semiramida) and suffered defeat from her troops at the foot of this mountain. Turks call it Agri Dagi = 'crooked mountain' and Persian name is Kūh-e Nūḥ = 'Noah's mountain' (according to Bible story, Ark came to rest on mountain).

Archangel
City and seaport on *White Sea*, north-west USSR
Named after monastery of St Michael the Archangel, founded here in 12th century. City was built in 1584 by order of Ivan IV with original name of Novokholmogory. Name was changed in 1613 to Arkhangelsky and subsequently to present Russian Arkhangelsk.

Arctic
Icy landmass and sea surrounding North Pole
From Greek arktikos = 'northern', in turn from arktos = 'bear' as territory lies under constellation of Great Bear.

Ardennes
Forest in south *Belgium, Luxembourg* and north-eastern *France*

Possibly from Celtic ardu = 'dark', or Breton ar-Den = 'the oak' (for abundance of them here), or Celtic Arduenna = 'high land'. Roman writers called forest Arduenna silva, reflecting last of these.

Argentina
Republic in south of South *America*

In 1526 English explorer Sebastian Cabot, leading Spanish expedition, named the river where he bartered with the Indians for silver Rio de la plata = 'river of silver', not knowing that the silver was not got locally. When country achieved independence in 1826 name became Argentina, from Latin argentina = 'silvery'. (See also *Plate, River.*)

Arizona
State in south USA

From Indian (Papago) ali = 'little' + shonak = 'spring', ie 'place of the little spring'. Original Spanish name was Arizonac, but 'c' was later dropped to sound more like genuine Spanish name. Original 'little spring' is now south of the border, in *Mexico.*

Arkansas
State in south central USA

Original name of a river, from Indian Akenzea, of unknown meaning; later became name of whole state. River name was given final 's' to match that of neighbouring state of *Kansas.*

Arles
Town in south-west *France*

From Roman name Arelate, derived from Gaulish ar = 'by' + lait = 'marsh'. Town is situated on low-lying land beside River *Rhône.*

Armenia
Republic of USSR south of *Caucasus Mountains*

Name is ancient, though of uncertain origin. Known as early as 6th century BC. Legend tells of one Armenak, supposed forefather of all Armenians.

Arnhem

City in *Netherlands* on River *Rhine*, south-east of *Utrecht*

From Roman name Arenacum, in turn from Celtic ar = 'marshland'. (Compare *Arles*.)

Arno, River

River of central *Italy* flowing west through *Florence* and *Pisa* into Ligurian Sea

From Indo-European er = 'to move' or ar = 'to flow'. Sanskrit arna = 'flowing'.

Arras

Town in north-east *France*, south-west of *Lille*

Former capital of Atrebates, whose name derived from root word trebo = 'people'. (See also *Artois*.)

Artois

Historic province in north-east *France*

Roman name was Artesia, from Gaulish tribe of Atrebates, with name = 'people, dwellers' (see *Arras*). (Latin name survives in English 'Artesian well', first adopted here.)

Ascension Island

In South *Atlantic*, midway between *Brazil* and *Angola*

Discovered by Portuguese navigator João da Nova Castella on Ascension Day, 1501, and named after this feast.

Ashkhabad

Capital of republic of *Turkmenia*, USSR

From Turkmenian uskh = 'pleasant' + Iranian abad = 'town'. From 1919 to 1927 was Poltoratsk.

Asia

Largest continent in world, east of *Europe*

Has been interpreted as deriving from Assyrian asu = 'sunrise, east', in contrast to ereb = 'sunset, west' (see *Europe*). Originally 'Asu' was only east coast of *Aegean Sea*. Name then spread gradually—in 1st century BC Asia was name of Roman province—to whole continent. (Compare *Levant, Japan*.)

Assam

State in north-east *India*

In 13th century one of Thai peoples (Ahomi) set up state here called Ahom = 'invincible'. This sounded like 'Assam' to neighbouring tribes and came to denote whole region of valley of River *Brahmaputra*. Not likely to be connected with Sanskrit a-sama = 'incomparable'.

Astrakhan

City and port on delta of River *Volga*, inland from *Caspian Sea*, in south-west USSR

Of uncertain origin; perhaps from an Iranian language or from Tatar hajji = 'one who has made a pilgrimage to Mecca' + tertkhan = 'high rank awarded by a khan (of the Golden Horde)', giving general sense of 'town belonging to a highly venerated man' (who according to legend was one Asha).

Asturias

Historic region in north-west *Spain*

Named after River Asturia, in turn with name derived from Basque asta = 'rock' + ura = 'water'.

Asunción

Capital of *Paraguay*, South *America*

Spanish explorers built fort here on 15 August, feast-day of Assumption, 1536, giving it full name Nuestra Señora de la Asunción = 'Our Lady of the Assumption'. Last word gives present name.

Atacama

Desert in South *America*, largely in *Peru* and *Chile*

From an Indian word = 'desert land'.

Athens

Capital of *Greece*

According to ancient Greeks, city was named after Athene, its patron goddess, but name may be of pre-Greek origin, from language of Pelasgians (who inhabited south part of *Balkan* Peninsula before 3000 BC), with meaning = 'hill, height'.

Athos, Mount
In north-east *Greece*, in *Macedonia*

From Greek thoos = 'sharp, pointed': mountain is like tall pointed tower over *Aegean Sea*. Modern Greek name is Hagion Oros = 'holy mountain'.

Atlanta
State capital of *Georgia*, USA

Not named directly after *Atlantic Ocean*, but after Western and Atlantic Railroad, for which town was terminus; name was given in 1845 by rail engineer J. E. Thomson.

Atlantic Ocean
Between *America* on the west and *Europe* and *Africa* on the east

Name given by ancient Greeks after *Atlas Mountains* in North-West *Africa*.

Atlas Mountains
North-West *Africa*

Named by ancient Greeks after legendary giant who stood here bearing the heavens on his shoulders. Name may possibly have more factual link with Berber adrar = 'mountain'.

Auckland
City, seaport and former capital of *New Zealand*, on North Island

Founded in 1840 and named, even before it was built, after Lord Auckland, patron of 1st governor, Captain William Hobson, who selected city as capital. Capital transferred to *Wellington* in 1865.

Augsburg
City in south of West *Germany*, north-west of *Munich*

Founded as Roman fortified town in 12 BC with name Augusta Vindelicorum, in honour of Emperor Augustus. (The 2nd word is name of tribe Vindelicii, possibly meaning 'fortunate ones, fair ones'.) Name was shortened to 1st element + German suffix burg = 'town'.

Augusta
Town and river port in *Georgia*, USA

Named in honour of Princess Augusta, daughter-in-law of English king George II (reigned 1727–60).

Austin
State capital of *Texas*, USA
Named after Stephen F. Austin (1793–1836), Texan coloniser.

Australia
Continent and great island between Indian Ocean and *Pacific*
From Latin australis = 'southern'. Originally Terra Australis Incognita (= 'unknown southern land') and so marked on Ptolemy's map in 2nd century AD; then—though still undiscovered—Terra Australis. Northern coast was sighted by Dutch explorers in 1st half of 17th century and given name New Holland, but in 1814 English explorer Matthew Flinders proposed name should be simply Australia, and this received official backing in 1817.

Austria
Republic in central *Europe*
Name is latinised version of original Germanic name meaning 'eastern kingdom' (compare modern German name Österreich). Region developed from eastern border territory formerly held by Charlemagne.

Auvergne
Historic province in central *France*
From Roman name Arvernicum, after Gaulish tribe Arverni who inhabited region before Roman conquest of Gaul in 1st century BC. Tribal name derives from Celtic ar = 'good' + vern = 'warrior'.

Avignon
Town in south *France* on River *Rhône*
Name derives from Roman Avennio, perhaps a personal name, + suffix (Latin -onem) indicating possession.

Azerbaijan
Republic in USSR south-east of *Caucasus Mountains*
Of uncertain origin. Popular theory is that name means 'land of fire' (natural combustible gases are found in north, and around them grew up temples of fire-worshippers).

Azores
Islands in North *Atlantic*, west of *Lisbon*, *Portugal*
From Portuguese Ilhas dos açores = 'islands of hawks';
Portuguese explorers who discovered islands in 1431 noticed
a large number of these birds here. Islands were in fact
known earlier to Carthaginians and also to Arabs and
Norsemen, who called them 'Bird Islands'.

Azov, Sea of
Arm of *Black Sea*, USSR
Probably from town of Azov, at mouth of River *Don*. Name
of town said to derive from Polovtsian prince Azum or
Azuf, killed when Polovtsy (Turkish nomadic tribe) cap-
tured town in 1067.

B

Baden
Region, former state, in south-west of West *Germany*
As with many German and Swiss towns and spas of similar name, from German bad = 'springs, baths'. (See *Baden-Baden*.) Region forms part of modern 'Land' of *Baden-Württemberg*.

Baden-Baden
Famous spa in south-west of West *Germany*, south-west of *Karlsruhe*
Best-known of the various Badens, so named as it was capital of former state of *Baden*, ie it was the 'Baden' Baden as distinct from any other Baden. Roman name of town was Aquae Aureliae = 'waters of Aurelius', in honour of Emperor Aurelius.

Baden-Württemberg
'Land' in south-west of West *Germany*
Formed in 1952 from 'Länder' of *Baden*, Württemberg-Baden, and Württemberg-Hohenzollern. (For origin of these see *Baden, Hohenzollern, Württemberg*.)

Badlands
Region in South *Dakota*, USA
Probably translation of French name Terres mauvaises; region is infertile, rocky and desolate.

Baffin Bay
Between north-east *Canada* and *Greenland*
Named in honour of English navigator William Baffin (1584–1622) who discovered bay in 1616 when leading an expedition in search of the North West Passage from the *Atlantic* to the *Pacific*.

Baghdad
Capital of *Iraq*
According to popular theory, from Iranian bag = 'God' + dad = 'gift', ie 'God's gift'.

Bahamas
Group of islands in *Atlantic*, off south-east *Florida*, USA

Origin unknown. Bahama was originally the name of a small stream in northern *Cuba*; later the strait between *Cuba* and *Florida* was called the New Bahama Straits (now the Straits of Florida), and eventually the name of the strait became that of the islands. Popular theory sees name as deriving from Spanish bajamar = 'shallow water'.

Bahia Blanca
City and seaport in *Argentina*, South *America*

Spanish = 'white bay'. Bay gave name to town.

Bahrain
Emirate and group of islands in Persian Gulf

Name is Arabic al-Baḥrayn, meaning 'two seas', in sense either of a country possessing not one sea but two, or referring to position of islands in between two seas.

Baikal, Lake
In south-east *Siberia*, north of *Mongolia*

Possibly from a Mongolian word of uncertain meaning, but perhaps from native (Yakut or Buryat) word = 'big'. Chinese name is Pai-hai = 'northern sea'. Early Russian settlers named it Holy Sea.

Baku
Capital of republic of *Azerbaijan*, USSR

Popular theory explains name as deriving from Arabic through Persian with meaning 'windswept' (Persian baadku = 'mountain wind'). Possibly from Iranian abad = 'town' + ku = 'fire' (with reference to practice of fire-worship). True origin still uncertain.

Balaklava
Port in south *Crimea*, USSR, on *Black Sea*

Possibly from Turkish balik = 'fish' + yuva = 'nest'; bay of Balaklava is one of richest fishing areas in *Black Sea*. Or perhaps from former town Palakion, situated here in 2nd–1st centuries BC, named in honour of Palak, son of Scythian king Scilur (although this name was not known before Turks captured town in 1475).

Balaton, Lake
Large lake in *Hungary*, south-west of *Budapest*
Not likely to be derived from Slavonic boltno (Russian boloto) = 'marsh'. Possibly from Illyrian pelso = 'forest'.

Balboa
Port at *Pacific* end of *Panama* Canal
Named after Spanish explorer Vasco Nuñez Balboa (1475–1517) who was 1st European to cross *Panama* isthmus (in 1513) and sight the *Pacific*.

Balearic Islands
Off east coast of *Spain*, in *Mediterranean*
Possibly from Phoenician words = 'islands of the sling' (compare Greek ballein = 'to throw, to sling'), and in fact inhabitants fought for Romans as stone-slingers. But name may be of pre-Phoenician origin.

Balkans
Range of mountains in *Bulgaria*
Name possibly connected with Slavonic balka = 'gorge, ravine', imported by Turkish-speaking Bulgarians from southern *Caucasus*, but borrowed by themselves from Slavs. Or possibly linked with Old Turkish balak = 'high, tall'. Bulgarian name is Stara Planina = 'old mountains'.

Baltic Sea
In northern *Europe*, bounded largely by *Sweden, Poland* and north-west USSR
Of uncertain origin. Roman author Pliny writing in 1st century AD mentions an island called Baltia, from where amber was obtained. Possibly connected with Lithuanian baltas = 'white' or Russian boloto = 'marsh'. Other links could be with Latin balteus, Swedish and Danish balte = 'belt' (in sense of sea 'girding' part of earth).

Baltimore
City and seaport in state of *Maryland*, USA
Town was established in 1729 and named after Lord Baltimore (?1580–1632), founder of *Maryland*.

Baluchistan
Region of *Pakistan* bounded by *Afghanistan*, Arabian
Sea and *Iran*
Name means 'place of the Baluch people', whose own name
may mean 'tufted-hair folk'.

Bamako
Capital of *Mali*, West *Africa*
Name is that of a Soninke chief who formerly lived here,
Bamma, + particle ko = 'behind'. Place was thus founded
on a site 'behind Bamma's village' (which was itself called
Motibadougou).

Bandar Seri Begawan
Capital of *Brunei*
Name was given to former Brunei (town) in 1970 by Sultan
of Brunei in honour of his father, Sir Omar Ali Saifuddin
('Umar 'Ali Saif-ud-Din), who abdicated in 1967 in favour
of his son. Bandar = 'town', and Seri Begawan was honorary
title of the abdicating sultan, literally = 'illustrious, blessed'.

Bangkok
Capital of *Thailand*
According to one popular theory, name derives from bang
= 'village, district' + makok = 'wild plums'. Thais call city
Krung Thep = 'city of angels'.

Bangladesh
Republic between *India* and *Burma*
From Bengali = 'Bengal nation'. Before 1971 was East
Pakistan.

Banjul
Capital of *Gambia*, West *Africa*
Name was formerly that of the island of St Mary here, and
is said to mean 'rope mats'. Until 1973 was called *Bathurst*.

Banks Island
Most westerly island of North-West Territories,
Canada, in *Arctic* Ocean
Discovered in 1819 and named, as are Banks Island, British
Columbia and Banks Peninsula, *New Zealand*, in honour of
English naturalist Sir Joseph Banks (1743–1820), a member
of Cook's 1st expedition.

Barbados
Independent state, one of *Windward Islands, West Indies*
Discovered by Spanish explorers, probably in 1518, who named it Los Barbados = 'the bearded', with reference to fig-trees from which hung trails of moss.

Barbary Coast
Coast of North *Africa* from *Morocco* to *Libya*
Named after principal inhabitants, Berbers, whose name has meaning 'man' (ie belonging to one people). Not likely to be connected with English 'barbarian', which derives from Greek barbaros = 'foreign'.

Barcelona
Province and its capital in north-east *Spain*
Said to have been founded by Carthaginian general Hamilcar Barca in 230 BC.

Barents Sea
Part of *Arctic* Ocean, bounded by *Norway* and north-west USSR
Named after Dutch explorer Willem Barents (1550−97) who in 1594 made 1st of 3 attempts to find North-East Passage from *Atlantic* to *Pacific*. He died here, his ship caught in the ice off *Novaya Zemlya*.

Bari
City and seaport on *Adriatic* in province of *Apulia*, south-east *Italy*
Roman name was Barium, from Latin baris = 'boat, barge' (ie harbour for boats).

Barrow Strait
In north Canada on route from *Baffin Bay* through *Arctic* Ocean to *Beaufort Sea*
Named in honour of English explorer Sir John Barrow (1764−1843), 1st of the searchers for the North-West Passage. Strait was discovered by Parry in 1819.

Basle
City in north-west *Switzerland*
Founded in AD 44 as Robur, from Latin roburetum = 'oak grove'. In 374 renamed Basilia, from Greek basileus = 'king': town was fortress for Roman emperor Valentinian I.

Basque Provinces
North-east *Spain*
Named after Basques, whose own name derives from
Basque vasok = 'man' (ie one native to this region and
speaking a different language from surrounding peoples).

Bass Strait
In South *Pacific* between *Australia* and *Tasmania*
Named in honour of English navigator George Bass who in
1798–99 explored south coast of *Australia* and *Tasmania*.

Basutoland
Former name of *Lesotho*
Named after Basuto or Suto (Sotho) people who are its
native inhabitants. Their name forms main element of
Lesotho, name of country since 1966.

Bathurst
Former name of *Banjul*, capital of *Gambia*, West *Africa*
Named, as are Bathurst, town in *New South Wales, Australia*,
and Bathurst, port in north-east *Canada*, after Lord Bathurst,
British Colonial Secretary 1812–28.

Baton Rouge
State capital of *Louisiana*, USA
From French bâton rouge = 'red stick'. According to one
story, when French claimed territory here in 17th century
they set up a red pole, like an Indian totem pole, to mark
boundary between Indian territory and their own. Another
version says French found pole already existing to mark
boundary between hunting grounds of two Indian tribes.
Name may also perhaps be translation of name of Indian
chief.

Bavaria
'Land' in south of West *Germany*
Named after Celtic tribe Boii, with their own name derived
from Indo-European buoi = 'warriors', who settled here in
6th century AD.

Bayonne
Town in south-west *France*, near Bay of *Biscay*
Name may be based on Low Latin baia = 'bay'.

Bayreuth

Town in *Bavaria*, West *Germany*, north-east of Nuremberg

From name of tribe Boii (who gave their name to *Bavaria*) + Old High German riuti = 'to clear (a wood)', ie 'place cleared by the Boii'.

Beaufort Sea

In *Arctic* Ocean, between north *Alaska* and *Banks Island*

Named after English admiral Sir Francis Beaufort (1774–1857), hydrographer to Royal Navy (who also gave his name to Beaufort Scale on which wind speed is measured).

Bechuanaland

Former name of *Botswana*

From name of native inhabitants, Bechuans, with their own name (more correctly, Tswana) meaning 'equal'.

Beira

Seaport in *Mozambique*, South-East *Africa*

Named by Portuguese after Portuguese province of Beira, with meaning = 'shore'.

Beirut

Capital of *Lebanon*

Perhaps from Aramaic berotha = 'pine trees' or from Roman name for city, Berytus, itself from Phoenician word beroth = 'wells'.

Belfast

Capital of Northern *Ireland*

From Irish Béal Feirste = 'mouth of the sandbank'; sandbank is one at mouth of little river Farset where it flows into larger Lagan.

Belfort

Town in central eastern *France*, between *Jura* Mountains and *Vosges*

From French bel = 'fine' + fort = 'fortress'. Feature of town is castle on high rock which was used for defence as recently as 20th century (it commands route between *Vosges* and *Jura* Mountains).

Belgium
Kingdom in north-west *Europe*
Named after Celtic tribe Belgae, conquered by Caesar in 1st century BC. They inhabited not only modern Belgium but also *France*. Their name derives from Celtic belg, bolg = 'brave, warlike', probably related to English 'bellow'.

Belgrade
Capital of *Yugoslavia*
From Slavonic = 'white fortress'; first fortress here was built by Celts in 4th century BC.

Belize
Independent British colony in Central *America*, formerly British *Honduras*
From River Belize, with Indian (Maya) name of uncertain meaning. Capital from 1970 is *Belmopan*. (Belize was name of capital before this.)

Belle Isle
Island at east end of strait of same name between *Newfoundland* and *Labrador*, east *Canada*
French = 'beautiful island'. Discovered and named by French explorer Jacques Cartier in 1535, who by sailing through Belle Isle Strait proved that *Newfoundland* was an island.

Bellingshausen Sea
Part of *Pacific* west of *Graham Land*, *Antarctic*
Named after Russian explorer F. F. Bellingshausen (1778–1852) who led expedition which discovered sea in 1821.

Belmopan
Capital of *Belize*, formerly British *Honduras*
From name of former capital *Belize*, destroyed by hurricane in 1961, + River Mopan, tributary of River Belize, on which it stands. City is situated 80 km (50 miles) inland; founded in 1967, government began transfer here in 1970.

Belorussia
Alternative spelling of *Byelorussia*

Benares
City in south-east *Uttar Pradesh, India,* on River *Ganges*
Native name is Varanasi, of which Benares is a corruption.
Name derives from that of River Varana (Barna) and River
Asi, which flow into River *Ganges* at point where city is
situated. Benares is ancient sacred Hindu city, with flights
of steps leading down to river called 'ghats' (see *Ghats*).
This explains false derivation sometimes given—from San-
skrit varanasi = 'town of best water'.

Bengal
Historic territory in north-east *India*
From Hindi Bang-alaya = 'habitation of the Bangs' (who
once lived here).

Benghazi
Former joint capital, with *Tripoli,* of *Libya,* North
Africa
Named after Moslem saint Ben-Ghazi (Ben-Rhasi) who is
venerated here and buried near here.

Benin
Republic, Central West *Africa*
Before 1975 was *Dahomey.* Present name comes from that of
former Edo-Bini kingdom here, whose territory extended
much further than present state, so that Bini people are
more closely connected with southern *Nigeria.*

Bergamo
Province and city in north *Italy*
Roman name was Bergomum, and Greek Pergamon. Origin
may lie in Venetian dialect word with meaning 'strange
speech', relating to that of local inhabitants.

Bergen
City and seaport in south-west *Norway*
From Norwegian Björgvin = 'mountain pasture'.

Bering Sea

Part of *Pacific* between *Siberia* and *Alaska*, with Bering
Strait to the north
Named in memory of Danish navigator Vitus Bering (1680
−1741) who explored territory for Peter the Great of Russia
in 1725−28 and who died on one of the *Komandorskiye
Islands* (now named Bering Island). Name was proposed by
G. Foster, member of Cook's expedition, in 1778, but came
into use only in 19th century, before which was known as
Kamchatka Sea.

Berkeley

City in *California*, USA, near *San Francisco*
Named in honour of Irish bishop George Berkeley (1685−
1753), a pioneer of American education (Berkeley is a
famous university city) and author of the line 'Westward
the course of empire takes its way'. City was founded in
1865.

Berlin

Largest city in *Germany*, politically divided into east
and west, with East Berlin the capital of East *Germany*
Origin not yet finally established. Many suggestions have
been made, with words from Germanic, Celtic and Slavonic
languages proposed with meanings as varied as 'lake',
'hill', 'dam', 'place of judgement', 'customs post', 'sandy
place', etc, as well as from personal name Berla. First
known as Berlin in 1244. Popular theory relates name to
word for 'bear', as reflected in city's coat of arms.

Bermudas

Group of islands in West *Atlantic*, south-east of *New
York*, USA
Discovered in early 16th century by Spanish explorer Juan
Bermudez, who named them 'Islands of devils' (with ref-
erence to strong winds). In 1519 renamed after him in his
honour by a Spanish compatriot.

Berne

Capital of *Switzerland*

Origin uncertain; possibly from Indo-European ber = 'marshy place'. In attempt to explain name, legend arose of count who, deciding to found the city but not knowing what to call it, met a bear while out hunting and so decided on 'Bear Town' (from German Bär = 'bear'). One theory relates name to that of *Verona*, claiming that Swiss city, founded in 12th century, was northern version of Italian city. Cities are relatively close to each other.

Berry

Historic province in central *France*, south of *Paris*

From Roman Biturica, after Gaulish tribe Bituriges, with their own name derived from Celtic bith, bed = 'marshland'.

Besançon

City in central east *France* at foot of *Jura* Mountains

Roman name was Vesontio, from Gaulish beron = 'river'. Besançon was capital of Gaulish tribe Sequani, whose name = 'water-dwellers' (see *Seine*).

Bessarabia

Region in USSR with north and south parts in *Ukraine* and main part in *Moldavia*

Named either after local ruler Bessara or after Wallachian land Basarab, both names deriving from Thracian tribe Bessi who overran it in 7th century.

Bethlehem

1 Town in west *Jordan*, near *Jerusalem*

Arabic name is Bayt Laḥm = 'house of meat'; Hebrew is Bet Leḥem = 'house of bread'. Both names refer to fertile plain here.

Bethlehem

2 Town in *Pennsylvania*, USA, north-west of *Philadelphia*

After town in *Jordan*, occurring (in Biblical sense) in a German carol sung at the founding of the town on 24 December 1741.

Beverly Hills
Suburb of west *Los Angeles*, south *California*, USA
Name suggested from account of 1907 that American president Taft was staying at a place called Beverly Farms. Name was originally Beverly, but from 1911 Beverly Hills. Ultimately derived from English town of Beverley, Yorkshire. American name has assumed connotation of luxury: Beverly Hills is home of film stars.

Bhutan
Kingdom in east *Himalayas* bounded by *Tibet*, *India* and Sikkim
From Sanskrit bhot = 'country' (ie Tibet).

Biafra
Former independent republic in *Nigeria*, West *Africa*
State formed in 1967 when East *Nigeria* seceded from *Nigeria*, taking name from Bight of Biafra, bay between delta of River *Niger* and Cape Lopez in *Gabon*. Ceased to exist in 1970.

Biarritz
Town and resort on Bay of *Biscay*, in south-west *France*
Name is of Basque origin, perhaps = 'two rocks'; from bi = 'two' and harri = 'rock'.

Bihar
State in north-east *India*
From Sanskrit vihāra = '(Buddhist) monastery', though not clear whether territory was named after a town with a famous monastery, or because it contained many monasteries. Name was given by Muslim invaders in about AD 1200.

Bilbao
City and seaport in north-west *Spain*
From Latin bellum vadum = 'good ford'; city is near mouth of River Nervión.

Birmingham
City in *Alabama*, USA
Founded in 1871 and named after English city with reference to its iron and steel industry, for which American town was soon to be noted.

Biscay, Bay of
In North *Atlantic*, off west coast of *France* and north coast of *Spain*

Name is rendering of Spanish province of Vizcaya, around *Bilbao*. Province name derives from Basque bizkar = 'hill, slope', applying to section of *Pyrenees* here.

Bismarck
State capital of North *Dakota*, USA

Named in 1873 after German chancellor, Otto von Bismarck (1815−98), as compliment for German financial support for construction of railway here.

Bismarck Archipelago
In South-West *Pacific*, east of *New Guinea*

Discovered by English in 1700 and named New Britain (still the name of the largest island of the group); in 1884 became German protectorate and renamed after Chancellor Otto von Bismarck.

Bissau
Capital of *Guinea*-Bissau, West *Africa*

Name is that of island on which town arose, itself named after people (tribe) who lived here, taking their own name from a former chief.

Bizerta
Port on *Mediterranean* in *Tunisia*

City was originally Phoenician outpost Hippo Diarrhytus, in time corrupted to Hippo Zarytus and eventually, under Arab rule, to Bizerta. Roman name was Hippo regius = 'royal fort', after King Hala (Gala) who set up colony here in 1st Punic War (264−241 BC).

Black Forest
Mountainous forest in west of West *Germany*

Translation of German Schwarzwald. 'Black' because mountains are covered with dark-leaved pines. Roman name was Silva Nigra, with same meaning.

Black Sea
Between *Europe* and *Asia*, bounded by USSR, *Turkey, Bulgaria* and *Romania*

'Black' not because of colour of water but because stormier than southern seas. Greek name was Pontos Melas, with same meaning, but was also known as Pontos Axeinos = 'inhospitable sea, unfriendly sea', 2nd word sounding like ancient Iranian name Ahshaena = 'dark'. From this in turn derived similar-sounding Greek name Pontos Euxinos, but with opposite meaning = 'hospitable sea, friendly sea' (English name was Euxine Sea). Could, however, be 'black' in sense of 'north', as many Asian languages have colour names for different parts of the world (see *Red Sea*).

Blantyre
City in *Malawi*

Named after birthplace of Scottish explorer Livingstone, Blantyre in Lanarkshire, *Scotland*. City was founded in 1876, 3 years after death of Livingstone while exploring Central *Africa*.

Bloemfontein
Capital of *Orange Free State*, South *Africa*

From Dutch (Boer) = 'flower spring', probably in sense of 'spring among flowers'. Alternative theory, not so likely, is that land belonged to farmer named Jan Bloem.

Blue Mountains
Range in south-east *Australia*, in *New South Wales*

From bluish haze seen on clear days over uplands on which grow dense eucalyptus forests.

Bogotá
Capital of *Colombia*, South *America*

Founded by Spanish explorer Gonzalo Jiménez de Quesada in 1538 on 6 August, feast-day of Transfiguration (Spanish Santa Fé, literally = 'holy faith'), with name Santa Fé de Bogotá. Santa Fé was also Quesada's birthplace in *Spain*. Main part of name is rendering of Indian Bacatá, which was probably name of tribal chief here.

Bohemia
Historic kingdom in central *Europe*; province of *Czechoslovakia*
From Germanic Bai-haimoz = 'land of the Boii' (tribe who settled here, and in *Bavaria*, in 6th century). Their own name derives from Indo-European buoi = 'hunters'.

Boise
State capital of *Idaho*, USA
From French rivière boisée = 'wooded river'; city derives name from that of river on which it stands, also Boise.

Bolivia
Republic in central South *America*
Before 1825, when a Spanish colony, was known as Upper Peru. Liberated from *Spain* in this year by Simón Bolívar (1783–1830) in South American War of Independence, and renamed after him.

Bologna
City and province in central *Italy*
In 4th century BC known as Bononia, after Boii (see *Bavaria, Bohemia*), with first 'n' later changing to 'l'.

Bombay
2nd largest city in *India*, on west coast
From name of goddess Mumba, wife of Siva (Shiva), to whom temple was built here. Portuguese explorers of 15th century named city Bombain instead of Mumbain.

Bonn
Capital of West *Germany*
Probably from Celtic bona = 'town', or perhaps with other meaning = 'good'. Roman name for town was Castra Bonnensia, based on Celtic.

Boothia
Peninsula in north *Canada*
Discovered and explored by Sir James Ross in 1829–33, who named it after his Scottish patron Sir Felix Booth. Region was originally called Boothia Felix.

Bordeaux
Chief port of south-west *France*
Latin name was Burdigala, probably from Gaulish tribe Bituriges Vivisci, but this is not likely to be taken, as sometimes stated, from bordigala, diminutive of bordo (borda) = 'fish-pond'.

Borneo
Largest island in *Indonesia*, in Malay Archipelago
Portuguese explorers who discovered it in 1521 named it after *Brunei*, north-west part of island. Indonesians call it Kalimantan, said to mean 'land of mangoes'.

Bornholm
Island in *Baltic Sea*, off south-east *Sweden*
Originally known as Burgendaland = 'land of the Burgundians', ie of the people who gave *Burgundy* its name. Later, final element -land was replaced by Danish holm = 'island', with 'born' wrongly taken to mean 'stream', as in English Bournemouth.

Bosnia
Republic in north *Yugoslavia*
Named after River Bosna, in turn with name derived from Illyrian bhogi-na = 'flowing'.

Bosporus
Strait linking *Black Sea* with Sea of *Marmara*
Popular origin is from Greek bos poros = 'ox ford' (with which is linked legend of Greek priestess Io, loved by Zeus, who swam across it in the form of a heifer). Name may, however, be of pre-Greek origin, from Thracian Bos-para, corresponding to Phrygian Bos-poros = 'bright river'.

Boston
State capital of *Massachusetts*, USA
Founded by English Puritans in 1630 who named it after English town Boston, Lincolnshire, from which many of them had come.

Botany Bay
Inlet on coast of *New South Wales, Australia,* south of
Sydney
Discovered by Cook's expedition in 1770, botanist members of which are said to have found 400 new species of
plants here in less than 3 weeks. Cook had originally called
bay Stingray Bay, but changed this because of great variety
of plants discovered.

Bothnia, Gulf of
In *Baltic Sea,* between *Sweden* and *Finland*
Named after former region of *Scandinavia* called in what is
now *Sweden* Westerbotten = 'west (valley) bottom' and in
what is now *Finland* Osterbotten = 'east bottom'. The 2nd
element of these two names gave present name of gulf.

Botswana
Republic in southern *Africa*
Named after native inhabitants, Tswana (Batswana), group
of Bantu tribes, from whom was also derived name of
country before 1966—*Bechuanaland.*

Bougainville
Largest of *Solomon Islands,* South-West *Pacific*
Named after French navigator who sighted it in 1768 during
his voyage round the world, Louis-Antoine de Bougain-
ville (1729–1811).

Boulogne
Port in north *France,* on English Channel
Named by Roman emperor Constantine after Italian city
Bononia (modern *Bologna*).

Bounty Islands
In South *Pacific,* south-east of South Island, *New Zea-
land*
Named after ship *Bounty,* whose captain, British admiral
William Bligh, discovered them in 1788.

Bouvet Island
In South *Atlantic,* south-west of *Cape Town,* South
Africa
Named after Jean-Baptiste-Charles Bouvet de Lozier (1705
–86), French naval officer who discovered it in 1739.

Brabant

Historic province between *Belgium* and *Netherlands;* modern province in *Belgium*

Precise origin uncertain, although 2nd element is Germanic banti = 'region'. Roman version of name, recorded in 7th century, was Pago Pracbatinse.

Brahmaputra, River

River in South *Asia*, rising in *China* and flowing through *Pakistan* and *India* into Bay of *Bengal*

Perhaps from Sanskrit words = 'son of a brahmin', but more likely to be derived from an older, unknown word.

Brandenburg

City in East *Germany*, south-west of *Berlin*

Originally thought to derive from Slavonic branibor = 'defending forest' (ie dividing Slavonic tribes from Germanic), with German name— = 'burnt town'—as attempt to explain Slavonic name (though could also be vice versa). Most recent theory is that name may derive from Celtic brandobriga = 'peak town', or may possibly be connected with Slavonic root word brenna = 'marshy' + German burg = 'town'. (Yet another—Canadian—theory is that name may be connected with that of Irish missionary Brendan, who converted Slavs to Christianity.)

Brasília

Capital of *Brazil*

Named after country, Portuguese for which is Brasil, + suffix -ia. Before 1960 capital was *Rio de Janeiro*.

Brazil

Republic in South *America*

Named after red dye (in Portuguese braza, from brassa = 'heat, coals') got from brazil-wood. Word itself is probably corruption of some eastern word, as Latin brasilium referred to red dyewood brought from the East. Brazil was discovered by Portuguese navigator Cabral in 1500. Original name of newly discovered land was Vera Cruz, Portuguese = 'true cross'.

Brazzaville
Capital of *Congo*, Central *Africa*
Named after Pierre de Brazza (1852–1905), French explorer of Italian extraction who founded it in 1883, + French ville = 'town'.

Bremen
City and port on River *Weser*, north-west of West *Germany*
From Old High German brem = 'marshy shore'. (Word is related to English 'brim'.)

Brest
City and seaport in west *Brittany*, north-west *France*
Probably based on Breton bre = 'hill', as for Irish town Bray. Romans had military post and fort here.

Brindisi
Province and port on *Adriatic*, south *Italy*
Roman name was Brundisium, from Illyrian brentas = 'deer', either because winding coast looked like deer's head with antlers or because deer were once plentiful here (perhaps they had been herded on to one of the headlands).

Brisbane
Capital of *Queensland, Australia*
Named in honour of former English governor of *New South Wales*, Sir Thomas Brisbane, who founded it in 1824.

Britain
Name used for *Great Britain*
From Roman name Britannia, from Celtic tribe of Britons who once inhabited south-west *England*. Their own name possibly derives from Celtic brith = 'speckled', from Indo-European brit = 'marshy place', or from Phoenician Baratanak = 'land of tin'. (See also *Brittany*.)

Brittany
Historic province in north-west *France*
Name arose in 5th century AD when Britons fled here from *Britain* to escape Germanic invaders (Angles, Saxons and Jutes). Roman name was Britannia minor = 'little Britain', in contrast to Britannia major = 'great Britain'. Breton name of Brittany is Breiz, of same origin, as is 'Breton' itself.

Brno
City in *Czechoslovakia*, south-east of *Prague*
Possibly derives from Roman name Eburodunum, mentioned by Ptolemy writing in 2nd century AD. Other theories: 1. from German Brunnen = 'well, spring'; 2. from Hungarian personal name Burin; 3. from Slavonic brnie = 'mud, clay'. Some modern toponymists relate name to Celtic brynn = 'hill'.

Broken Hill
Town in *New South Wales, Australia*
Humpbacked range here was first explored and named in 1844 by Charles Sturt. Present town was founded in 1883 after discovery of lead and silver.

Brooklyn
Borough of *New York* city, USA, on *Long Island*
Founded by Dutch settlers in 1645 from small town of Breukelen, near *Amsterdam*. Name re-spelt by English who occupied it in 1664.

Brooks Range
Mountains in north *Alaska*, USA
Named after geologist Alfred H. Brooks, who led survey work here from 1903 to 1924.

Bruges
City in west *Belgium*
From Dutch brug = 'bridge', possibly in sense of 'town with many bridges', but more likely referring to one bridge by which town arose, as was the case with many towns in Middle Ages. There was originally a Roman bridge here over the Rei River.

Brunei
Sultanate in north-west *Borneo, formerly in Malaysia*
Name may be of Sanskrit origin and mean simply 'land', although some interpret it as a Malay word meaning 'plant' (ie mangoes). See also *Borneo*.

Brunswick

City in north of West *Germany*, former capital of historic duchy of Brunswick

From name of Saxon count Bruno, son of Duke Ludolf of *Saxony*, + Old High German wik = 'settlement'. German name is Braunschweig, not as close to original name as English.

Brussels

Capital of *Belgium*

Name was originally Bruoc-sella = 'settlement in the marshes', in sense of 'town built on a marsh'; city was originally built on an island in marshes of River Senne, tributary of River *Scheldt*.

Bucharest

Capital of *Romania*

Said to have been founded in 15th century by shepherd named Bucur, but in fact city existed before this. May be connected with Albanian bucur = 'pleasant, beautiful', or with Romanian = 'to rejoice'.

Budapest

Capital of *Hungary*

Name was given to city when two independent towns merged in 1872: Buda, on right bank of River *Danube*, and Pest on left bank. Both names are of Slavonic origin: Buda may = 'building' or 'water'; Pest (Pesht) may = 'cave' or 'hearth'. Romans called military town and camp here Aquincum, with this name of Celtic origin = 'ample water'.

Buenos Aires

Capital of *Argentina*, South *America*

Founded by Spanish settlers in 1536 with full name of Ciudad da la Santisima Trinidad y puerto de nuestra señora la virgen Maria de los buenos aires = 'City of the Most Holy Trinity and port of Our Lady the Virgin Mary of Good Winds'. Name has nothing to do with the climate: 1st half of name was given because city was founded on Trinity Sunday; 2nd half because Virgin Mary was patron saint of sailors (who prayed that she would send favourable winds for their ships). By 19th century only last two words remained as name, and these are today often shortened even further to Baires.

Buffalo
City in *New York* state, USA
Name given in 1816, either after nearby Buffalo Creek, or after name of Indian chief. Some have linked name to French beau fleuve = 'beautiful river', although this origin unlikely.

Buganda
Region of Uganda, East *Africa*
From name of native inhabitants—Ganda— + prefix bu-. Name of whole country derives from it.

Bulawayo
City in *Zimbabwe*, Central *Africa*, south-west of *Harare*
From native Gubulawayo = 'place of killing'; city was founded on site of kraal, burned down in 1893, of Matabele chief Lobengula.

Bulgaria
Republic in south-east *Europe*
From name of native inhabitants, Bulgars, originally Turkish-speaking tribe in north-west *Caucasus*. Their own name possibly derives from Turkish bulga = 'to mix' or Old High German belgh = 'to increase'. Popular origin is in name of Bolgar, eponymous folk hero of Bulgarians.

Burgos
Province and its capital in north *Spain*
From Gothic baurgs = 'barricade of wagons, laager'; in 884 a number of settlements united here in their defence against the Arabs.

Burgundy
Historic province in east central *France*
From Germanic tribe Burgundii who settled here in 5th century, with their name derived from Gothic baurgjans = 'dwellers in fortified places'. They had originally settled on *Bornholm*.

Burkina Faso

Republic, West *Africa*

Before 1984, country was called Upper *Volta*, after river whose upper reaches were in its territory. New name is properly Burkina = 'honest men', with Faso = 'country' and corresponding to English title 'Popular and Democratic Republic of'.

Burma

Republic in South-East *Asia*

From Sanskrit mranma, bama = 'strong ones' (ancient name of native inhabitants). Burmese name for country is Bama.

Burundi

Republic in Central *Africa*

With independence of Ruanda-Urundi in 1962, Burundi (otherwise Urundi) remained a monarchy, while Ruanda (now *Rwanda*) became a republic. Burundi became a republic in 1966, with name derived from majority population, Barundi.

Byelorussia

Republic in west USSR

Otherwise White Russia, from Russian byely = 'white', supposedly because White Russians were originally fair-haired race with light grey eyes who wore white garments. More likely explanation of 'white' is in sense of 'free', with reference to liberation of White Russians from Tatar yoke. Another derivation may be from River Belaya, tributary of River Narev. ('White' has no connection with later Russian meanings of 'counter-revolutionary, anti-Communist'.)

Byrd Land

Territory in *Antarctic* between *Bellingshausen Sea* and Ross Sea

Name given in 1929 by American explorer Richard Byrd (1888–1957). Territory was originally named Marie Byrd Land, after explorer's wife.

C

Cádiz
Province and its capital in south *Spain*
From Phoenician gadir = 'wall', ie city surrounded by walls.

Caen
City in *Normandy*, north *France*
From Gaulish catu = 'battle' + magos = 'field'.

Cairo
Capital of *Egypt*
English version of last element of Arabic name Misr-al-Qahirah = 'Mars the victorious'; city was founded in 969 when *Egypt* was conquered by Arabs, who in 641 had founded El Fustat, now Old Cairo (this name being derived from Byzantine fortress of Fossatum, from Latin fossa = 'moat'). (Planet Mars, god of war, was said to be visible on night city was founded.)

Calabria
Region in extreme south of *Italy*
Possibly from Gaulish root kal = 'white', though not easy to see in what sense, and perhaps derived from Indo-European kal = 'watercourse', as region is mountainous. Alternatively, some trace name back to people called Calabri who lived here, with their own name perhaps = 'rock dwellers'.

Calais
Town and seaport in north-east *France* on Straits of Dover
Named after Belgian/Gaulish tribe Caleti, whose name = 'dwellers by the sea', from Gaulish cul = 'channel'. Otherwise name could perhaps derive from pre-Celtic root kal = 'rock'.

Calcutta

Largest city in *India* and capital of Western *Bengal*

Many possible origins: most likely is from Sanskrit Kalikata = 'abode of Kali'—a Hindu goddess, wife of Siva (Shiva). Less likely are origins in Sanskrit kola = 'pig', for abundance of pigs near here, or in kali = 'slaked lime', referring to village industry.

Calgary

City in south *Alberta, Canada*

Named in 1876 by Scottish colonel James MacLeod after his native Scottish village of Calgary on Isle of Mull.

California

State in south-west USA

True origin uncertain. Said to have been named by Spanish explorer Cortez in 1535, either from Spanish Caliente fornalla (Latin calida fornax) = 'hot furnace', referring to powerful heat of sun, or after legendary isle of Greek mythology ruled by Queen Caliphia. In fact Cortez also named it Santa Cruz = 'holy cross', but this name was already widespread in *America* and did not last.

Calvados

Department in north *Normandy*, north *France*

Named at end of 18th century after ledge of rocks off coast here, in turn from Latin calvus = 'bald' + dossum (French dos) = 'back', referring to reef. Popular origin derives name from that of the ship 'Salvador', wrecked on rocks here in rout of Spanish Armada in 1588. But reef was known and named well before this.

Cambodia

Republic in south *Indochina*

Said to be named after mythical forefather of all Khmers who are its native population—Cambu (which is also name of River *Mekong* in Cambodia). Republic was renamed Khmer Republic 1970, and name has been officially Kampuchea since 1977. Latter is more accurate native (Khmer) spelling, with Cambodia a Portuguese corruption.

Cameroon
Republic in West *Africa*

Named after River Cameroon, in turn with name derived from Portuguese camarões = 'prawns', observed in it by Portuguese sailors who discovered it.

Campania
Region in south *Italy*, on *Tyrrhenian Sea*

From Latin campus = 'field, plain'; region is flat and fertile.

Canada
Country occupying almost whole of North *America*, north of USA

Originally name of one of a number of Indian settlements, then of regions surrounding it, and eventually of whole country. Probably from Indian (Huron) kanata = 'cabin, lodge'. Not likely to be from Spanish cañada = 'canyon' or Portuguese = 'path', since neither Spanish nor Portuguese ruled here. During French rule was called New France (French La Nouvelle France).

Canary Islands
In North *Atlantic*, off north-west coast of *Africa*

Known in ancient times to Phoenician, Greek, Carthaginian and Roman sailors (the latter calling them Insulae Fortunatae = 'fortunate islands'). The 1st 'modern' discovery was by Spanish explorers in 1402 who called them Islas Canarias = 'dog islands', as they had heard of legendary islands in the West said to be populated by men with dogs' heads and, on landing, heard (wild) dogs barking in the woods. Islands in turn have given name to canaries, found as wild birds here.

Canaveral, Cape
Cape in east *Florida*

From Spanish = 'canebrake' (thicket of reeds), probably referring to cape's appearance as seen from the sea by Spanish sailors in the 16th century. Renamed Cape *Kennedy* from 1963 to 1973, in honour of John F. Kennedy (1917–63), 35th US President.

Canberra
Capital of *Australia*, in *New South Wales*
Although of recent foundation (1913), origin of name is uncertain. Region where city was founded was named Limestone Plain, but town assumed native name of Canberra. Perhaps derived from aboriginal word = 'meeting-place'.

Cannes
Seaport and resort on *Mediterranean* in south *France*
Probably from Latin canna = 'reed' (French word is plural), or perhaps from pre-Indo-European can = 'height'; old town of Cannes is at foot of low hills.

Cantabrian Mountains
North *Spain*
Named after Cantabri, Iberian tribe defeated in Cantabrian War of 29−19 BC by Augustus. The tribal name may = 'rock dwellers'.

Canterbury
Province on South Island, *New Zealand*
Named after Canterbury Association, Anglican society (with Archbishop of Canterbury as president) whose members settled here in 1850 with aim of planting colony on similar lines to those of Presbyterian settlement set up two years earlier at *Dunedin*. See also *Christchurch*.

Canton
Former name of *Kwangchow/Guangzhou, China*
English version is in fact corruption of name of province Kwangtung/Guangdong of which Canton (*Kwangchow/Guangzhou*) is the capital.

Cape Province
In south of South *Africa*
Full name is Cape of *Good Hope* Province, named (1910) after famous headland here. (Before this was Cape Colony.)

Cape Town
Capital of South *Africa* and of *Cape Province*
Founded by Dutch in 1652 with name Kaapstad, of which Cape Town is English translation (ie 'Cape of Good Hope Town').

Cape Verde Islands
Republic in *Atlantic*, west of *Senegal*, West *Africa*
Named after Cape Verde (originally Portuguese Cabo Verde = 'green cape') in *Senegal*, to west of which they lie.

Capri
Island off coast of *Campania, Italy*, near *Naples*
Not likely to be derived from Latin capra = 'goat'—this is merely attempt to explain name—but perhaps from Greek kapros = 'boar' (island was former Greek colony), or from Etruscan capra = 'burial ground'.

Caracas
Capital of *Venezuela*, South *America*
Founded by Spanish explorers in 1567 and named after warlike Indian tribe Caracas, with full name of town Santiago de León de Caracas. 'Santiago' is Spanish for 'Saint James', ie in honour of the apostle, who is the patron saint of Spain; León is in honour of Don Pedro Ponce de León, who was the provincial governor.

Cardiff
Capital of *Wales, Great Britain*
From Celtic caer = 'fortress' + personal name Didius (ie 'Didius' castle') or + Dydd, Welsh name of River Taff on which city stands. (Welsh name of city is Caerdydd.)

Caribbean Sea
Part of *Atlantic* bounded by *West Indies* and coasts of Central *America, Venezuela* and *Colombia*
Named after Caribs, Indian tribe with their own name = 'heroes, brave ones', who inhabited *West Indies* and were encountered by Columbus when he landed here in 1492. Tribal name is related to English word 'cannibal'.

Carinthia
Province in south *Austria*
Named after Celtic tribe who lived in the *Alps* here BC, with their own name derived possibly from Illyrian karant = 'rock, cliff', or from Celtic karantos = 'friendly ones'. German name is Kärnten.

Carolina
Two states, North and South, in south-east USA
French coloniser Jean Ribaut established settlement of
Huguenots here in 1560 and named it in honour of French
king Charles IX, with name La Caroline. With time this
name fell out of use, and in 1629 territory was granted to
English coloniser Robert Heath who named it Carolina
after English king Charles I. In 1663 state was re-granted to
9 proprietors by English king Charles II, for whom name
Carolina was just as suitable. State divided into North and
South in 1712, with separate governor for each.

Caroline Islands
In West *Pacific*, west of *Marshall Islands*
Spanish explorers who discovered them in 1528 called
them Islas de los Barbados = 'islands of the bearded' (ie
Polynesians); in 1542 they became Islas de los Jardinos =
'islands of the gardens'; finally, in 1686, they received their
present name, given in honour of Spanish king Charles II.

Carpathian Mountains
In East *Europe*, between *Alps* and *Balkans*
Name is probably of Thracian/Illyrian origin, either after
inhabitants Carpi or connected with Albanian karpe =
'rock, cliff'.

Carpentaria, Gulf of
In north *Australia*, in *Arafura Sea*
Named in honour of General Pieter Carpentier, Governor
General of Dutch East Indies, in 1623. Discovered by Tas-
man in 1606.

Carrara
Town in *Tuscany*, north-west *Italy*, near Ligurian Sea
Probably from Latin quadraria = 'quarry' (town is famous
for marble quarried here), or possibly from pre-Indo-
European cara = 'rock'.

Carson City
State capital of *Nevada*, USA
Named in honour of Christopher (Kit) Carson (1809–68),
famous frontiersman. Original name of settlement here
was first Eagle Station, then Eagle Ranch.

Casablanca
City and seaport in *Morocco*, North-West *Africa*
Roman name was Anfa. Portuguese founded Casablanca on site of Roman city in 1515 with name = 'white house' (Portuguese casa branca). Present form of name is Spanish casa blanca, with same meaning. Arabic name is Dar el-Beida, with same meaning. Reference is to white houses here generally, not individual one.

Cascade Range
Mountains in north-west USA, parallel to *Pacific*
Named about 1820 after cascades of River Columbia, which cuts through it.

Caspian Sea
Largest inland sea in world, between south USSR and *Iran*
Named after Caspi, race formerly inhabiting territory south of *Caucasus Mountains,* with their own name perhaps related to Cushites (ancient inhabitants of North-East *Africa*) + suffix -pi denoting plural.

Castile
Historic province in central and north *Spain*
From Latin castellum = 'fortress', ie 'land of castles' (built for defence against Moors).

Catalonia
Historic region in north-east *Spain*
Origin uncertain. Not likely to be derived from Got-Alania, ie from Goths and Alani.

Catania
Province and its capital in east *Sicily*, south *Italy*
Possibly connected with Phoenician katon = 'small' (ie by comparison to *Syracuse*), although according to archaeologists original population consisted of Sekeloi (who gave name to *Sicily*), from whose language name is more likely to derive—but with unknown meaning.

Caucasus Mountains
Range in south USSR between *Black Sea* and *Caspian Sea*

Mentioned by Greek classical writers Aeschylus and Herodotus, and explained by Roman author Pliny as deriving from Scythian word = 'snow-white'. Possibly connected with Gothic hauhs = 'height', Avestan kahrkasa and Lithuanian kaukas = 'bump' or, more likely, with Iranian words = 'ice-glittering'. But name may actually be that of people who lived here.

Cayenne
Capital of French *Guiana*, north of South *America*

French form of *Guiana* (*Guyana*), from Indian word probably = 'respected' (ie 'we who demand respect').

Cayman Islands
North-west of *Jamaica, West Indies*

From caymans (South American kind of alligator) found in *Caribbean* here. Islands are more famous for turtles, and Columbus who discovered them in 1503 named them Islas de las Tortugas = 'islands of turtles'.

Cévennes
Mountain range in central south *France*

From Gaulish cebenna = 'ridge, crest'.

Ceylon
Former name of *Sri Lanka*

Original name was Singhala, from Sinhalese inhabitants, in turn with name derived from Sanskrit sinha = 'lion' (ie in sense of 'brave'). Name changed in 1972 to *Sri Lanka.*

Chad
Lake, and republic named after it, in north-west Central Africa

Probably from Bornuan word with basic meaning = 'large expanse of water'. Three Britons who sighted lake in 1823 named it Waterloo, after famous victory of 1815 and also with semi-punning reference to 'water'.

Chamonix
Town and resort in *Alps*, east *France*
From Roman name Campimontium = 'mill field' (from Latin campus = 'field' + molentium = 'mill'). Or possibly from Latin campus munitus = 'fortified field' (because region is naturally protected in valley).

Champagne
Historic province in north-east *France*
From Latin campus = 'field, plain' (French champ). Region is flat, especially in north.

Charleston
1 City in South *Carolina*, USA
Named as Charles Town in 1670 in honour of English king Charles II (see *Carolina*); name shortened to Charleston in 1783.

Charleston
2 State capital of West *Virginia*, USA
Founded in 1794 as Charlestown, but name soon changed to Charleston; given by founder, George Clendenin, as tribute to his father Charles.

Chartres
City in north *France*, south-west of *Paris*
Roman name was Autricum, probably from Celtic name of River Autura (modern Eure), but in 4th century was re-named Carnotum, after Carnutes (Gaulish tribe who inhabited this region).

Chatham Islands
In South *Pacific*, south-east of *Wellington, New Zealand*
Discovered in 1791 by English lieutenant William R. Broughton, who named them after expedition's ship, the *Chatham*.

Cherbourg
Seaport on English Channel, north *France*
Popular origin is usually given as Latin Caesaris burgus = 'Caesar's town', but name is more likely based on woman's personal name of Germanic origin.

Chesapeake Bay
Large inlet on *Atlantic* coast, USA, off *Maryland* and *Virginia*
Possibly from Indian (Delaware) k-che-seipogg = 'great salt water', or (Algonquian) che-sipi-oc = 'big-river-at', with this originally name of village here. Certain element is che = 'big'.

Cheyenne
State capital of *Wyoming*, USA
For name of Indian tribe, said to = 'red talkers'. When *Wyoming* was created as a state in 1868, name was proposed for it but rejected because believed to mean 'snakes'. It did become that of state capital, however.

Chicago
3rd largest city in USA, in *Illinois*
Name found in form Chigagou in French text of 1688; from Indian (Algonquian) word = 'stinking', probably referring either to wild onion growing here, to stench of stagnant water (of marshland round Lake *Michigan*), or to skunk (whose fur is valuable). Origin, as with many Indian words, not certain, but may have been she-kang-ong. Name has never been popular, and when city was founded in 1803 it was named Fort Dearborn, after Henry Dearborn, American Secretary of War. This name was not adopted, however, and from 1830 official name was Chicago.

Chile
Republic on west coast of South *America*
Probably from Indian (Araucanian) chili = 'cold, winter' (not connected with English 'chilly', however). Explanation of name is that Peruvian Incas, who conquered part of country, found climate cool compared to their native equatorial land.

Chimborazo, Mount
Inactive volcano in *Andes*, *Ecuador*, South *America*
Named after River Chimbo + Peruvian rasu = 'snow'; volcano is permanently snow-capped.

China
Republic in South-East *Asia*
Present spelling of name is due to Portuguese influence, introduced from *India* in 16th century, deriving either from Ch'in dynasty of 3rd century BC or from Ji-nan = 'south of the sun'. Chinese name for China is Chung-hua = 'middle land'.

Chios
Island in *Aegean Sea* belonging to *Greece*, off west coast of *Turkey*
Turkish name is Sakis-Adasi = 'island of mastic', ie island on which mastic tree grows (whose resin is used for varnish and incense).

Christchurch
City on South Island, *New Zealand*
Founded in 1848 by John Godley of the Anglican Canterbury Association (see *Canterbury*) and named by him after his college at Oxford, Christ Church.

Christmas Island
In central *Pacific*, just north of equator
Discovered by Cook on Christmas Eve, 1777.

Cincinnati
City in *Ohio*, USA
Founded in 1788, originally with artificially concocted name Losantiville (from L for 'Licking' + Latin os = 'mouth' + Greek anti = 'opposite' + French ville = 'town', ie 'town opposite the mouth of the Licking Creek'). In 1790 renamed Cincinnati in honour of General Arthur St. Clair, President of the Pennsylvania Society of the Order of Cincinnati, a group of Republican army officers elected on a system based on that of Roman farmer-general Lucius Quinctius Cincinnatus.

Ciudad Real
Province and its capital in central *Spain*
Spanish = 'royal city'; founded in mid-13th century by King Alfonso X of *Castile*.

Clermont-Ferrand
City in central *France*, in *Auvergne*
In Roman times was Augusta Nemetum, after Emperor Augustus + name of local Gaulish tribe, with their own name derived from Gaulish nemeton = 'sanctuary'. In 3rd–4th centuries town was named Arverni, after Gaulish tribe whose capital it was (see *Auvergne*). Finally, in Middle Ages, town became Clermont (French clair mont = 'bright mountain'), a popular French name. In 1731 Clermont combined with Montferrand, of which first 'mont' was dropped to avoid reduplication. Latter place is named after Ferrand, lord of nearby castle.

Cleveland
City in *Ohio*, USA
Founded in 1796 and named after landowner Moses Cleaveland (1754–1806), who planned it. Name re-spelt without first 'a' from 1832.

Coblenz
City in west of West *Germany*, on River *Rhine*
From Latin confluentes = 'confluence'; city is situated at point where River *Moselle* flows into River *Rhine*.

Cochin-China
Former French colony of *Indochina*
Name originated with Portuguese who turned local name Koe Chin, of uncertain meaning, into Cochin, and then added 'China' to distinguish this region from that of Cochin on *Malabar* Coast, south-west India.

Cocos Islands
In Indian Ocean, north-west of *Perth, Australia*
Islands are covered with coconut palms. Alternative name for them is *Keeling Islands.*

Cod, Cape
Long peninsula in south-east *Massachusetts*, USA
Discovered in 1602 by English explorer Bartholomew Gosnold, who recorded 'near this cape ... we took great store of codfish'.

Cologne
City in West *Germany*, on River *Rhine*
From Latin Colonia Claudia Agrippina = 'colony of Claudia Agrippina' (wife—and murderess—of Roman emperor Claudius, and mother of Nero), who ordered a fort to be built here in AD 50. City was founded in 38 BC by Roman general Agrippa.

Colombia
Republic in north-west of South *America*
Coast here said to have been visited by Columbus in 1502, after whom country was named in 1863. Spanish settlers of 16th century had called it New Granada.

Colombo
Capital of *Sri Lanka*
Name has nothing to do with Columbus. Sinhalese called port here Kolamba, and Portuguese derived this from Sinhalese kola = 'leaves' and amba = 'mango'. However, native word more likely means simply 'port'.

Colón
2nd largest city in *Panama*, Central *America*
Name in Spanish = 'Columbus' (in sense of 'Columbus's town'). Founded in 1850 with name Aspinwall, after one of railway builders. Renamed Colón in 1890. Twin port of Cristóbal, to south of Colón, bears first name of Columbus, ie 'Christopher'.

Colorado
State in west USA
State named after River Colorado, in turn from Spanish Rio Colorado = 'red river' (waters are reddish with clay washed down from canyons).

Columbia, District of
In east USA, with capital *Washington*
Named in 1791 in honour of Columbus. Also named after him are Columbia, capital of South *Carolina* (1786), Columbia River (by American captain Robert Gray, sailing in ship 'Columbia') in north-west USA (1792) and British Columbia (1858). (See also *Colombia, Colón, Columbus.*)

Columbus
State capital of *Ohio*, USA
Named in honour of Columbus in 1812. City of same name in *Georgia* was named in 1828.

Como
Lake and city in north *Italy*
From Celtic camb, comb = 'valley' (compare English 'coomb', Welsh 'cwm').

Comoro Islands
Republic in Indian Ocean, between north *Mozambique* and north *Madagascar*
Original Greek name, mentioned by Ptolemy in 2nd century AD was Ore Selenaie = 'moon mountains' (Latin montes Lunae). Arabic name reflects this as al-Komair, from ḳamar = 'moon'.

Conakry
Capital of *Guinea*, West *Africa*
City derives name from village here inhabited by Susu people. In their language name = 'over the waters', 'on the other bank'. City is on Tombo Island, at end of Kaloum Peninsula.

Concepción
City in south *Chile*; city in *Paraguay*, South *America*
Spanish = 'Conception': both cities were founded on 8 December, Feast of Immaculate Conception (1st city in 1550 by Pedro de Valvivia on a site 11 km (7 miles) north-east of present city).

Concord
State capital of *New Hampshire*, USA
Founded in 1725 as Pennycook, from Indian (Algonquian) word probably = 'descent'. In 1763 renamed Concord after city of same name in *Massachusetts*, whose immigrants settled it. Name may have been given to mark peaceful agreement drawn up between two factions.

Coney Island
Resort in south-west of *Long Island, New York* City, USA
From English version of Dutch konijn = 'rabbit'; animals once bred and lived here in natural state.

Congo
Republic in Central *Africa* and great river there
Republic named after river, in turn named probably from
Bantu kong = 'mountains' (through which it flows). River
is also known as *Zaïre*.

Connecticut
State in *New England*, north-east USA
From Indian (Algonquian) kuenihtekot = 'long-river-at'.
River gave name to state. The 2nd 'c', which is silent, was
probably inserted by an English scribe thinking of word
'connect'.

Constance, Lake
Bordering on *Austria*, West *Germany* and *Switzerland*
Named after town of Constance, in turn with name derived
from Roman Constantia, after Emperor Constantine I.
German name of lake is Bodensee, from German Boden =
'bottom' (in sense of 'low-lying valley') + See = 'lake'.

Constantinople
Former name of *Istanbul*
Founded, as New Rome, by Constantine the Great in AD
330 as capital of Roman empire on site of ancient Byzantium. Name therefore derives from Constantine + Greek
polis = 'town'. Renamed *Istanbul* in 1930.

Cook Islands
In South *Pacific*, east of *Tonga*
Named in honour of Cook, who discovered some of them
in 1773. Cook himself named islands Hervey, in honour of
Augustus John Hervey, a lord of the Admiralty.

Copenhagen
Capital of *Denmark*
From Danish kiopman = 'merchant' + havn = 'harbour', ie
'merchants' harbour'.

Cordova
Province and its capital in *Andalusia*, south *Spain*
Possibly from Arabic karta-tuba = 'big town'. Spanish
spelling of name is Córdoba.

Corfu

Island and town on it in *Ionian Sea*, off west coast of *Greece*

Probably from Greek name Kerkyra = 'winding' (referring to its coast), or possibly from Greek kerkouros = 'boat' (originally name of bay on east Corfu).

Corinth

Town and port on Gulf of Corinth, west of *Athens*, south *Greece*

Has been explained as deriving from Greek koronis = 'crown' (ie mountain peak), but name is of pre-Greek origin. Modern Corinth was founded in 1858 on site of ancient Corinth, which was founded about 1350 BC.

Cork

County and its capital in *Ireland*, on south coast

From Irish corcaigh = 'marsh', on edge of which town was founded in 7th century.

Corsica

Island in *Mediterranean*, north of *Sardinia*

True origin uncertain: possibly from Phoenician horsi = 'wooded' (Phoenicians built their ships from wood out of Corsican pine forests), or perhaps from Greek name Kyrnos, from Phoenician keren = 'horn, cape, rock', or again perhaps from tribe of Corsi who lived here.

Cortina d'Ampezzo

Resort on slopes of *Alps*, north *Italy*

From Italian cortina = 'yard, smallholding' + dialect word ampezzo, from Italian in pezzo = 'in the field', ie 'smallholding in the field'.

Corunna

Province and its capital in *Galicia*, north-west *Spain*

Not likely to be from Latin columna = 'column', referring to Roman Tower of Hercules off Cape Corunna, a famous lighthouse. Probably from mediaeval name Coronium, although Roman name was Brigantium.

Costa Blanca

Coast of east *Spain* between *Alicante* and *Valencia*

Spanish = 'white coast' (referring to light-coloured sand).

Costa Brava
Coast of east *Spain* from French frontier to *Barcelona*
Spanish = 'wild coast' (referring to rugged coastline).

Costa del Sol
Coast of south *Spain* with *Málaga* as its central resort
Spanish = 'sunny coast' (ie the Spanish Riviera).

Costa Dorada
Coast of west *Spain* from *Barcelona* to *Valencia*
Spanish = 'golden coast' (with abundance of sun and sand).

Costa Rica
Republic in Central *America*
Spanish = 'rich coast'. When Columbus landed here in 1502 he named the region Costa del Oro = 'coast of gold' because of gold ornaments worn by natives and offered to him as gifts.

Costa Smeralda
Coast of north-east *Sardinia*
Italian = 'emerald coast' (from bright green vegetation).

Costa Verde
Coast of north *Spain*, extending west from French frontier to *Corunna*
Spanish = 'green coast'; region is green and fertile.

Côte d'Argent
Coast of south-west *France*, on Bay of *Biscay*, between *Biarritz* and mouth of River Adour
French = 'silver coast' (from brightness of sand, sun and sea).

Côte d'Azur
South coast of *France*, on *Mediterranean*, from Italian frontier westwards to *Marseilles*
French = 'azure coast' (from deep blue colour of sea and sky); otherwise the (French) *Riviera*.

Côte d'Émeraude
Coast of north *Brittany, France,* centring on *Dinard* and *St Malo*
French = 'emerald coast' (from colour of sea here).

Côte de Nuits
North region of *Côte d'Or, France*
From French côte = 'hill, slope' + name of town Nuits-St Georges, first element of which is of uncertain origin: not French = 'nights' but perhaps from Latin nauda = 'marshy place'.

Côte d'Or
Plateau in *Burgundy*, central *France*
French = 'golden slope' (region is famous for vineyards).

Côte Vermeille
Section of coast of south *France* adjoining Spanish frontier
French = 'vermilion coast' (from bright red colour of rocks and earth).

Cotonou
Political capital and chief town and port, *Benin*, Central West *Africa*
Origin is disputed. One theory derives it from African words ku = 'death' + tonu = 'lagoon', another traces name back to Okotonou = 'bank of the lagoon called Okou'.

Cotopaxi, Mount
Highest active volcano in world, in *Andes, Ecuador*, South *America*
From Indian (Quechua) cotto = 'mass, mountain' + pacsi = 'shine, brilliance', ie 'shining mountain' (though this may be attempt to explain older name of unknown meaning).

Cremona
Town in *Lombardy*, north *Italy*, south-east of *Milan* on River *Po*
From Celtic tribe Cenomani, whose own name derives from Celtic cen = 'ridge, crest'.

Crete
Island in *Mediterranean*, to south of *Aegean Sea*
Name is very old, from tribe that once inhabited island. May be connected with Candia, former capital (present Heraklion, Iraklion), and originally name of canal dug in AD 820. Name spread to town and then perhaps by Venetians to whole island.

Crimea
Peninsula on north side of *Black Sea*, USSR
Many possible explanations: most likely is from Stary Krym or Solkhat, former capital of khanate here (though name of town is of unknown origin), or possibly from Turkish kurum = 'ditch, moat' (narrow isthmus at head of peninsula had channel dug across it). Other less likely derivations are: 1. from Turkish kerman = 'fortress'; 2. from Mongolian herem = 'rampart'; 3. from some Russian word such as kroma = 'boundary' or kremen = 'flint'.

Croatia
Republic in north-west *Yugoslavia*
From Croats, who settled here in 7th century AD, with their own name of uncertain origin; perhaps derived from shar-vatas = 'armed' or Slavonic gor = 'mountain', or connected with the name of *Carpathians*.

Crozet Islands
In south-west Indian Ocean, south of *Madagascar*
Discovered in 1772 by French captain Nicolas-Thomas Marion-Dufresne, and named after one of his officers.

Cuba
Island republic in *West Indies*, Central *America*
Was originally name of settlement on island, noted by Columbus in 1492. Name is from (extinct) Indian language of unknown meaning (though 'district' has been suggested).

Curaçao
Island in *West Indies*, off north coast of *Venezuela*
Discovered by Spanish explorer Hojeda in 1449 who called it Isla de los Gigantes = 'island of giants'. Later, in 1499, Spanish colonisers abandoned here several sailors suffering from malaria; some years later another Spanish expedition was surprised to find them recovered and living among native Indian inhabitants. Thus name perhaps derived from Spanish curación = 'cure'.

Cyprus
Island republic in *Mediterranean*, south of *Turkey*
Possibly from groves of cypress trees, imported here from *Lebanon*. Famous in ancient times for its copper mines; Greek name for island, Kypros, is related to English 'copper'.

Czechoslovakia
Republic in central *Europe*
Name of country formed in 1918 from two main groups of inhabitants, Czechs and Slovaks. Czechs derive their name from Czech četa = 'body of men, army'. (For Slovaks see *Yugoslavia*.)

D

Dacca
Capital of *Bangladesh*
Named perhaps after Durga, wife of Siva (Shiva) and goddess of fertility, or else refers to ḍhāk tree, once common here. Official spelling of name is now Dhākā.

Dahomey
Former name of *Benin*, republic in Central West *Africa*, on Gulf of *Guinea*
Probably from personal name Dag + west Sudanese word = 'inside, intestines'. Negro prince Dag had his belly ripped open by member of his retinue in 17th century and capital was named 'Dag's belly', possibly with metaphorical sense of 'inside Dag' (ie 'in possession of Dag').

Dairen
Former name of *Talien/Dalian*
Japanese variant of *Talien* (former Russian name being *Dalny*); now, with *Lüshun*, forms great port of *Lü-ta/Lüda* *China*.

Dakar
Capital of *Senegal*, West *Africa*
Probably from African (Wolof) word = 'tamarind tree'; and originally the name of a native village of the Lebu tribe here.

Dakota
Two states, North and South, in north USA
From name of Indian (Sioux) tribe who once inhabited region here. Indian (Omaha) dakota = 'allies', ie members of tribal union. State divided into North and South in 1889.

Dallas
City in north *Texas*, USA
Named in 1845 after George M. Dallas, Vice-President of USA 1845–49.

Dalmatia
Strip of *Adriatic* coast in *Croatia, Yugoslavia*
Formerly (BC) Illyria. Then named Dalmatia after town Dalmion, with name perhaps connected with Albanian dalmium = 'sheep pasture'. As Roman province, under Augustus, was officially Illyricum, but Dalmatia was name that prevailed.

Dalny
Former name of *Talien/Dalian*
From Russian = 'far, distant'; port was founded in 1860 in extreme east of Russian empire.

Damascus
Capital of *Syria*
Name is very old and has been known at least 3,000 years, but meaning is uncertain. Perhaps = 'industrious'.

Dampier Archipelago
Off north-west coast of Western *Australia*
Named in 1803 after English explorer William Dampier (1652—1715) who discovered them in 1699. Mountains in South Island, *New Zealand*, are also named after him.

Danube, River
2nd longest river in *Europe*, flowing generally south-east through 8 countries, into *Black Sea*
Possibly from Sanskrit danus = 'damp', or from Avestan danu = 'current'. From same root as River *Don*.

Dardanelles
Strait connecting *Aegean Sea* with Sea of *Marmara, Turkey*
Formerly Hellespont (explained as Greek = 'Helle's sea', from name of daughter of Athamas, who drowned in it). From Greek town of Dardanus, in turn named after its inhabitants, with name perhaps connected with Albanian dardhe = 'pear' (though this may be a mere coincidence and connection is hard to see).

Dar es Salaam
Capital of *Tanzania*, Central *Africa*
From Arabic = 'house of peace', ie place where merchants could trade freely.

Darjeeling
Town in West *Bengal*, north *India*, north of *Calcutta*
Many unlikely explanations of meaning, as 'far island of meditation', 'land of the lama's sceptre', 'place of thunder' and 'region of precious stones'. Most likely derivation is from Tibetan dar = 'spread' + gjas = 'broad' + ling = 'island, land', ie 'far spreading land'.

Darling, River
Longest tributary of *Murray* River, *Australia*
Named in 1828 by Captain Charles Stewart, first European to sight it, after Sir Ralph Darling, Governor of *New South Wales*, 1825—31.

Darmstadt
City in central West *Germany*, south of *Frankfurt*
In 8th century was Darmundestadt = 'town of Darmund' (personal name in itself shortened from Darmundolf). Then, through similarity of 2nd element of name with German Munde = 'mouth', came to mean 'town at the mouth of the Darm', but River Darm was first recorded only in 1759.

Darwin
Capital of Northern Territory, *Australia*
Founded in 1869; at first named Palmerston, after English prime minister (1784—1865), but in 1911 renamed in honour of Charles Darwin, who had visited coast here in 1836 on his voyage to *New South Wales*.

Dauphiné
Historic province in south-east *France*
Ceded to French king Philip VI in 1349 when it became official property (appanage) of king's eldest son, Charles of Valois (future king Charles V), heir to the throne, who had title of 'dauphin' (from family name, Delphinus, of lords of Valois, whose crest had dolphins).

Davis Strait
In North *Atlantic*, between *Baffin Island, Canada*, and *Greenland*
Named after English explorer John Davis (1550—1605) who discovered it in 1587 when in search of the North West Passage from the *Atlantic* to the *Pacific*.

Davos
Resort in east *Switzerland*
From Romansch davo = 'behind'; valley in which town lies turns and goes back to north, thus sheltering it from wind. So named in 13th century by huntsmen of Baron von Vatz, who discovered it.

Dawson
Former capital of *Yukon* territory, north-west *Canada*
Founded in 1896 in *Klondike* gold rush; named after Canadian explorer and geologist George M. Dawson. Now a 'ghost' town; population at height of gold rush was 25,000 —in 1981 only 1320.

Dayton
City in state of *Ohio*, USA
Named after one of founders, Jonathan Dayton (1760–1824). Town first settled in 1796.

Dead Sea
Between *Israel* and *Jordan*
Contains no organic life because of high salt and mineral content. Hebrew name is Yam ha-Melah̲ = 'salt sea', and Arabic al-Bah̲r al-Mayitt = 'sea of death'.

Death Valley
In east *California* and south *Nevada*, USA
Named in 1849 by party of gold-seeking 'forty-niners', some of whom died of thirst and exposure when trying to cross it.

Deauville
Resort in *Calvados* department, north *France*
Probably from Latin de = 'belonging to' + Germanic auwa = 'damp plain' + Latin villa = 'village'.

Deccan
Plateau of south peninsula of *India* between Eastern and Western *Ghats*
From Sanskrit dakshina-patkha = 'southern country', original meaning being 'right road'.

Delaware
State on east coast of USA
Named after Delaware River and Bay, in turn named in honour of Thomas West, Lord de la Warr (1577–1618), appointed Governor of *Virginia* in 1609. (Bay was named by Sir Robert Carr in 1644.)

Delft
Town in south *Netherlands*, south-east of *The Hague*
From Old Dutch delf = 'canal' (word is related to English 'delve'): town is on Schie canal.

Delhi
Capital of *India*, and union territory in north *India*
Founded in 10th century on site of ancient city of Indraprastha. Name is of uncertain origin, although Hindi dilli = 'threshold' (perhaps with reference to Hindustan). Old Delhi is also called Shahjahanabad, after Mogul emperor Shah Jahan who rebuilt it in 17th century. New Delhi, just south of Old Delhi, was chosen as capital in 1912 and became capital in 1947.

Denmark
Kingdom in north *Europe*
Named after Germanic tribe, Danes + mark = 'territory'. Danes derive their name from Old High German tenar (Sanskrit dhann) = 'sandbank'.

Denver
State capital of *Colorado*, USA
Founded as gold-mining centre in 1858 with Latin name Auraria = 'golden'. Following year renamed Denver in honour of General James W. Denver, governor of the territory.

Des Moines
State capital of *Iowa*, USA
City named after river, in turn from French Rivière des moines = 'river of the monks', perhaps with reference to Trappist monks who had settled here or, more likely, from name of Indian tribe, recorded in French text of 1673 as Moingouena, shortened to (plural) Moings.

Detroit
City in *Michigan*, USA
From French détroit = 'strait', referring to narrow sound between Lake St Clair and Lake *Erie*. City was founded by French settlers in 1701, with name probably translated from Indian. Original full name was Fort-Pontchartrain du Détroit, after Comte de Pontchartrain, Louis XIV's minister of state who was patron of city's founder, French trader Antoine de la Mothe Cadillac.

Dieppe
Port and resort on English Channel, north *France*
Probably from Saxon word deop = 'deep', referring to mouth of River Arques on which town is situated.

Dijon
City in central east *France*
From Roman name Diviodunum = 'hill of Divio'; 2nd element of name is Celtic.

Dinard
Resort on English Channel in north *Brittany*, *France*
From Celtic din = 'hill' + (perhaps) Breton arzh = 'bear'.

Djibouti
Republic and its capital, North-East *Africa*
Original name of country was French Somaliland (see *Somalia*). From 1967−77 was Afars and Issas, after two main ethnic groups here. Present name, which has always been that of capital, is said to derive from Afar word gabouri = 'plate' (one woven from doum-palm fibres and raised on pedestal for ceremonial purposes).

Dnieper, River
River in USSR flowing south and west through *Ukraine* into *Black Sea*
Latin name was Danapris, from Sarmatic don = 'river' + ipr (probably also) = 'river'.

Dniester, River
River in USSR rising in *Carpathians* and flowing south-east through *Ukraine* into *Black Sea*
Latin name was Danaster, from Sarmatic don, dan = 'river' + (probably) Indo-European is-ro = 'to flow'.

Dodecanese
Group of islands in south-east *Aegean Sea*
From Greek = 'twelve islands' (dodeka = 'twelve', nesos = 'island'). Largest island in group is *Rhodes*.

Dogger Bank
Sandbank in *North Sea*, east of north *England*
Named after 'doggers'—two-masted Dutch fishing vessels which formerly used region as one of their chief fishing grounds.

Dolomites
Region of *Alps* in south-east *Tyrol*, north *Italy*
Named after French mineralogist Dieudonné de Dolomieu (1750–1801) who carried out extensive work here.

Dominica
Republic and one of *Windward Islands, West Indies*
So named by Columbus, who discovered it on Sunday (Latin (dies) dominica) 3 November 1493.

Dominican Republic
East part of island of *Hispaniola, West Indies*
In 1697 named Santo Domingo (Spanish = 'holy Sunday'), its capital from 1844, but originally settled by Spanish explorers on a Sunday (see *Dominica*) in 1496.

Don, River
River in USSR flowing into Sea of *Azov*, north of *Black Sea*
From Sarmatic dan, don = 'river'. Word appears as chief element in name of a number of rivers, eg *Danube, Dnieper, Dniester* (and English River Don).

Dordogne
Department and river in central south *France*
Probably from Celtic dour = 'river'.

Dortmund
City in West *Germany*, north-east of *Essen*
In 890 was known as Throtmenni, from name of channel, in turn derived from Old High German word = 'throat'. Not likely to be connected with Old High German tros = 'heath', and certainly not = 'mouth of the Dort' as no such river exists.

Douai
Town in north *France*, south of *Lille*
Of uncertain origin. Perhaps from Gaulish personal name Dous.

Drakensberg
Chief mountain range of South *Africa*
From Dutch drake = 'dragon' (from wild and dangerous nature of mountains) + berg = 'mountain'. Native name is Quathlamba = 'piled-up rocks'.

Dresden
City in south of East *Germany*
Named after Slavonic tribe, Drezhdane, with their own name from Slavonic drezga = 'forest' + ending -ane = 'dwellers'.

Dublin
Capital of *Ireland*
From Irish dubh = 'black' + linn = 'lake' (equivalent to English Blackpool). Irish name is Baile Átha Cliath = 'town of the ford of the hurdle'. Both names relate to the Liffey River, on which city is located.

Dubrovnik
Resort and seaport in *Dalmatia*, west *Yugoslavia*
From Slavonic dubrova = 'oak wood'. Older name Ragusa does not derive from Slavonic rogoza = 'reed-mace' (kind of tall grass) but from earlier form Rausim, of unknown origin.

Dunedin
City and seaport on south-east coast of South Island, *New Zealand*
Founded in 1848 by Scottish Presbyterian settlers, who first wished to call town New Edinburgh. Provost of *Edinburgh*, publisher Sir William Chambers, then suggested name Dunedin, old Celtic name of *Edinburgh*, understood to mean 'Edin's fort'.

Dunkirk
Port in north-east *France*, on *North Sea*
From Flemish duine = 'dune' + kerk = 'church', ie 'church on the dunes'. Town grew up round church of St Éloi, built here in 7th century.

Durban
City and seaport in *Natal*, South *Africa*
Founded in 1824 as Port Natal, after former name of Durban Bay, originally sighted by Portuguese explorer Vasco da Gama on Christmas Day (Portuguese Natale) 1497. In 1835 renamed Port D'Urban, later simplified to Durban, after Sir Benjamin D'Urban, Governor of Cape Colony (1777–1849).

Dushanbe
Capital of republic of *Tadzhikistan*, USSR
Probably named after village on this site in 7th century with same name—Tadzhik = 'Monday' (ie market day). From 1929 to 1961 was Stalinabad (= 'Stalin town').

Düsseldorf
City in west of West *Germany*, on River *Rhine*
City is situated at point where small River Düssel (with name perhaps from Celtic dur = 'river') flows into River *Rhine*, + German Dorf = 'village'.

E

Easter Island
In South *Pacific*, west of *Chile*
Discovered by Dutch navigator Jacob Roggeveen on Easter Sunday (or possibly Monday) 1722 (although English pirate Edward Davis claimed to have landed here in 1695).

East London
Seaport in *Cape Province*, South *Africa*
Town lies on east coast and is named after British capital *London*. Earlier name was Port Rex, after George Rex, said to be illegitimate son of English king George III. Name changed to East London in 1847.

Ebro, River
River in north *Spain* flowing south-east into *Mediterranean*
From Roman name Iberus, in turn from Basque ebr, Celtic iber = 'river'. (See also *Iberia*.)

Ecuador
Republic on north-west coast of South *America*
Before 1830 name was *Quito*, that of present capital. Since then called Ecuador—Spanish = 'equator' (which crosses it).

Edam
Town in north *Netherlands*, north-east of *Amsterdam*
From Dutch = 'dam on the (River) Ee'. (Compare *Amsterdam, Rotterdam*).

Edinburgh
Capital of *Scotland, Great Britain*
Popular explanation is that city was founded in 617 as fortress for Edwin, King of Northumbria, with name = 'Edwin's (Edin's) castle'. (Compare *Dunedin*.) More recent theory says name derives from Eidyn = 'steep slope', on which was situated din (= 'fortress') of ancient kingdom of Manau Gododdin in 6th century.

Edmonton
Capital of province of *Alberta, Canada*
Named in 1877 after Fort Edmonton, built in 1795 about 30 km (18 miles) further down River *Saskatchewan*. Fort, which was destroyed by Indians in 1807 and rebuilt following year where Edmonton now is, was in turn named by William Tomison of Hudson Bay Company after Edmonton near *London, England*, probably as compliment to his clerk, John Peter Pruden, who was born there.

Edward, Lake
Between *Zaïre* and *Uganda, Africa*
Discovered by English explorer H. M. Stanley in 1888 and named after Prince of Wales, later King Edward VII. In 1970s was renamed Lake Idi Amin Dada, after Ugandan head of state 1971−78.

Egmont, Mount
Extinct volcano in west of North Island, *New Zealand*
Named by Cook in 1770 in honour of English Earl of Egmont, First Lord of Admiralty. Native name, Taranaki, is used for surrounding province.

Egypt
Republic in North-East *Africa*
Possibly from Ga-Ka-Pta = 'house of the god Pta' (patron god of ancient capital Memphis), or from Phoenician kapthor = 'island' (ie surrounded by waters of River *Nile*), or from Greek aia koptos = 'land of the Copts'. Another proposed derivation is from Arabic kemi = 'black land' (with 'black' referring either to colour of inhabitants' skin, waters of *Nile*, or earth). In 1958 official name became United Arab Republic, and from 1972 Arab Republic of *Egypt*.

Éire
Irish name of *Ireland*

Elba
Island off west coast of *Italy*, east of north *Corsica*
Greek name was Aethalia = 'smoky place', probably referring to smelting furnaces, then Latin Ilva from which modern form of name, Elba.

Elbe, River
River in Central *Europe* flowing through *Germany* into
North Sea
From Indo-European alb = 'to go, to flow', from which
Scandinavian elv = 'river'. Or possibly from Indo-
European alb = 'white'.

Elbruz
Extinct volcano, highest mountain in *Caucasus*, USSR
Perhaps from Iranian aitibares = 'high mountain', but
more likely from Iranian = 'sparkling' (referring to snows
in the sun). Armenian name is Alberis, which may be
connected with name of *Alps*.

Élisabethville
Former name of Lubumbashi, *Zaïre*
Founded in 1910 and named after Belgian queen Élisabeth,
wife of King Albert I, + French ville = 'town'. Renamed
Lubumbashi (after river here) in 1966.

Elizabeth
City in state of *New Jersey*, USA
Called Elizabethtown until 1740. Named after wife of Sir
George Carteret, who founded it in 1664 (also perhaps with
reference to Castle Elizabeth, *Jersey*, from which island
Carteret had come).

Ellesmere Island
In *Arctic*, north *Canada*
Named after Francis Egerton, Earl of Ellesmere, by Sir E. A.
Inglefield, who first explored it in 1852.

Ellice Islands
Former name of Tuvalu, in South *Pacific*, between *Fiji*
and *Gilbert Islands* (*Kiribati*)
Named after head of Canadian shipping firm, Alexander
Ellice, who owned ship *Rebecca* on board which Captain de
Peyster discovered them in 1819. Independence achieved
in 1978.

Ellis Island
In *New York* Bay, USA
Named after Samuel Ellis, *Manhattan* merchant who bought
it in 18th century.

El Salvador
Republic in Central *America*
Spanish = 'the Saviour' (ie Christ); name was given by Spanish settlers to their fort here in 1524 and then spread to whole territory.

Endeavour Strait
South part of *Torres Strait* between Cape *York, Queensland, Australia,* and *Prince of Wales Island*
Named after Cook's ship *Endeavour* which passed through strait on his return voyage in 1770.

Enderby Land
Most westerly part of Australian Dependency, *Antarctic*
Discovered in 1831 by John Biscoe, who named it after English whaling firm of Samuel Enderby & Sons who had financed his expedition.

England
South and chief part of *Great Britain*
Named after Germanic tribe of Angles who invaded country and settled here in 5th−6th centuries AD. Angles derive their name from Old High German angul = 'angle, corner': they came from 'corner' of what is now extreme north *Germany*, between Flensburg Fjord and River Schlei.

Erebus, Mount
Active volcano on Ross Island in Ross Sea, *Ross Dependency, Antarctic*
Discovered by Sir James Ross in 1841 and named after one of expedition's two ships, the *Erebus* (name of legendary Greek god, personification of darkness). Other ship, the *Terror*, gave her name to another volcano here.

Erie, Lake
One of Great Lakes between USA and *Canada*
Named after Indian (Iroquois) tribe who once inhabited territory round lake. Their name = 'panther', tribe's totemic animal.

Eritrea
Territory in *Ethiopia* bordering on *Red Sea*
From Greek erythros = 'red', referring either to *Red Sea* or to colour of soil.

Esbjerg
Port on *North Sea* in south-west *Denmark*
Possibly from Danish = 'fish bait' or 'mountain range', but more likely corruption of Eskebjerg = 'ash-tree hill'.

Escorial
Small town north-west of *Madrid, Spain*
From Spanish escoria = 'slag, clinker', ie piles of slag left from old mine-workings. Town is famous for fine buildings and art treasures.

Essen
City in north-west of West *Germany*
In 897 was known as Astnida = 'hills, smelting furnace', from Indo-European as = 'to dry, to burn', with name changing gradually from this to present form. Explanation of meaning is difficult: perhaps in sense of 'woodland cleared by burning'.

Estonia
Republic in north-west USSR, on Gulf of *Finland*
From Esthes, ancestors of modern Estonians. They were a Finno-Ugrian people with name probably derived from Baltic word aueist = 'dwellers by the water'.

Estremadura
Historic region in west *Spain*; province in west *Portugal*
From name of Roman province Extrema Durii, from Latin extremum ab Duera = '(land) farthest from the (River) Duero'. Roman territory on Spanish Peninsula extended from *Mediterranean*, so Estremadura was at its western extremity.

Ethiopia
Independent state in North-East *Africa*
According to popular origin, from Greek aithos = 'burnt' + ops = 'face', ie 'people with sunburnt faces'.

Etna, Mount
Highest volcano in *Europe*, in east *Sicily*, south *Italy*
From Greek aitho = 'burn'. Sicilian name is Mongibello, popularly derived from Italian monte bello = 'beautiful mountain' or from Arabic jebel = 'mountain'.

Euphrates, River
River in South-West *Asia*, joining River *Tigris* in *Iraq* to flow into Persian Gulf
Assyrian name was Purattu, possibly from bur = 'vessel' or, more likely, from ur = 'river', + at = 'father, powerful', ie in sense of 'father of rivers' or 'mighty river'. Present spelling Greek in origin.

Eurasia
Europe and *Asia* regarded as one continent
From Eur(ope) + Asia. Name dates from mid-19th century.

Europe
Continent west of *Asia*
Name is very old: mentioned in Greek hymn to Apollo written in 6th century BC. Originally name applied only to part of *Balkan* Peninsula: north *Greece, Albania* and *Macedonia*. Name may have originated in Near East, from Assyrian ereb = 'darkness, west', ie 'land of the setting sun' (compare *Asia*). However, modern theory derives name from word meaning simply 'mainland'.

Eureka
Port in north-west *California*, USA
Named by first settler, James Ryan, who on landing here in 1850 is said to have exclaimed 'Eureka!' (Greek = 'I have found it'). Not clear whether he meant land or gold.

Everest, Mount
Highest mountain in world, in *Himalayas*, on frontier of *Nepal* and *Tibet*
Named in 1865 after Sir George Everest (1790−1866), Surveyor-General of India, said by some newspapers of the time to have had 'more to do with papers than with mountains'. Tibetan name is Chomolungma = 'mother goddess of the earth'.

Extremadura
Historic province in *Spain*
Alternative name for *Estremadura*.

Eyre, Lake
South *Australia*, north of *Adelaide*
Named after English explorer Edward J. Eyre (1815−1901), who discovered it in 1840.

F

Fairbanks

Town in *Alaska*, USA, north-east of *Anchorage*

Named in 1902 after Charles Warren Fairbanks, American politician from *Indiana*, later vice-president of USA.

Falkland Islands

In South *Atlantic*, east of *Magellan Strait*

Originally Davis Land (discovered by Captain John Davis in 1592), then named Hawkins Maidenland in 1594 by Sir Richard Hawkins in honour of English queen Elizabeth I (the 'Maiden' queen). Finally named by Captain John Strong in 1690 after Viscount Falkland, chief minister of state of Charles I, who had financed Strong's expedition.

Farewell, Cape

1 In extreme south of *Greenland*

Point of departure of English explorer John Davis in 1586 on his voyage of discovery to *Canada*.

Farewell, Cape

2 In extreme north of South Island, *New Zealand*

Point of departure of Cook in 1770 on his voyage of discovery to east *Australia*.

Faroe Islands

In North *Atlantic*, between *Iceland* and *Shetland Islands, Scotland*

Probably from Danish faar = 'sheep' + öe = 'island'; islands were settled by Norsemen in 861.

Fernando Póo

Former name of island of Bioko, now a province of Equatorial *Guinea, West Africa*

Named after Portuguese explorer Fernão do Pó, who discovered it in 1471 (though he himself named it Formosa—Portuguese = 'beautiful').

Ferrara
Province and its capital in north-east *Italy*
Popularly derived from Italian ferraria = 'forge, ironworks'. But may come from Roman name Forum Alieni, understood as 'market of the foreigner'.

Fiji
Group of islands in South-West *Pacific*, north of *New Zealand*
Of uncertain origin. Perhaps derived from native name of main island, Viti, applied by European explorers to whole group.

Finger Lakes
In *New York* state, USA
So named because of their long, narrow shape.

Finistère
Department of west *Brittany*, *France*
From Old French = 'end of the earth' (Latin finis terrae), ie promontory, in same sense as Cape *Finisterre* and peninsula Land's End in Cornwall, *England.*

Finisterre, Cape
Headland in north-west *Spain*
From Spanish fin de tierra (Latin finis terrae) = 'end of the earth'. (Compare *Finistère*, for which spelling Finisterre is not correct.)

Finland
Republic in north-west *Europe*
Name is of Swedish origin = 'land of the Finns', whose own name is of uncertain origin: perhaps from Germanic finden = 'to seek', ie 'seekers, nomads'. Finns call their own country Suomi, from word probably = 'lake, swamp': Finland has over 60,000 lakes.

Flanders
Historic region in west *Belgium* and north-east *France*
From Flemish Vlaanderen, probably = 'low-lying marsh'. Not likely to be from Roman division of Franks into Fluminarii = 'river-dwellers' (said to have inhabited modern Flanders) and Ripuarii = 'shore-dwellers'.

Flinders, River
Queensland, Australia
Named after English navigator Matthew Flinders (1774–1814) who explored coasts of *Australia* and also gave his name to Flinders Chase, Island and Range.

Florence
City in central north *Italy*
In 200 BC Etruscan name was Faesulae or Fiosele, and in 82 BC Roman name was Colonia Florentia = 'flowering colony', either in literal sense ('with many flowers') or in sense of 'flourishing'. Benvenuto Cellini had theory that name was originally Fluentia = 'flowing', as town was on River *Arno*.

Florida
State in south-east USA
From Spanish Pascua florida = 'flowering Easter'; territory was first sighted, probably on Palm Sunday but perhaps on Easter Sunday, by Spanish expedition of Ponce de León in 1513. Name could also have had literal sense of 'flowering' (as with *Florence*).

Flushing
Seaport in south-west *Netherlands,* at mouth of River *Scheldt*
English version of name is corruption of Dutch Vlissingen = 'fortress on the water'.

Foggia
City in south-west *Italy*, north-west of *Bari*
Possibly from Latin foveae = 'pits, cellars' (on the Piano delle Fosse = 'plain of pits'), or from Italian dialect word fosse = 'cisterns, tanks' (used for watering flocks of sheep).

Fontainebleau
Town in central north *France*, south-east of *Paris*
Early name was Fons Bleaudi. First word is Latin = 'fountain'; second ultimately derives from Indo-European bla = 'to gush, to spout'. Meaning therefore is 'gushing fountain'. Town is famous for hunting-lodge built here in 998 by French king Louis I and for palace of Francis I which developed from it in 16th century.

Formosa
Alternative name of *Taiwan*
Portuguese = 'beautiful'; name was given to island by Portuguese explorers in 1516.

Fort Lamy
Former name of *N'Djamena*, capital of *Chad*, Central *Africa*
Founded by French colonisers in 1900 and named after French soldier and explorer François Lamy (1858–1900).

Fort Worth
City in *Texas*, USA, west of *Dallas*
Named after American major-general William J. Worth, hero of Mexican War of 1846–48.

France
Republic in west *Europe*
Named after Franks, Germanic people who settled in what was Gaul in 5th century AD, with their own name = 'freemen'.

Franche-Comté
Historic province in east *France* near Swiss frontier
French = 'free county'; name was given in 12th century to county of *Burgundy* (as distinct from duchy), to which special privileges were accorded. Geographical extent of region was greater then than now.

Frankfurt
1. City in West *Germany* on River *Main*; 2. City in East *Germany* on River *Oder*
The 2nd city took name from 1st, = 'ford of the Franks', ie 'ford where Franks crossed the river'. Name later acquired meaning of 'free ford', in sense of city offering access to south *Germany*. (Franks in fact never inhabited 2nd city. For origin of name of Franks, see *France*.)

Franklin
District of North-West Territories of north *Canada*, in *Arctic*

Named in memory of English polar explorer and admiral Sir John Franklin (1786–1847), who died in the *Arctic* while searching for the North West Passage. Many places in *Canada* are named after him, including mountains, lakes, islands, strait, cape.

Franz Josef Land
Group of islands in *Arctic*, north of *Novaya Zemlya*, USSR

Discovered by an Austrian-Hungarian expedition led by Julius von Payer and Karl Weyprecht in 1873, and named after Austrian emperor Franz Joseph I (1848–1916).

Frascati
Town and resort in central west *Italy*, south-east of *Rome*

Named after church of St Mary and Sebastian 'in the bushes' (Italian in frascata), built here in 9th century.

Fraser, River
In British *Columbia*, north-west *Canada*

Named after Scot Simon Fraser who crossed Rocky Mountains in 1806–08 and set up a trading station on Fraser Lake.

Freetown
Capital of *Sierra Leone*, West *Africa*

Founded in 1787 as English settlement for liberated slaves. (Compare *Liberia* and *Libreville*.)

Fremantle
City and seaport in Western *Australia*, south-west of *Perth*

Founded in 1829 by English governor James Stirling, who named it after Captain Sir Charles Fremantle who had made survey here before him and annexed the territory.

Friendly Islands
Alternative name for *Tonga*

Name given in 1773 by Cook for friendly welcome accorded him by natives. Islands had been discovered by Dutch expedition of Cornelius Schouten and Jakob LeMaire in 1616 and explored by Tasman in 1643.

Frisian Islands
Off west coasts of *Netherlands,* West *Germany* and *Denmark*

From inhabitants, Frisians, with name probably derived from Old High German fri = 'free' (compare *France*), or possibly from Old Frisian frisiaz = 'frizzled (hair)' or from Indo-European fer, fars = 'coast'.

Frunze
Capital of republic of *Kirghizia,* USSR

Founded as fortress in 19th century with name Pishpek. In 1926 renamed Frunze in honour of Russian revolutionary leader M. V. Frunze (1885−1925), who was born here.

Fujiyama
Extinct volcano, highest mountain in *Japan,* west of *Tokyo*

The 1st element is of uncertain meaning; 2nd is Japanese yama = 'mountain'. Name has been variously interpreted as 'mountain of immortality', 'mountain of abundance' and even 'beauty of the long slope hanging in the sky'. The 1st element could perhaps be from Ainu word = 'fire'.

Furneaux Islands
In *Bass Strait* off north-east *Tasmania,* south of *Australia*

Named after Tobias Furneaux (1735−81), captain of one of Cook's ships, who discovered them on Cook's 2nd expedition of 1772−74.

G

Gabon
Republic in West *Africa*
Named after River Gabon, whose estuary was discovered by Portuguese explorers in 1485 and named Gabão = '(sailor's) cape', perhaps because of appearance of clothing worn by natives here.

Gaborone
Capital of *Botswana*
Name is that of chief Gaborone Matlapin, who reigned here when town was founded in 1890s.

Galápagos Islands
In *Pacific,* on equator west of *Ecuador*, South *America*
From Old Spanish galápago = 'tortoise'; Spanish explorers who discovered islands in 1535 were impressed by large numbers of giant tortoises (*Testudo elephantosus*), which have since become almost extinct.

Galicia
1 Historic region in *Carpathians*, modern *Ukraine* and west *Poland*
Name is Latin form of Old Russian Galich, of uncertain origin; perhaps from Slavonic root gala = 'mountain', or from Lettish and Lithuanian gals = 'end, peak', or from Polish hala = 'mountain pasture'.

Galicia
2 Historic kingdom in north-west *Spain*
Named after Iberian-Celtic tribe, with their own name from Celtic cala = 'waterway', ie 'dwellers by the water'.

Galilee
Sea and region in north *Israel*
From Hebrew galil = 'district' (ie of Gentiles, not Jews). Sea is also called Lake Tiberias, after town on shore, itself named after Roman emperor Tiberius.

Gallipoli
Peninsula in north-west *Turkey* on *Dardanelles*, and port here
From Greek kalliopolis = 'beautiful city'. Turkish name, Gelibolu, is corruption of this.

Gambia
Republic in West *Africa*, surrounded by territory of *Senegal*
Named after River Gambia, in turn named by Portuguese who discovered it in 15th century and who had corrupted native name Ba-Dimma = 'river'.

Gambier Islands
In South *Pacific*, south-east of *Society Islands, Polynesia*
Discovered in 1797 by Captain James Wilson and named after English admiral Lord James Gambier (1756–1833).

Ganges, River
Long river of *India* and *Bangladesh*, flowing into Bay of *Bengal*
From Sanskrit and modern Hindi ganga = 'river'.

Garda, Lake
In north *Italy*, east of *Milan*
From lakeside town with name = 'watch-tower, guard-post'. Roman name was Benacus, probably from Latin bi(-n-)aqua = '(place on) two waters', ie situated at point where lake divides into two bays.

Garonne, River
In south-west *France*
Possibly from pre-Indo-European karr = 'rock, stone' + Gaulish onno = 'river'. From Garonne derives name of *Gironde* department.

Gascony
Historic province in south-west *France*
Latin name was Vasconia, from inhabitants Vascs (Basques), who in 6th century were driven out of their territory in south *Pyrenees* by Western Goths and settled here.

Gaza
Town in south-west *Palestine*
From Hebrew azah = 'strong' (ie 'fortress').

Geelong
Seaport in *Victoria, Australia,* south-west of *Melbourne*
Said to derive from Aboriginal word jillong = 'place of the native companion', this referring to a long-legged water bird common here.

Geneva
City and lake in *Switzerland*
From Celtic gena = 'mouth'. City stands on Rhône at point where it flows out of lake, but 'mouth' is that of little river Avre, which joins Rhône here also.

Georgetown
Capital of *Guyana*, South *America*
Founded by British in 1781 and named after George III. Under Dutch occupation (1784–1812) was called by them Stabroek = 'standing pool'. British then regained control and renamed town Georgetown.

George Town
Capital of Penang state, north *Malaya*
Named after English king George IV in whose reign (1820–30) it was founded.

Georgia
1 State in south-east USA
Became British colony in 1732 and was named in honour of English king George II (reigned 1727–60).

Georgia
2 Republic in south USSR, south of *Caucasus*
Ancient name (BC) of west part of territory was Colchis, and later Iberia. Eastern people were known as Gurz or Gurdzh, of unknown meaning, and this gave Russian name Gruzia, anglicised as Georgia. Russian Orthodox Christians like to relate name to St George, country's patron saint.

Germany

Country of Central *Europe*, divided into East (German Democratic Republic) and West (Federal Republic of Germany)

Named after Germans, people whose name spread BC to other peoples and later to whole family (Germanic) of languages. Roman name for territory between River *Rhine* and River *Danube* was Germania, after inhabitants, whose own name has many possible origins, eg german = 'greedy hands', ermana = 'big (strong) hands'. German name of country is Deutschland, from Old High German thiuda = 'people' + land = 'country'. French name, Allemagne, is from tribe Alemanni (Alamanni), with name = 'all men'.

Gettysburg

Small town in south *Pennsylvania*, USA, south-west of *Harrisburg*

Named after James Gettys, who planned the town + German burg = 'town'. Famous as site of Battle of Gettysburg and Abraham Lincoln's Gettysburg Address (both 1863).

Ghana

Republic in West *Africa*

Before 1957 was *Gold Coast*; then took name of former Negro country which existed here in 4th–13th centuries but covering much larger territory (corresponding to that of modern *Mauritania* and west *Mali*). Name is that of tribal leader, and amounts to royal title, ie = 'king'.

Ghats

Mountain ranges of *India*—Eastern Ghats and Western Ghats—running parallel with coast

Name is Hindi word ghat = 'mountain pass' or 'river landing stairs'. Word also has regular use to refer to river banks terraced for bathing on religious occasions, as those of *Ganges* at Varanasi (*Benares*).

Ghent

City in east *Flanders, Belgium*

Probably from Celtic condati = 'confluence'; town is situated at point where River *Scheldt* flows into River Lys.

Gibraltar
Rocky mountain and British colony at its foot in extreme south of *Spain*
From Arabic Jabal Ṭāriq = 'mountain of Tarik' (Arab general Ṭāriq ibn Ziyād who crossed to territory from *Africa* in 711 and captured it).

Gilbert Islands
Former name of *Kiribati*, in South-West *Pacific*, northeast of *Papua New Guinea*
Discovered by Cook and named after Thomas Gilbert, captain of one of his ships, the *Resolution*, who explored them in 1788.

Gippsland
District in south-east *Victoria, Australia*
Named by Polish explorer Count Strzelecki in 1840 after Sir George Gipps, Governor of *New South Wales*.

Gironde
Department in south-west *France*, forming estuary of River *Garonne* and River *Dordogne*
Name is variant of *Garonne*, of same origin.

Goa
Territory on west coast of *India*
Probably corruption of local name Goe moat = 'fruitful land'; territory was Portuguese province from 1510 to 1961.

Gobi
Desert in Central *Asia*, largely in *Mongolia* and north *China*
From Mongolian gobi = 'desert', though Mongolians have no name for whole desert but only for sections of it. Chinese name is Shamo = 'sandy sea'.

Godwin-Austen, Mount
2nd highest mountain in world, in *Karakoram* range, north *Kashmir, India*
Named after Lieutenant-Colonel Godwin-Austen of Survey of India, who first sighted it in 1865. Alternative name is *K2*.

Gold Coast
Former name of *Ghana*
Name was given by Portuguese in 1471, with reference to gold found as natural deposit here in rivers. Name changed to *Ghana* in 1957.

Golden Gate
Strait at entrance to *San Francisco* Bay, *California*, USA
Strait was probably seen by Drake in 1579, but actual discovery first recorded by Spanish a century later, when they named it La Boca del Puerto de San Francisco = 'the mouth of the port of San Francisco'. Present name given in 1846 by American general and explorer John Charles Frémont, taking it from Turkish *Golden Horn*. Name became increasingly significant with Californian gold rush two years later.

Golden Horn
Inlet of *Bosporus* forming harbour of *Istanbul, Turkey*
So named because of abundance of fish, especially tunny, which are trapped here on entering bay from *Black Sea*. 'Golden' refers to 'richness' of fish; 'Horn' to shape of harbour, which is branched and winding like antlers.

Good Hope, Cape of
Headland in south-west *Cape Province*, South *Africa*
First rounded by Portuguese navigator Bartolomeu Dias in 1488, who named it Cabo Tormentoso = 'stormy cape' (it is here that waters of *Atlantic* and Indian Ocean meet). But Portuguese king John II regarded such a harsh name unpromising for possible future trade with *India* and renamed it Cabo da Bõa Esperança = 'cape of good hope'.

Gorky
City and port on River *Volga*, east of *Moscow*, USSR
So named in 1932 in honour of Russian writer Maxim Gorky, born here in 1868. Earlier name was Nizhny Novgorod = 'lower Novgorod' (ie situated 'lower'—further south —in country than *Novgorod* in north-west USSR).

Gotland

Island in *Baltic Sea*, off south-east coast of *Sweden*

Possibly from Germanic word = 'god' (island was centre of heathen cult), or from word = 'water current'. More likely to be derived from name of Goths, who inhabited Sweden early AD, with their own name probably deriving from Old Norse gotnar = 'men'.

Graham Land

Peninsula in *Antarctic*, west of *Weddell Sea*

Discovered by John Biscoe in 1832, who named it after Sir James Graham, First Lord of Admiralty.

Grahamstown

Town in *Cape Province, South Africa*, north-east of *Port Elizabeth*

Named after Scottish colonel John Graham, who founded it in 1812.

Granada

Province and city in *Andalusia*, south *Spain*

Said to be from Spanish = 'pomegranate', not because many grow here, but because town is situated on 4 hills divided like the divisions of a pomegranate. Or perhaps from Moorish name Karnattah, said to = 'hill of strangers'.

Gran Chaco

Large plain in South *America*, largely in north *Argentina* and south *Paraguay*

From Spanish gran = 'big' + Indian (Guarani) chaco = 'hunting field'.

Great Barrier Reef

Greatest coral reef in world, off north-east coast of *Queensland, Australia*

So named by Cook in 1770. Reefs and islands form great natural breakwater (barrier) stretching nearly 2300 km (1200 miles).

Great Bear Lake

In *Mackenzie*, North-West Territories, *Canada*

Probably translation of Indian name (through French Lac du grand ours), given to lake on account of large number of bears here.

Great Britain
Kingdom of *England, Scotland* and *Wales*, west *Europe*
'Great' as opposed to 'Little' Britain, ie *Brittany*.

Great Slave Lake
In south *Mackenzie*, North-West Territories, *Canada*
Named after Indian tribes who once inhabited its shores
and were driven north by Cree Indians who called them
Awokanak = 'slaves'.

Greece
Republic in south-east *Europe*
Name is of Italic origin; Greeks were small tribe living in
Aipiros (region in modern north-west *Greece* and south
Albania), nearest part of *Balkan* Peninsula to *Italy*. Name
then spread to whole country. Name of people probably
derives from Indo-European gra = 'venerable'.

Greenland
Large island belonging to *Denmark* off north-east coast
of North *America*
Name is of Scandinavian origin and is literal = 'green
land'. Given by Norseman Eric the Red in 982 with aim of
attracting settlers here, though country is in fact largely
cold and infertile.

Grenada
Independent state and one of *Windward Islands, West
Indies*
Discovered in 1498 by Columbus who named it Conception, after religious feast of Immaculate Conception. Present name is that of Spanish *Granada*, although identity of
namer is still uncertain.

Grenoble
City in south-east *France*
Latin name was Gratianopolis = 'town of Gratian' (Roman
emperor who founded it in 4th century). Modern name
derives from this.

Guadalquivir, River

River of south *Spain* flowing south-west through *Seville* into *Atlantic*

From Arabic Wādī al-Kabīr = 'river of great water'. (Guada- is common 1st element of many Spanish names, from Arabic wadi = 'river, ravine'.)

Guadeloupe

One of *Windward Islands, West Indies*

Discovered by Columbus in 1493 who named it Santa Maria de Guadelupe after monastery on River Guadelupe in *Estremadura*, west *Spain*.

Guam

Largest of *Mariana Islands*, West *Pacific*

First sighted by Spanish explorers led by Magellan on St John's Day 1521 and named San Juan (= 'St John'). Present name is native corruption of this.

Guatemala

Republic in Central *America*

Name is Spanish version of Indian (probably Tuendal) uhatzmalha = 'mountain that gushes out water' (referring to volcano Agua), though earlier explanation of origin had been from Aztec quauhtemellan = 'land of the eagle' (tribal totemic bird).

Guernsey

2nd largest of Channel Islands, west of *Normandy, France*

Possibly from Old Norse gron(-s-)oy = 'green island', or perhaps from Breton guern = 'alder-tree'. Roman name may have been Sarnia or perhaps Lisia.

Guiana

Name of various countries in north-east of South *America*: 1. British Guiana (now *Guyana*); 2. Dutch Guiana (now Surinam); 3. French Guiana

Discovered by Columbus in 1498 and explored in 1499 by Vespucci and Hojeda, latter naming territory after people, the Guaizas, whose own name = 'respected' (ie 'we who must be respected').

Guinea
3 republics in West *Africa*: Guinea, Equatorial Guinea, and Guinea-*Bissau*
Probably from Berber aguinau = 'black (-skinned people)'. Name was general one for this area of Africa, and in turn gave name of coin called guinea, originally made from gold from Guinea.

Gulf Stream
Warm ocean current in North *Atlantic*
Originates in Gulf of *Mexico*; name was suggested in 1772 by American statesman Benjamin Franklin. Earlier name was *Florida* Stream.

Guyana
Republic in north-west of South *America*
Same word as *Guiana*; until 1966 was British *Guiana*.

Guyenne
Historic province in south-west *France*
Corruption of Latin Aquitania (French *Aquitaine*); in 12th century province consisted of duchy formed from *Aquitaine* and *Gascony*. (Name also spelt Guienne.)

H

Haarlem

City in north *Netherlands*, west of *Amsterdam*
From Dutch dialect haar = 'hill' + lem = 'clay'.

Hague, The

City—seat of government but not capital—in west *Netherlands*
Originally hunting-lodge of Dutch counts, set in a wood, from Dutch gravenhage = 'count's enclosure' (Old High German hagan = 'hedge').

Haifa

Chief seaport of *Israel*, on *Mediterranean* north-east of *Tel Aviv*
Probably from Hebrew keph = 'cliff'. City is on Mount Carmel.

Haiti

Republic in west part of island of *Hispaniola*, *West Indies*
From native (Caribbean) name, probably = 'mountainous', or perhaps 'rocky, high'.

Halifax

City and seaport in *Nova Scotia*, east *Canada*
Founded by English settlers in 1749 and named in honour of Earl of Halifax (1661–1715), who as President of Board of Trade had actively supported British colonisation.

Hamburg

City in north of West *Germany*, at mouth of River *Elbe*
From Germanic ham = 'inlet' + burg = '(fortified) town'. Or perhaps from Hammaburg = 'fortress in a wood'. City was founded by Charlemagne in 811.

Hamilton

1 City in *Ontario, Canada*
Founded in 1813 by George Hamilton, who had bought farmland here the previous year.

Hamilton
2 City in state of *Ohio*, USA
Named in honour of Alexander Hamilton (1757—1804),
American statesman and officer in War of Independence.
Various other American towns are also named after him.

Hamilton
3 City on North Island, *New Zealand*
Named after English captain John Hamilton, killed here in
1864 in war against Maoris.

Hanoi
Capital of *Vietnam*
Original name was Kecho = 'capital'. Present name came
into use only in 19th century, = 'surrounded by a river' (ie
by *Red River*).

Hanover
City and former province in central West *Germany*
Original name was Honovere = 'high bank' (ie built on
banks of navigable River Leine). Historic original site is
now referred to in German as am hohen Ufer = 'on the
high bank', and this is modern equivalent of name.

Harare
Capital of *Zimbabwe*, south-east Central *Africa*
Name is that of small hill here (kopje) on which present city
was founded as Fort *Salisbury* in 1890. Hill took name from
chief Neharare, who is said to be buried here.

Harpers Ferry
Small town in West *Virginia*, USA
Named after Robert Harper, who started ferry service here
about 1748. Town lies at confluence of River *Potomac* and
River Shenandoah.

Harrisburg
State capital of *Pennsylvania*, USA
Named after English Quaker John Harris, whose son
founded city in 1785, + German burg = 'town'.

Hartford
State capital of *Connecticut*, USA
Originally named Newtown when founded by English
settlers in 1635; renamed Hartford in 1637 after English
town Hertford (but spelt with 'a' to reflect pronunciation).

Harz Mountains
Range in West *Germany* between River *Elbe* and River *Weser*

From Old High German hart = 'wood, forest' (not from modern German Harz = 'resin'). Mountains are well wooded and were once 90% covered with trees.

Havana
Capital of *Cuba*

Of unknown origin, perhaps from Indian tribal name. Founded in 1514 by Spanish explorer Diego Velásquez with name San Cristóbal de la Habana (= 'St Christopher of Habana') in honour of Christopher Columbus.

Hawaii
Group of islands in North *Pacific*, a state of USA

Discovered by Spanish explorers in 1527 and given native (Polynesian) name = 'place of the gods', referring to two volcanoes Mauna Kea and Mauna Loa, regarded as abode of the gods. In 1778 Cook (murdered here the following year) named them *Sandwich Islands*. Name reverted to Hawaii in 1898.

Hawke's Bay (Hawke Bay)
Province on North Island, *New Zealand*

Named in 1769 by Cook after Admiral Sir Edward Hawke, First Lord of British Admiralty. Name originally given to bay, after which province was named.

Hebrides
Group of islands off west coast of *Scotland, Great Britain*

Of unknown origin; mentioned by Pliny as Hebudae and by Ptolemy as Eboudai. Norsemen named them sudur öer = 'southern islands' (ie in relation to *Norway*); 1st element of this name is preserved in name of bishopric of Sodor and Man, which formerly included Hebrides. Suggestion has been made that 'u' of original spelling became 'ri' by error of transcription.

Heidelberg
City in West *Germany*, south-east of *Mannheim*

Probably from German Heidelbeere = 'bilberry', or possibly from Heid = 'heath' + Berg = 'mountain'.

Helena

State capital of *Montana*, USA

Named after home town Helena, *Minnesota*, of one of gold-seekers here in 1864, when town was founded.

Heligoland

Island in *North Sea* off north-west coast of West *Germany*

From Old High German heilag = 'holy' + land; there was once a heathen shrine on the island. But could also perhaps be from Old Friesian halik = 'steep' (island has steep cliffs) + land.

Helsinki

Capital of *Finland*

Founded by Swedes in 1550 with name Helsingfors, from name of tribe, Helsingi, + Swedish fors = 'waterfall' (of River Wanda, near which town was built). In 1648 town was moved to present site on Gulf of *Finland*. Helsinki is Finnish version of Swedish name.

Hercegovina

With *Bosnia* forms north republic of *Yugoslavia*

From Serbian = 'duke land' (from Old High German herizoge = 'duke'); country became dukedom (duchy) in 1448 and kept name while under Turkish rule from 1483 to 1878.

Hessen

'Land' in west of West *Germany*, former grand duchy

Probably from name of Germanic tribe Hatti who inhabited central *Germany* early AD. Their name comes from Germanic hattu = 'hat', with reference to Turkish-style turbans that they wore. In 8th century name became Hessii, then Hessia.

Himalayas

Mountain system in Central *Asia*, largely in south *Tibet*

Probably from Sanskrit hima = 'snow' + ālaya = 'abode', although another explanation gives derivation of name from goddess Shimalia (= 'mistress of the white mountain').

Hispaniola
Island in *West Indies*, divided into (west) *Haiti* and (east) *Dominican Republic*
Discovered by Columbus in 1492 who named it La Isla Española (Spanish = 'the Spanish island), although native name of whole island then was *Haiti*. This was later corrupted to Hispaniola.

Hobart
Capital of *Tasmania, Australia*
Until 1881 was Hobarttown; named after English Secretary of State Lord Hobart who founded city in 1804 and used island as penal colony.

Ho Chi Minh City
City in south *Vietnam* and former capital of South Vietnam
Name was given to former *Saigon* in 1976 when North and South Vietnam were united as single Socialist Republic, and was tribute to Ho Chi Minh, president of North Vietnam 1954–69.

Hohenzollern
Ancestral castle of Hohenzollern dynasty on Mount Zollern, south-west of *Stuttgart*, West *Germany*
From German hoch = 'high' + name of Mount Zollern, from Old German zolra = 'sugar-loaf mountain' (ultimately from Indo-European tul = 'mountain, height'). Name Hohenzollern (that of Swabian family which became successively Electors of *Brandenburg* (1415–1701), kings of *Prussia* (1701–1918) and German emperors (1871–1918)) combined with that of *Württemberg* to form 'Land' of Württemberg-Hohenzollern in 1945. (See also *Baden-Württemberg*.)

Hokkaido
North island of *Japan*
Japanese = 'land of the northern sea' (hoku = 'north', kai = 'sea', dō = 'division')

Holland
Used as alternative name for *Netherlands*, but properly name of two provinces: North Holland and South Holland

Possibly from Dutch holt = 'grove' + land, ie 'wooded land'; or perhaps from hal = 'low' + land, with same meaning as *Netherlands*.

Honduras
Republic in Central *America*, with *Belize*, formerly British Honduras, to the north of it

From Spanish = 'depths'; story is that when Spanish sailors reached coast of Honduras in 1524 they thanked God for having brought them safely over the depths of the *Atlantic*; sea off the coast here is in fact very deep and for many years a good harbour could not be built.

Hong Kong
British crown colony on coast of south *China*, chiefly an island

From Chinese Hiangkiang = 'fragrant water', 'good harbour'.

Honolulu
State capital of *Hawaii*, USA

From Hawaiian hono = 'harbour' + lulu = 'quiet, calm', ie 'sheltered harbour'.

Honshu
Largest of islands forming *Japan*

Japanese = 'chief province' (hon = 'main, principal' + shū = 'province, state').

Hook of Holland
Seaport in south *Netherlands*, west of *Rotterdam*

From Dutch hoek = 'point, edge'; port is at south-west extremity of province of South *Holland*.

Horn, Cape
Rocky headland in extreme south of South *America*

First rounded in 1616 by Dutch navigator Willem Schouten, who named it after his native town in the *Netherlands*, Hoorn (in province of North *Holland*).

Houston
City in state of *Texas*, USA
Founded in 1836 and named after General Samuel Houston (1793–1863), who gained independence of *Texas* from *Mexico*.

Hudson Bay
Gulf in north *Canada*
Named after English explorer Henry Hudson (1550–1611), who discovered it in 1610. The previous year he had explored Hudson River, which he had named North River.

Humboldt, River
In state of *Nevada*, USA
Named after German scientist Alexander von Humboldt (1769–1859), who had explored North *America* in 1799–1804. After him are also named Humboldt Bay (*California*), Humboldt Sea, Humboldt Mountains.

Hungary
Republic in south-east of Central *Europe*
Possibly from name of people, Ugrians, who originally lived on River Ugra, in basin of River *Danube*. Hungarians call themselves Magyars, from kär = 'man' + prefix ma = 'land', ie 'landsmen, natives'.

Huron, Lake
One of Great Lakes, between USA and *Canada*
From name of Indian Huron tribe who once lived on its shores. French settlers named them thus from their bristly hair, which was like that of a boar (French hure = 'boar's head'), perhaps also with reference to their 'bristly' nature.

Hwang Ho/Huanghe, River
2nd longest river in *China*, also known as *Yellow River*
Chinese = 'yellow river'.

Hyderabad
City in central south *India*
From Persian name Haidar, through Arabic, + Iranian abad = 'town', ie 'Haidar's town'. (Personal name = 'lion', regarded as ruler's title.)

I

Ibadan
City in south-west *Nigeria*, West *Africa*
From Arabic ibada = 'divine service'; city has long been a centre of Islam.

Iberia
Ancient name for peninsula of *Portugal* and *Spain*
From name of River *Ebro*, formerly Ebros, which flows through it. (See *Ebro, River.*)

Ibiza
One of *Balearic Islands* in *Mediterranean*, off east coast of *Spain*
Name is Phoenician, given by Carthaginians when they settled on these islands in 654 BC. Probably from Phoenician word = 'island', or perhaps connected with Basque ibis = 'stream'. Could also be from Phoenician ibrusim = 'island of fir trees'.

Iceland
Island republic in North *Atlantic*
Name is literal = 'ice land'. Given, in form Island, by Viking Floki who landed on island in 960s, although another Viking had landed on opposite coast nearly 100 years before him and had given island name of Snjoland = 'snow land'.

Idaho
State in central east USA
An Indian (Kiowa-Apache) name of uncertain meaning: possibly = 'fish-eaters' or 'mountain gem' (referring to deposits of gold and silver in mountains).

Île de France
Historic region in north *France* with *Paris* as centre
French = 'island of France', either because region is watered by many important rivers (eg *Marne, Seine, Oise*) or because it was administrative centre from which early French kings ruled.

Illinois
State in central east USA

Named after River Illinois (tributary of *Mississippi*), in turn named after Indian Illini tribe, with name derived from Algonquian word = 'people, men, warriors'. Final 's', indicating plural, was added by French settlers who conquered territory in 1673.

India
Republic in South *Asia*

Named after River *Indus*, which flows through what is now Pakistan.

Indiana
State in central east USA

Latin-type name was given by French settlers in 1702 after Indian tribes who formed population of territory, and was officially adopted about 1765 by land developers here known as the Indiana Company. State was formed in 1816, though by 1830s not one native Indian was left.

Indianapolis
State capital of *Indiana*, USA

Name was given to city when it was founded in 1820, from Indiana + Greek polis = 'town'.

Indonesia
Republic of South-East *Asia*

From name of *India* + Greek nesos = 'island', ie 'island India'.

Indus, River
Great river of *Pakistan*, flowing into Arabian Sea

From Sanskrit sindhu = 'river'. Romans and Greeks left off initial 's' when pronouncing name.

Innsbruck
City in west *Austria*

From German Brücke = 'bridge' + name of River Inn, on which city stands. Name of river is probably from Celtic enos = 'water'.

Interlaken
Resort in *Alps, Switzerland*
From Latin inter = 'between' + lacus = 'lake'. Town is situated between Lake Thun and Lake Brienz. Name is of Latin origin, not Germanic, as town arose by Augustinian monastery in 1130.

Ionian Sea
Part of *Mediterranean* between south *Italy* and *Greece*
Named after Greek people, Ionians, who settled on most of islands in *Aegean Sea*, with their own name = 'wanderers, rovers'.

Iowa
State in central USA
Named in 1846 after River Iowa, tributary of *Mississippi*. Name is of Indian (probably Sioux) origin, possibly = 'cradling', or from tribal name Ayuba = 'sleepy' (nickname given to tribe, in sense 'sleepy', by neighbouring Dakotas). French map of 1673 records name in form Ouaouiatonon.

Iran
Republic in South-West *Asia*
From Sanskrit aria (Iranian ariya) = 'worthy'. Name originally applied to Indo-European people who had settled here several thousand years BC and from whom Iranian family of languages originated. Name of country until 1935 was *Persia*.

Iraq
Republic in South-West *Asia*
Name is Arabic ʿiraq = 'the well-rooted country'. Classical name for region here was *Mesopotamia*.

Ireland
Republic west of *Great Britain*
Name is in English form = 'land of the Irish'. Irish name of country is Éire, from Old Irish eirin (compare poetic name Erin) = 'western' or possibly 'green' (compare name Emerald Isle, used in poetic or familiar sense).

Irrawaddy, River

Main river of *Burma*, flowing south-west through entire length of country

Name is thought to derive from Hindi airāvatī = 'elephant river', and connection with Arabic wadi = 'river' is unlikely.

Irtysh, River

Rises in *China* and flows west through USSR to join River *Ob*

Perhaps from Mongolian ertis = 'river', or from Kazakh ir = 'land' + tysh = 'to dig' (though name existed before Kazakhs settled upper reaches of river). Also perhaps from Bashkir yrtysh = 'rushing' (though river is largely slow-flowing). Most likely is connected with Turkish ir = 'to flow'.

Islamabad

Capital of *Pakistan*

Iranian = 'city of Islam' (Islam + Iranian abad = 'city').

Ismailia

City on *Suez* Canal, *Egypt*

Named after Ismail Pasha, Turkish khedive (viceroy) of *Egypt* from 1863 to 1879. Under his rule *Suez* Canal was completed (1869).

Israel

Republic in South-West *Asia*

From name of Hebrew tribe, Israelites, in turn with name derived from Israel = 'god Isra'. In 10th century BC was name of Jewish country in *Palestine*. In Bible Israel is 2nd name of Jacob and is interpreted as 'God's warrior' (with reference to Genesis 32:28), from Hebrew sara = 'to fight' + El = 'God'.

Istanbul

City in *Turkey*, on *Bosporus*

Many possible meanings; among them are: 1. from Turkish islam-bul = 'city of Islam'; 2. from Greek eis ten polis (dialect is tan polin) = 'into the city'; 3. (most likely) from Turkish corruption of *Constantinople*, its name to 1930.

Istria

Peninsula in north-west *Yugoslavia*, near Italian frontier

From Latin name Histria = 'land of the Istrians' (Illyrian tribe warring against *Rome* in 3rd century BC). Greek writers saw connection between Istria and their name for River *Danube*—Istros—but this link is not clear.

Italy

Republic in south *Europe*

Name arose about 500 BC as Vitalia and originally applied only to *Calabria*, where the Vitali, tribe from the north, had settled, with their own name taken to be connected with Latin vitulus = 'calf', but this may merely be attempt to explain unknown word. In 2nd–1st centuries BC name gradually spread and with rise of Roman empire was established to apply to whole *Apennine* Peninsula.

Ithaca

One of islands in *Ionian Sea*, off west coast of *Greece*

Letter 'i' which begins many *Mediterranean* names derives from Phoenician word = 'island, land'. Original name was Thiaki, of uncertain meaning. (Ancient Ithaca in *Odyssey* was not this island but Levkas. When name 'transferred' is not clear.)

Ivory Coast

Republic on Gulf of *Guinea*, West *Africa*

Ivory (elephant tusks) was traded here by Portuguese from 1447, later in keen competition with the East India Company. English name is translation of French Côte d'Ivoire, in turn translated from original Portuguese.

J

Jackson
State capital of *Mississippi*, USA
Named after Andrew Jackson (1767–1845), 7th president of the USA. (Named after him also is Jacksonville, *Florida*.)

Jaffa
Seaport in *Israel*, on *Mediterranean*
From Arabic yafe = 'bright, visible' (ie visible from afar). In 1949 incorporated with *Tel Aviv*.

Jakarta
Capital of *Indonesia*, on north-west coast of *Java*
Perhaps from Sanskrit jaya-kerta = 'place of victory', or from Iranian kert = 'built (place)'. Dutch settlers who built fort here in 1619 called it Batavia, after their homeland on delta of River *Rhine*, but city reverted to name Jakarta in 1949.

Jamaica
Independent island state in *Caribbean Sea*, south of *Cuba*
From native (Arawak) name Xaymaca = 'island of springs', with reference to plentiful supply of water on island. Columbus, who landed on island in 1494 named it Santiago as landing was made on St James's Day (Spanish San Jago), 25 July, but native name was one that was adopted.

Jamestown
Town in *New York* state, USA
Named after James Prendergast, an early settler who selected this site for his mill in 1811 (unlike Jamestown, *Virginia*, named in 1607 in honour of English king James I).

Jan Mayen
Island in *Arctic* between *Iceland* and *Spitsbergen*
First discovered by Hudson (see *Hudson Bay*) in 1607; rediscovered by Dutch captain Jan Mayen in 1611 and named after him.

Japan
Country in East *Asia*
From Chinese name of country Ji-pen-kue = 'land of the rising sun'. Japanese name of country is Nihon (conventional Nippon).

Java
Island in *Indonesia*, south-east of *Sumatra*
From Sanskrit java dvipa = 'barley island'. Settlers here BC from *India* and *Ceylon* found rich barley fields on island.

Jefferson City
State capital of *Missouri*, USA
Named after Thomas Jefferson (1743–1826), 3rd president of the USA.

Jericho
Town in *Jordan*, north-east of *Jerusalem*
From Hebrew j'richo = 'scented place' (with Hebrew addition ir hall' marim = 'of the palm-trees').

Jersey
Largest of Channel Islands, west of *Normandy, France*
Possibly from Old Frisian gers = 'grass' + Scandinavian ey = 'island', or from personal name of Viking who seized the island—Geirr—or from Old Norse jarl = 'lord' (compare English word 'earl'). Unlikely that name is a corruption of Roman Caesarea (after Julius Caesar) since it has not been finally proved that this name applied specifically to Jersey (though it did to some island between *Orkney* and *Ushant*).

Jerusalem
City in *Palestine*, since 1948 politically divided between *Israel* and *Jordan* but since 1967 recognised as capital of *Israel* (although not by United Nations)
In Assyrian cuneiform was Urusalimmi, and in Egyptian hieroglyphics Shalam. Probably from Old Hebrew shalem = 'peace' (derived from root word = 'stone') + ieru = 'house, people', ie 'house of peace' or 'house of stone'.

Jodhpur
City in north-west *India*, south-west of *Delhi*
From Sanskrit = 'military town'.

Johannesburg
City in *Transvaal*, South *Africa*
Founded by gold-seekers in 1886. Probably named after Johannes Rissik, government surveyor of *Transvaal* + Dutch burg = 'town', or possibly after Johannes Meyer, mining commissioner of the time.

Jordan
Kingdom in South-West *Asia*
Named after River Jordan, with its own name of unknown origin: perhaps from Hebrew jarden = 'drain, channel' or jarda = 'to rush, to roar'.

Juan de Fuca Strait
Separates *Vancouver* Island, *Canada*, from state of *Washington*, north-west USA
Discovered in 1592 by Greek sailor Apostolos Valerianos, serving *Spain* with name of Juan de Fuca, and named after him.

Juneau
State capital of *Alaska*, USA
Named in 1881 after Joseph Juneau, one of first gold-seekers here the previous year.

Jungfrau
Mountain in Swiss *Alps*, south-east of *Interlaken*
German = 'maiden', either because silhouette of mountain has appearance of nun or girl in white or, more likely, so named in contrast to neighbouring dark Mönch (= 'monk') Mountain.

Jura
Mountains on frontier between *France* and *Switzerland*, and French department here
Name describes nature of mountains, and means 'forest', from Gaulish juria, itself ultimately related to Slavonic gora = 'mountain'. Mountains also gave name to Jurassic period of geological time.

Jutland
Peninsula in north *Europe* consisting of south *Denmark* and north of West *Germany*
Named after Jutes, Germanic tribe who settled here BC, with their own name derived from Old Norse jotar, ytar = 'people'.

K

K2
Alternative name of Mount *Godwin-Austen*
So named from initial of *Karakoram* range, in which it was
the 2nd to be measured. (It is also the 2nd highest in the
world.)

Kabalega Falls
At north end of Lake *Albert* on River *Nile*, *Uganda*,
Central *Africa*
So named in 1972 after former king of Bunyoro, *Uganda*,
who fought against British. Earlier name was *Murchison
Falls*.

Kābul
Capital of *Afghanistan*
On River Kābul, with name of uncertain origin: perhaps
from Iranian word = 'storehouse' (unlikely, as town was
named after river), or from similar word = 'red' or 'horse'.

Kalahari
Desert chiefly in *Botswana*, southern *Africa*
Probably from Bechuana (Tswana) word kgalagadi = 'desert', although one theory derives source from native name
Karri-karri = 'torture, suffering'. Element -ri is regarded as
variant of Hottentot -di. Boers (Dutch colonisers of South
Africa) called it Bosjeveld = 'thorn field', from which Bush-
men (aboriginal race of South African hunters) derive their
name.

Kalgoorlie
Town in Western *Australia*, north-east of *Perth*
From aboriginal name of native shrub.

Kamchatka Peninsula
In north-east USSR, between Sea of *Okhotsk* and *Bering Sea*
Originally name of river. Various explanations of name, all equally unlikely: eg from name of brave warrior Khonchat, from mythical lovers Kam (son of a mountain) and Chatka (daughter of a volcano) who threw themselves to their death here, from local name of Khonchalo tribe, from dialect word = 'cape, peninsula'.

Kampala
Capital of *Uganda*
Name that of hill here on which town was built, itself probably meaning 'impala hill', and referring to former custom of grazing tame impala on its slopes.

Kanchenjunga
3rd highest mountain in world, in *Himalayas*, on *Nepal-Sikkim* border
Said to be from Tibetan kang = 'snow' + chen = 'big' + dzo = 'treasure' + nga = 'five', ie '(mountain of) five big snowy treasures' (referring to its 5 peaks).

Kandy
Town in *Sri Lanka*, north-east of *Colombo*
From Sinhalese kandi = 'mountain' (ie 'town in mountain country').

Kansas
State in central USA.
Named after River Kansas, in turn named after Indian (Sioux) tribe, Kansa—although perhaps tribe was named after river. Tribal name said to mean 'south wind', ie tribe living where south wind blows. Final 's' is probably plural, added by French settlers (compare *Arkansas*)

Karachi
City and seaport on Arabian Sea in *Pakistan*, of which it is former capital
In 18th century was only small fishing village. Name derives from Baluchi tribe of Kulachi (see *Baluchistan*), itself probably named after its headman.

Karakoram Range
Mountain system in north *Kashmir*, Central *Asia*
From Turkish kara = 'black' + korum = 'mountain, rocks'.

Karlovy Vary
Resort and spa in *Czechoslovakia*, north-west of *Prague*
Czech = 'Charles's springs'. Holy Roman emperor and king of Germany Charles (Karl) IV (1316–78) discovered warm mineral springs here in 1347 when building a hunting-lodge. German name is Karlsbad, with same meaning.

Karlsruhe
City in West *Germany*, north-west of *Stuttgart*
German = 'Charles's rest'. German count Karl Wilhelm von Baden-Durlach built a hunting-lodge here in 1715, thus founding present city.

Kashmir
State in north-west *India*
Said to be from Sanskrit Kasyapa-mira = 'sea of Kasyapa' (legendary hero who, according to story, cut pass through mountains here to link up mountain lake with River *Indus*).

Kassel
City in West *Germany*, north-east of *Frankfurt*
From Latin castellum = 'castle'. Name in 913 was Chassala. (Castle was that of Roman fortress.)

Katanga
Province in south-east *Zaïre*, Central *Africa*
From African (Hausa) name = 'walls, buildings', referring to former capital, Yoruba. In 1972 renamed Shabu, Swahili = 'copper'.

Katmandu
Capital of *Nepal*
Name comes from Nepalese kāṭh = 'wood' + mandir = 'temple', apparently referring to wooden temple said to have been built from a single tree in 1596 by Raja Lachmina Singh.

Kattegat
Strait between *Sweden* and *Jutland, Denmark*
From Old Scandinavian kati = 'ship, vessel' + gata = 'way'. Old Dutch maps name it as *Skagerrak*, and *Skagerrak* as Nordzee (= 'north sea').

Kazakhstan
Republic in south USSR, in Central *Asia*
Named after Kazakhs + Iranian stan = 'country'. Kazakhs, people of Turkish origin, have name probably = 'freemen'.

Keeling Islands
Alternative name for *Cocos Islands*, Indian Ocean
Discovered in 1609 by Captain William Keeling of East India Company.

Keewatin
East district of North-West Territories, *Canada*
From Indian (Cree) word = 'north wind', ie tribe living where north wind blows. (Compare *Kansas.*)

Kennedy, Cape
Now *Cape Canaveral*, on east coast of *Florida*, USA
Originally *Cape Canaveral*. Renamed in 1963 in honour of John F. Kennedy (1917–63), 35th president of the USA. Officially reverted to *Cape Canaveral* in 1973.

Kentucky
State in central south USA
Named after River Kentucky, in turn with name derived either from Indian kan-tuk-kee = 'land dark with blood' (referring to inter-tribal wars), or from kan-tuc-kec = 'land of green reeds', or, most likely, from Iroquois ken-take = 'plain, meadow-land'. Latter origin would mean that river was named after land here.

Kenya
Republic in East *Africa*
Named after Mount Kenya, with name of uncertain origin: possibly simply Swahili = 'mountain', although some see source in Kikuyu kerenyaga = 'mountain of whiteness', referring to glaciers on it.

Kerguelen Islands
In Indian Ocean, south-east of South *Africa*
Named after French navigator Yves Joseph de Kerguélen-Trémarec (1734–97), who discovered them in 1772.

Kermadec Islands
In South-West *Pacific*, north-east of *Auckland, New Zealand*
Named after one of his ships by French navigator Antoine Raymond Joseph de Bruni d'Entrecasteaux, who discovered some of them in 1793.

Khartoum
Capital of *Sudan*
Headland between River White *Nile* and River Blue *Nile*, where city was founded in 1822; Arabic name is Al-Khurṭūm = 'elephant's trunk', referring to its outline.

Khmer Republic
Former name of Kampuchea: see *Cambodia*
Named after native population, Khmers, whose name is of uncertain meaning, but known to be very old. Originally, final 'r' was not pronounced.

Kicking Horse Pass
Through Rocky Mountains, on frontier between *Alberta* and British *Columbia, Canada*
Discovered in 1858 by Sir James Hector, English geologist, who was kicked by his horse while making his way through it.

Kiel
City in *Schleswig-Holstein*, in north of West *Germany*
In 10th century name was recorded as Kyle, probably = 'ford' or 'spring', and related to English 'keel'.

Kiev
Capital of republic of *Ukraine*, USSR
Probably named after legendary ferryman Kiy, said to have founded city on River *Dnieper*; or perhaps after Prince Kiy, who came with Oleg to capture the city in the 9th century. Kiev is the most ancient of all Russian cities: Ptolemy mentions city called Metropolis on River *Dnieper* in 2nd century AD, and it is known as the 'mother of Russian cities'. Exact year when founded not known.

Kilimanjaro
Extinct volcano in north-east *Tanzania*, East *Africa*
From Swahili kilima = 'mountain' + njaro = 'god of cold'.

Kimberley
1. District in north of Western *Australia*; 2. Town in *Cape Province*, South *Africa*
Both named after English colonial secretary Lord Kimberley.

Kingston
Capital of *Jamaica, West Indies*
Founded in 1693 on site of earlier Port Royal, which was destroyed by earthquake in 1692 and named in honour of English king William III.

Kinshasa
Capital of *Zaïre*, Central *Africa*
From Bantu word of unknown origin. Name was that of African settlement where Sir H. M. Stanley founded *Léopoldville* in 1882; in 1966 name reverted to Kinshasa.

Kirghizia
Republic in south-east USSR, bordering on *China*
Named after its native inhabitants, Kirghiz, with their own name of Mongolian origin, perhaps from kir = 'plain' + kis = 'to wander', but this could be attempt to explain unknown name.

Kiribati
Island republic, South-West *Pacific*
Name is indigenous pronunciation of former name of island group, current until 1979, *Gilbert* (Islands). Similar corruption occurs in name of one of islands in group, Kiritimati, formerly Christmas Island.

Kishinev
Capital of republic of *Moldavia*, USSR
Possibly from Moldavian neu = 'new' + Turkish kishlah = 'winter quarters'.

Klondike, River
In *Yukon* Territory, north-west *Canada*
From Indian thron-diuck = 'hammer water', referring to manner in which Indians pounded sticks into river bed to support salmon nets. River gave name to famous gold-bearing region here.

Klyuchevskaya
Highest active volcano in *Asia*, on *Kamchatka* Peninsula, USSR
Named after nearby town of Klyuchi, in turn with name derived from Russian = 'springs'.

Knoxville
City in east *Tennessee*, USA
Originally founded in 1785 as frontier outpost named White's Fort, after James White, former officer of Revolutionary War. In 1791 renamed Knoxville, after Henry Knox, Secretary of War in Washington's cabinet.

Komandorskiye Islands
Between *Kamchatka* Peninsula and *Aleutian Islands*, east USSR
Discovered in 1744 by expedition led by Commander (Russian komandor) Bering, after whom are named one island of this group—Bering Island—and *Bering Strait*.

Korea
Peninsula in East *Asia* on which are situated two politically divided republics of North Korea and South Korea
Name is that of former dynasty from 10th to 14th century, Koryo, itself thought to mean 'high place'. After fall of this dynasty, country took name of Chosen, as Japanese pronunciation of Choson, name of next (Yi) dynasty. This is now used by North Korea, while South Korea calls itself Taehan, from Han, name of ancient states here.

Kosciusko, Mount
Highest mountain in *Australia*, in *New South Wales*, south-west of *Canberra*
Named after Polish hero and statesman Tadeusz Kosciuszko (1746–1817) by Polish explorer Strzelecki, who discovered it in 1839.

Krakatoa
Volcanic island in Sunda Strait, between *Java* and *Sumatra*
Native name is Kerakatau, from Javanese rekatak = 'to split, to crack' + prefix ke-. Volcano erupted violently in 1883, blowing entire north part of island away.

Krakow
2nd largest city in *Poland*, on River *Vistula*, south-west
of *Warsaw*
From personal name Krak or Krok (founder of city or lord of
castle here), whose name is of uncertain origin, possibly
from a Celtic word or from Slavonic krak = 'raven'.

Kuala Lumpur
Capital of *Malaysia*
From Malay kuala = 'mouth, estuary' + lumpur = 'mud'.
City is situated at mouth of River Kelang.

Kuril Islands
Chain of islands extending from south end of *Kamchatka* Peninsula, USSR, to *Hokkaido, Japan*
Number of possible explanations: 1. from Ainu kuri =
'cloud, mist'; 2. from Russian kurit = 'to smoke' (referring
to steam from volcanoes on islands); 3. from Ainu kur =
'people' (as name of inhabitants). Japanese name is Chi-
shima = 'thousand islands'.

Kuwait
Arab state and its capital on north-west coast of Persian Gulf
Arabic name is Al-Kuwayt = 'the enclosed', possibly referring to Portuguese fort built here in 16th century. Arabic
kūt = 'fort'.

Kwangchow/Guangzhou
City in south-east *China* on River Pearl
From Chinese kwan = 'broad, large' + chow, denoting
town of upper rank, ie 'capital of a large territory' (province
of Kwangtung). Former name of Kwangchow/Guangzhou
was *Canton*.

L

Labrador
Coastal territory in north-east *Canada*
Many theories concerning origin of name: 1. sighted by Portuguese navigator Gaspar de Cortereal in 1501 and named by him Terra de lavradores = 'land of ploughmen' (he saw natives as potential slaves working on plantations); 2. (less likely) named by Spanish or Portuguese explorers after Terre de Labour, a small territory in south France; 3. (least likely) from French le bras d'or = 'the golden arm', name given by optimistic gold-seekers. Originally settled by Norsemen in 10th century with name Hellaland = 'rocky land'; later named Vinland = 'land of grapes'.

Laccadive Islands
In Arabian Sea, west of coast of *Malabar*, south-west *India*
From Sanskrit lakshna = 'a hundred thousand' + dvipa = 'island' (there are in fact 14 coral islands and several reefs; perhaps name was meant to include *Maldives* as well).

Ladoga, Lake
Largest lake in *Europe*, in north-west USSR, north-east of *Leningrad*
Probably from Finnish aalto = 'wave' or ala = 'lower'.

Ladysmith
Town in *Natal*, South *Africa*, north-west of *Durban*
Named in honour of (Spanish) wife of Sir Harry Smith, British Governor of Cape Colony 1847–52. Nearby town of Harrismith bears his own name.

Lafayette
Cities in *Indiana* and *Louisiana*, USA
Named in honour of French soldier and statesman, Marquis de la Fayette (1757–1834), who in 1776 fought against British in American War of Independence.

Lagos
Capital of *Nigeria*
Name given by Portuguese in 16th century from lagoon (Portuguese lago) surrounding island on which city stands. Some derive name specifically from port of Lagos on south coast of Portugal.

Lahore
2nd largest city of *Pakistan*, north-east of *Karachi*
Said to have been founded by Lo (Sanskrit Lava), son of Hindu god Rama, but this is merely attempt to explain earlier name of unknown meaning.

Lampedusa
Island in *Mediterranean* between *Malta* and *Tunisia*
Popularly regarded as deriving from Italian lampada = 'lamp', referring to lighthouse here, but name is much older than this, and was recorded by Greek geographer Strabo in 1st century BC/AD as Lopadusa.

Landes
Region in south-west *France* extending parallel to Bay of *Biscay*
French = 'heathland, sandy waste', from Gaulish landa (related to English word 'land'). Region consists largely of moorland and sand-dunes.

Languedoc
Region and historic province in southern *France*
Name arose at end of 13th century, from French langue d'oc = 'language of oc': oc was French word for 'yes' in south of country, as distinct from oïl (later oui) in north.

Lansing
State capital of *Michigan*, USA
Named by emigrants from village of Lansing in *New York* state, in turn named after John Lansing (1754–1829?), politician and lawyer.

Laos
Republic in South-East *Asia*, between *Thailand* and *Vietnam*
Named after Thai people Lao (from Lava), with plural 's' added by Portuguese settlers.

La Paz
Capital of *Bolivia*, South *America*
Full name, given by Spanish in 1548 to mark peace concluded between two warring factions, was Pueblo Nuevo de Nuestra Señora de la Paz = 'new town of Our Lady of Peace'.

Lapland
Region in north *Europe* covering north of *Norway*, *Sweden*, *Finland* and extreme north-west USSR
Named after principal inhabitants, Lapps, whose own name derives from Finnish lappalainen = 'border dwellers'.

La Plata
City on estuary of River *Plate*, *Argentina*, South *America*
From Spanish name of river—Rio de la Plata (see *Argentina*).

Laptev Sea
Part of *Arctic* Ocean, in north central *Siberia*, USSR
Named in 1913 by Russian Geographical Society in honour of *Arctic* expedition of 1733—41 made by Lieutenants Dmitry and Khariton Laptev. Earlier name was Nordenskjöld Sea, after Swedish explorer Nils Nordenskjöld (1832—1901) who discovered North East Passage in 1878—79.

Las Palmas
Largest city in *Canary Islands*, *Spain*
Spanish = 'the palm-trees' (which are prolific here).

Las Vegas
City in south-east *Nevada*, USA
Spanish = 'the meadows' (referring to fields used as camp-sites on early trails).

Latin America
Term used for *Mexico*, Central *America* and South *America*
Comprises countries in which are spoken languages derived from Latin—Spanish and Portuguese—as opposed to North *America*, where chief language is English.

Latvia
Republic in north-west USSR on *Baltic Sea*
Named after principal inhabitants, Letts, whose name is of uncertain origin.

Lausanne
City on north shore of Lake *Geneva, Switzerland*
Original name was Lausonna or Leusonna, probably from Gaulish leusa = 'smooth stone'. Other theories trace name back to Celtic personal name Lousis or to Roman name of Celtic origin Lausodunum = 'fort on the river Laus' (with name of river = 'stony').

Lebanon
Republic in South-West *Asia*, south of *Syria*, on *Mediterranean*
Named after mountains, from Aramaic word laban = 'white', referring either to snow or to colour of limestone rock.

Leeuwin, Cape
Headland in extreme south-west of Western *Australia*
Named after Dutch ship, with name = 'lioness', whose crew discovered it in 1622.

Leeward Islands
In *West Indies*, extending south-east from *Puerto Rico* to *Windward Islands*
Islands are situated in position sheltered from prevailing north-east Trade Winds (in contrast to *Windward Islands*).

Leghorn
City and seaport in north-west *Italy*, south-west of *Pisa*
English name is corruption of Italian Livorno, named after Liburni, ancient inhabitants of modern *Croatia*. Element -orn seems to have been added by Illyrians. Town was once Portus Herculis = 'port of Hercules' (Greek god venerated along *Mediterranean* coast).

Le Havre
City and seaport in north *France* at mouth of River *Seine*
Founded by French king Francis I in 1517 as Le Havre de Grâce = 'the harbour of grace', as was on site of fishing village with chapel dedicated to Notre Dame de Grâce (Our Lady of Grace).

Leiden

City in south *Netherlands,* north-east of The *Hague*

Probably from leithen = 'canal' (city is on canal leading to *North Sea*), or from Gaulish Lugdunum (see *Lyons*). However, latter name may not be genuine Roman one at all, but devised in 16th century by statesman Janus Dousa (Johan van der Does).

Leipzig

City in East *Germany,* south-west of *Berlin*

From Slavonic name Lipsk, from lipa = 'lime-tree'. In 920 town was fishing village by lime-grove. In 11th century name was recorded as Urbs Libzi.

Le Mans

City in north-west central *France,* south-west of *Paris*

Roman name in 2nd century BC was Vindinon, from Gaulish vindo = 'white'. In 4th century AD took name of tribe of Cenomanni (perhaps = 'hill dwellers'), whose capital city it was. Name was shortened to Celmans, with 1st element confused with French le = 'the'. (See also *Maine* (2), *Cremona.*)

Lemnos

Island in north of *Aegean Sea,* between *Greece* and *Turkey*

From Phoenician = 'white': sailors were impressed by hills of white pumice-stone.

Lena, River

Longest river in USSR, rising near Lake *Baikal* and flowing north-east into *Arctic* Ocean

Name is from Evenki (Tungus) or Yakut word meaning simply 'river'.

Leningrad

2nd largest city in USSR, in north-west of Gulf of *Finland*

Named in 1924 after Russian revolutionary leader V. I. Lenin (1870–1924) + Slavonic grad = 'town'. From 1914 to 1924 was *Petrograd,* and before 1914, from founding in 1703, *St Petersburg.*

León
Province and its capital and historic kingdom in north-west *Spain*
From Latin legio = 'legion': town was station of Roman 7th legion.

Léopoldville
Former name of *Kinshasa, Zaïre*
Founded by English explorer Sir H. M. Stanley in 1882 and named in honour of Belgian king Léopold II (1835–1909), who financed his explorations, + French ville = 'town'. In 1966 renamed *Kinshasa*.

Lesbos
Island in *Aegean Sea* off west coast of *Turkey*, belonging to *Greece*
Name is almost certainly pre-Greek, perhaps = 'wooded'.

Lesotho
Kingdom in South *Africa*
Named after principal inhabitants, the Sotho (Basotho), as was name of country before 1966, *Basutoland*. Tribal name comes from Usutu river in *Swaziland*, and itself = 'brown'.

Levant
Name for coastal countries of east *Mediterranean*, usually extending from *Greece* to *Egypt*
From Italian levante = 'rising', ie lands in east, where sun rises.

Lexington
Town in *Kentucky*, USA, south-east of *Louisville*
Name ultimately derives from English village of Laxton, Nottinghamshire (once Lexin(g)ton), but was influenced by title of Lord Lexington (1661–1723) and brought to *Kentucky* in 1776 by hunters who had heard news of battle of Lexington in *Massachusetts* the previous year.

Liberia
Republic in West *Africa*
From Latin liber = 'free'; Liberia was established in 1822 as territory for liberated American Negro slaves.

Libreville
Capital of *Gabon*, Central *Africa*
From French libre = 'free' + ville = 'town'; town was founded in 1848 for freed slaves (compare *Liberia*, *Freetown*).

Libya
Republic in North *Africa*
Name is very ancient, and was known in Egyptian hieroglyphics of 2000 BC. As yet meaning is unexplained.

Lido
Resort just south-east of *Venice*, *Italy*
Italian = 'shore' (from Latin litus).

Liechtenstein
Principality in Central *Europe*, between *Switzerland* and *Austria*
Named after princes who founded it in 1719, their own family name deriving from ancestral castle of Lichtenstein, near *Vienna* (in turn from German lichten = 'to shine, to lighten' + Stein = 'stone', referring to light colour of buildings).

Liège
City and province in east *Belgium*
Name in 770 was Leodicum, from personal name (Leudi) of lord of castle here. Not likely to be connected with Indo-European leod = 'of the people'.

Liguria
Region in north-west *Italy*
Named after Ligures, tribe who inhabited this region BC (on north coast of Ligurian Sea).

Lille
City in extreme north-east of *France*
From Old French l'isle = 'the island'; city was built as a fortress surrounded by marshes.

Lilongwe
Capital of *Malawi*, Central *Africa*
Name is that of river here, = 'big river'.

Lima
Capital of *Peru*, South *America*
Founded in 1535 by Spanish explorer Francisco Pizarro who named it Ciudad de los Reyes = 'city of the kings' (town was founded on 6 January, Feast of Epiphany). With time, however, city acquired name derived from that of River Rimac (named after god with name = 'he who speaks'), on which it stands.

Limburg
Province in east of south *Netherlands*
First recorded in 1093 with name Lintburch = 'town of lime-trees'.

Limerick
County and town in south-west *Ireland*
English version of Irish Luimneach, from luimne, diminutive of lom = 'bare, poor', referring to barren earth.

Limoges
City in central *France*, west of *Clermont-Ferrand*
Name derives from Gaulish tribe Lemovices (who also gave their name to Limousin), with their own name perhaps = 'dwellers among the elm-trees'. Earlier name was Augustoritum, from name of Roman emperor Augustus + Gaulish rito = 'ford'.

Limpopo, River
In South *Africa*, rising in *Transvaal* and flowing through *Mozambique* into Indian Ocean
Of uncertain origin. Perhaps = 'crocodile river', its alternative name. However, modern theory derives name from Matabele ilimphopho = 'river of the waterfall', and this could well describe upper reaches in *Transvaal*.

Lincoln
State capital of *Nebraska*, USA
Named in honour of Abraham Lincoln (1809–65), 16th president of the USA.

Lions, Gulf of
Bay of *Mediterranean* extending from (west) French-Spanish frontier to (east) *Toulon*
Not connected with city of *Lyons*, but with lions, either because of statues of lions set up along coast here or, more likely, because of roaring of sea when mistral blows (compare *Sierra Leone*).

Lisbon
Capital of *Portugal*
Name is probably of Phoenician origin, perhaps from ippo = 'fence' or alis ubbo = 'joyful bay'. Not named after legendary hero Ulysses (Odysseus) said to have founded it. Phoenician name was recorded as Olisipo.

Lithuania
Republic in north-west USSR on *Baltic Sea*, bordering on *Poland*
Probably from Lithuanian lieti = 'to flow', ie 'land on flowing water' (*Baltic Sea*), or perhaps from Lithuanian lytus = 'rain'.

Little Rock
State capital of *Arkansas*, USA
From smaller of two rocks on banks of River Arkansas, named La Petite Roche (= 'the little rock') in 1722 by French explorer Bernard de la Harpe.

Lofoten Islands
Off north-west coast of *Norway*
Original meaning lost. Supposed derivation from lo = 'fox' + fot = 'foot' is only attempt to explain unknown name.

Loire, River
Longest river in *France*, flowing north-west from central *France* into Bay of *Biscay*
Roman name was Liger, from Indo-European lig = 'to flow, to run'.

Lombardy
Region in north *Italy*, bordering on *Switzerland*
From Germanic tribe of Langobards who settled here in 569. Their own name may = 'long beards' or 'long axes'.

London
Capital of *Great Britain*

Many possible explanations; some are: 1. from Celtic llwyn = 'wood' + dinas = 'town'; 2. from Celtic lon = 'hill' + dun = 'place'; 3. from Celtic llyn = 'water' + dun = 'place'; 4. from Celtic lhong = 'ship' + dinas = 'town, port'; 5. from Celtic londo = 'wild (people)'; 6. from tribal name Londinos. Most popular derivation is blend of last two.

Londonderry
County and town in north-west of Northern *Ireland*

Original name was Derry, from Irish doire = 'oak-wood'. Name Londonderry dates from 1609, when James I granted charter for settlement here to merchants from *London*.

Long Island
In *New York* state, USA

Name was originally given in 1614 by Dutch settlers. Island is 190 km (118 miles) in length.

Lorraine
Historic province in north-east *France*

From Latin Lotharii regnum = 'kingdom of Lothair'; in 843 empire of Charlemagne was divided by his grandsons: central territory (Francia media) went to one of them, Lothair I (795−855), who in turn partitioned it between his sons, the younger, Lothair II (reigned 855−69), receiving the north region, then extending west of River *Rhine* from *North Sea* to the *Alps*, and corresponding to modern Lorraine.

Los Angeles
2nd largest city in USA, in southern *California*

Full name given by Spanish missionaries, when they settled here in 1781, was El pueblo de Nuestra Señora la Reina de los Angeles de la Porciúncula = 'the city of Our Lady of the Angels of the Little Portion' (the Porciúncula is Franciscan shrine near Assisi, *Italy*). Name was originally given on 2 August 1769 (without first 3 words) to river by which expedition camped, previous day having been Feast of the Porciúncula. Name eventually contracted to Los Angeles and colloquially just to L.A. (for similar contraction compare *Buenos Aires*).

Louisiana
State in south USA, on Gulf of *Mexico*
Region was explored by French in 1677–82 and in 1681 was named in honour of French king Louis XIV. Name originally covered much wider territory than today.

Louisville
City in north *Kentucky*, USA
Founded by French in 1778; in 1780 named in honour of French king Louis XVI, in recognition of his support during American War of Independence.

Lourenço Marques
Former name of *Maputo*

Loyalty Islands
In South-West *Pacific*, east of *New Caledonia*
Two islands of group, Lifou and Ouvea, were discovered by French admiral Dumont d'Urville in 1827 and named by him Îles Loyauté with reference to trustworthiness of natives and friendliness of their welcome.

Luanda
Capital of *Angola*, South-West *Africa*
Native name may mean 'place of the net', referring to fishermen who inhabited island of Luanda. Early Portuguese name for this island was Ilha dos Cabras = 'island of goats'.

Lübeck
City and seaport in *Schleswig-Holstein*, north of West *Germany*
Probably from personal name of Slavonic prince Liuba + Slavonic suffix -ichi = 'descendants'. Name was later interpreted to mean 'little stream', from Old German lützel-bek, but this is unlikely derivation.

Lucerne, Lake
Central *Switzerland*
Named after town of Lucerne on its shore; name has several possible origins: 1. from Latin lucerna = 'lighthouse'; 2. from Latin lucius = 'pike-basket' (ie place where pike are plentiful); 3. from Romansch lozzerina = 'marshy place'; 4. after Benedictine monastery of St Leodegar, founded nearby about 740. German name of Lake is Vierwaldstättersee = 'lake of the four forest cantons' (ie Uri, Schwyz, Unterwalden and Luzern, which surround it).

Lugano, Lake
Partly in *Switzerland*, partly in *Italy*
From Gaulish Lakvannos = 'lake dwellers' (laku = 'lake'), name of people who once inhabited this region.

Lundy
Small island in Bristol Channel, south-west *England*
From Old Norse lundi = 'puffin'—bird for which island is famous.

Lusaka
Capital of *Zambia*, Central *Africa*
Name is that of former headman, Lusaakas, who was chief of village near railroad siding here at turn of century.

Lüshun
Port in north-east *China*
From Chinese lü = 'army' + shun = 'safely'. English name was *Port Arthur*. Later joined with *Talien/Dalian* to form new city of *Lü-ta/Lüda*.

Lü-ta/Lüda
City and seaport in north-east *China*, on *Yellow Sea*
From 1st elements of *Lüshun* and *Talien/Dalian*, which merged after World War II to form one city.

Luxembourg

Grand duchy and its capital in west *Europe*, bounded by West *Germany*, *France* and *Belgium*

In 963 name was Lucilinburhuc, from Old Saxon luttil = 'little' + burug = 'town'. Duchy is named after town.

Lvov

City in republic of *Ukraine*, USSR, south-west of *Kiev*

From personal name Lev (Leo), probably that of Galician prince who built fortress here in 13th century.

Lyons

3rd largest city in *France*, in central south-east, on River *Rhône*

Roman name was Lugdunum, possibly from Gaulish dun = 'fortress', with 1st element lugus = 'little', or perhaps from name of pagan Celtic god Lug or from Celtic lucodunos = 'bright mountain'. Town was founded in 43 BC.

M

Maastricht
Town in east *Belgium*, north-east of *Liège*
From Roman name, Trajectum ad Mosam = 'crossing over (river) Maas (*Meuse*)'.

Macao
Portuguese province in south-east *China*, west of *Hong Kong*
Name is Portuguese corruption (via Amagoa, Amacoa) of Chinese name Aomin, from Chinese ngao = 'bay' + men = 'gate'. Or perhaps derives from Chinese Ama-ngao = 'bay of Ama' (goddess worshipped by sailors).

Macedonia
South republic of *Yugoslavia*; historic region on *Balkan* Peninsula
Named after Macedonians, Slavonic people who settled here in 6th century AD, though earlier inhabitants had same name, perhaps from Greek makednos = 'tall, slender'. Or possibly from Old Illyrian maketia = 'castle'. True meaning uncertain, hence attempt to explain name by story of legendary king Macedo, son of Zeus, said to have reigned here.

Mackenzie
West district of North-West Territories, north *Canada*
Named after River Mackenzie, in turn named after British explorer Sir Alexander Mackenzie (1764–1820) who sailed up it in 1789 on his way to *Arctic* Ocean.

McKinley, Mount
In central *Alaska*, highest in USA
Named in 1896 after William McKinley (1843–1901), 25th president of the USA.

Madagascar
Island republic in Indian Ocean, off South-East *Africa*
Name is still not satisfactorily explained. Marco Polo recorded it in 13th century as Madeigascar. From 1958 to 1975
was officially known as Malagasy Republic, after name of
peoples here, who are not strictly African but Indonesian
in origin.

Madeira
Group of islands in North *Atlantic* off North-West
Africa, and chief island of this group
Islands have been 'discovered' 3 times by Europeans: 1. by
Romans who called them Insulae purpurrinae = 'islands of
purple dye' (got from trees here), though Carthaginian
name was Al Agnam = 'small animals' (ie goats); 2. by
Italian sailors, who took Carthaginian name as Italian leg-
name = 'timber'; 3. by Portuguese in 1420 who translated
Italian word into Portuguese, with same meaning, this
giving modern name Madeira.

Madison
State capital of *Wisconsin*, USA
Named in honour of James Madison (1751–1836), 4th pre-
sident of the USA.

Madras
State and its capital in south-east *India*
Various unlikely explanations of name, eg from Mandradsh
= 'country of Mand' (a god) or 'country of fools', but most
likely from Arabic madrasa = 'school' (ie of Moslems).

Madrid
Capital of *Spain* and central province of country.
Name evolved from that of Moorish fort here, Majrit. Various theories have been proposed to explain this, but none
is satisfactory.

Magdeburg

City in East *Germany* on River *Elbe*, south-west of *Berlin*

Name possibly derives from woman's name Magda (ie 'Magda's town'), but uncertain if she owned town or was venerated here. Or perhaps from Celtic pagan god Mogon. More likely derived not from personal name Magda but from German Magd = 'maid', referring to some pagan goddess.

Magellan Strait

In south *Chile*, between mainland of South *America* and *Tierra del Fuego*

Discovered in 1520 by Portuguese explorer in Spanish service, Fernando Magellan (Fernão de Magelhães).

Maggiore, Lake

In *Lombardy*, north *Italy*, with north end in *Switzerland*

Italian = 'greater (lake)': lake is longer and wider than neighbouring Lake *Como* and Lake *Lugano*.

Mahé

Largest island of *Seychelles*, Indian Ocean

So named in 1742 by French captain L. Picault in honour of governor of French possessions in India Mahé de la Bourdonnais. (In Tibetan Mahé = 'buffalo'.)

Main, River

In West *Germany* flowing west through *Frankfurt* to join River *Rhine* near *Mainz*

From Celtic or Illyrian name Moinas, perhaps derived from Celtic mo = 'slow' + enos = 'water', or from Indo-European moinia = 'marsh'. Could also be connected with Celtic magos = 'big'.

Maine

1 State in *New England*, north-east USA

Two possible explanations: 1. named by French settlers in 1635 after their native province of Maine—see *Maine* (2); 2. named by English settlers in 1607 with sense of 'mainland' or even 'open sea', to distinguish territory from offshore islands. But French name came after English and may have been attempt to interpret it. Also, English name could be connected similarly with French province Maine since English queen Henrietta, wife of Charles I, had claim to it.

Maine

2 Historic province in north-west *France*, south of *Normandy*

Ancient name was Cenomania, from Celtic cenn = 'hill', giving name of tribe Cenomanni (= 'hill-dwellers'). Last element gives present name. (Compare *Le Mans, Cremona*.)

Mainz

City in west of West *Germany* on River *Rhine*, south-west of *Frankfurt*

City is situated at confluence of River *Rhine* and River *Main*. Roman name was Mogontiacum, possibly from pagan god Mogon or some personal name (compare *Magdeburg*). Connection with River *Main* not proved.

Majorca

Largest of *Balearic Islands*, in west *Mediterranean*

Roman name was Majorica (insula) = 'greater (island)', ie in relation to *Minorca*. Spanish name, Mallorca, is variant of this.

Malabar

Coastal region in south-west *India*

From Sanskrit = 'mountain country' (Sanskrit malai = 'mountain'; compare *Malaya*). But possibly from Iranian bar = 'shore' (as in *Zanzibar*).

Malacca

State and its capital in south-west *Malaya*

Probably from Sanskrit maha = 'big' + lanka = 'island', or possibly from Malay word for a tree found here (*Emblica officinalis*).

Málaga
Province and its capital in south *Spain*
Name is of Phoenician origin, perhaps = 'queen', or less likely from malh, malahah = 'salt place' (ie place where fish are salted).

Malawi
Republic in Central *Africa*
From African (Chichewa) word = 'flames', after name of ancient Negro people, Maravi. Meaning probably refers to reflection of rising sun on Lake Malawi and on 3 smaller lakes in country.

Malaya
State forming part of *Malaysia*, peninsula in South-East *Asia* south of *Thailand*
Probably from Sanskrit malai = 'mountain'.

Malaysia
Elected monarchy in South-East *Asia*, consisting of peninsula of *Malaya* and northern *Borneo*
Probably, as *Malaya*, from Sanskrit malai = 'mountain', but perhaps more closely linked to name of *Malacca*.

Maldive Islands
In Indian Ocean, south-west of *Sri Lanka*
Many possible meanings. Probably from Sanskrit dwipa = 'island' or malai = 'mountain' (or both) or from maldiva = 'thousand islands' (there are in fact nearly 2,000).

Mali
Republic in West *Africa*, south of *Algeria*
Until 1960 was French *Sudan*, when reverted to Negro name of Mali, applied in 11th–15th centuries to much wider territory. Name is linked to that of native Malinke (Mandingo) people.

Mallorca
Spanish name, also used in English, for *Majorca*

Malmö
City and seaport in south *Sweden*
From Old Scandinavian malm = 'sandy land, sandy valley' + oe = 'island'. Town's original name was Malmhaug = 'sandpile', and in late Middle Ages German merchants from *Lübeck* settled here and called it Elbogen = 'elbow' after contour of coastline.

Malta
Island republic in *Mediterranean*, south of *Sicily*
Greek name was Melite, from Phoenician = 'shelter, refuge' (ie from sea). Latin name Melita has been falsely associated with Greek word meliteia = 'balm' (based on meli = 'honey').

Man, Isle of
In Irish Sea between north *England* and Northern *Ireland*
In ancient times was Monapia or Mona, probably from Celtic mennin = 'middle', in sense of island being halfway between *England* and *Ireland*, or possibly from Celtic men = 'rock'.

Manchuria
Region in north-east *China*
Named after inhabitants, Manchus, whose own name means 'pure'. Tribe descended from the Nü-chên Tartars.

Mandalay
2nd largest city in *Burma*, north of *Rangoon*
From Sanskrit mandala = 'circle', in sense of holy precinct. Mandalay is great centre of Buddhism.

Manhattan
Island in *New York* state, USA
From Indian (Algonquian) word probably = 'hilly island'. Two (colourful) theories are that name derives from: 1. mana-hac-te-neid = 'place of drunkenness', referring to incident in 1609 in which Henry Hudson (see *Hudson Bay*) liberally regaled Indian delegation with spirits on board his ship here; or from 2. (Iroquois) man-hei-tanana = 'place where we were cheated', referring to purchase of Manhattan from Indians in 1610 by Dutch settlers for absurdly low sum of 60 guilders.

Manila
Capital of *Philippines*
Probably from Tagalog may = 'to be' + nila = 'indigo', ie 'place where there is indigo'. Original name was recorded as Maynilad.

Manitoba
Province in central east *Canada*
Province is named after Lake Manitoba, in turn named after island in lake with Indian name Manatuapa = 'great spirit' (worshipped here by Cree tribe, who regarded island as spirit's abode). Or perhaps from Sioux mine = 'water' + toba = 'prairie'. French explorers who discovered lake in 1738 named it Lac des Prairies, as if translating Indian name.

Mannheim
City on River *Rhine* in West *Germany*
Possibly from personal name Mano + German Heim = 'abode, home'. Or perhaps from older form am-aha-heim = 'dwelling by the river'. The 1st element may by connected with Celtic man = 'boundary stone' (as in Breton word menhir = 'long stone').

Mantua
Town in *Lombardy*, north *Italy*, south-west of *Verona*
Founded in 325, with name probably from Etruscan god Mantus.

Maputo
Capital of *Mozambique*, South-East *Africa*
Name is that of river here, itself named after one of sons of local chief Nuagobe in 18th century. Before 1975, name of capital was Lourenço Marques, after Portuguese navigator who first explored region here in 16th century.

Maracaibo
Lake and city in north-west *Venezuela*, South *America*
Name given to town in 1499 by Spanish explorer Alfonso de Hojeda after lake, in turn named after local Indian chief (cacique).

Marathon

Village in south-east *Greece*, north-east of *Athens*

Greek = 'fennel', which once grew in abundance here. Name became famous for Battle of Marathon (490 BC) in which Persians were defeated by Athenians, and for subsequent long-distance run bringing news of this victory to *Athens*.

Marches, the

Region in central east *Italy* bordering on *Adriatic Sea*

From Italian marche = 'borderland' (ie of *Ancona*, its capital).

Mariana Islands

In West *Pacific*, north of *Papua New Guinea* and east of *Philippines*

Discovered by Portuguese explorer Magellan in 1521 who called them Islas de los Ladrones, Spanish = 'islands of thieves'. In 1668 islands were renamed in honour of Maria of Austria, wife of Spanish king Philip IV.

Marmara, Sea of

In north-west *Turkey*, between *Black Sea* and *Aegean Sea*

Named after Island of Marmara in Sea of Marmara, with name derived from Greek marmaros = 'marble': island is famous for its white marble used for building palaces of *Istanbul* and other cities.

Marne, River

In north-east *France*, joining River *Seine* just north of *Paris*

Said to be from Latin matrona = 'mother', in sense of 'mother of the gods'; more likely to be from either Ligurian ma = 'to roar' or possibly Indo-European mad = 'to flow down'.

Marquesas Islands

In South *Pacific*, north-east of *Tahiti*, in French *Polynesia*

Discovered by Spanish expedition in 1595 and named in honour of Spanish viceroy of *Peru*, Marquis (Spanish Marqués) de Mendoza.

Marrakesh
2nd largest city in *Morocco*, south of *Casablanca*
Founded in 1062 with name Marrakush, Berber = 'fortified'.
City gave name to *Morocco*.

Marsala
Town and seaport in West *Sicily*, south *Italy*
Name is from Arabic Mars-el-Allah = 'harbour of Allah'.
Arabs founded town in 9th century on ruins of Greek
Lilybaion = '(cape) overlooking Libya'.

Marseilles
2nd largest city in *France*, seaport on south coast
Earliest known form of name is Massalia (Latin Massilia).
City was perhaps founded by Phoenicians about 1000 BC
and named after tribe Massili, whose own name is of
uncertain origin, or more likely by Greeks about 600 BC. It
is possible, though, that mas- element may mean simply
'spring'.

Marshall Islands
In West *Pacific*, east of *Mariana Islands, Micronesia*
First sighted by Spanish navigator Álvarez de Saavedra in
1529; explored by English captain John Marshall in 1788
and named after him.

Martinique
One of *Windward Islands, West Indies*
Discovered in 1502 by Columbus on 15 June, St Martin's
Day. However, some toponymists derive origin from
Indian name Madiana = 'island of flowers' or Madinina =
'fertile island with luxuriant vegetation'.

Maryland
State in east USA on central *Atlantic* coast
Founded by English Baron Baltimore in 1632 and named in
honour of Queen Henrietta Maria, wife of King Charles I.

Maseru
Capital of *Lesotho*, South *Africa*
Name = 'place of red sandstone', describing rocky height
here where town arose in 1860s.

Massachusetts
State in *New England*, north-east USA
Of uncertain origin; perhaps from Indian (Algonquian) massud-ch-es-et = 'high hill, little plain', adopted by English from tribal name with 's' added for plural. Name was first given to Massachusetts Bay, then to state with original name Massachusetts Bay Colony.

Mato Grosso
State in central south-west *Brazil*, South *America*
Portuguese = 'big forest': much of territory is vast tropical rain forest.

Matterhorn
Mountain in Swiss *Alps* on Swiss-Italian border
From German Matte = 'mountain meadow' + Horn = 'peak'. French name is Mont Cervin, Italian is Monte Cervino, both = 'deer mountain' (from steep, horn-shaped peak).

Mauritania
Republic in North-West *Africa*
Name ultimately derives from Arabic, through Greek = 'land of the blacks', with word from same root as for Moors (and 'blackamoors').

Mauritius
Independent state and island in Indian Ocean, east of *Madagascar*
Named by Dutch admiral Van Neck in 1598 in honour of Prince Maurice (Latin Mauritius) of Orange, Stadtholder of United Provinces (modern *Netherlands*).

Mbabane
Capital of *Swaziland*, South-East *Africa*
City derives name from that of chief Mbabane Khunene, who held land here before arrival of Europeans. His own name comes from stream here, = 'thing that crushes', referring to erosion caused by its current.

Mecca
City in *Saudi Arabia*
Possibly from Phoenician makak = 'ruined', but more likely from Arabic makorab = 'shrine'; Mecca is holiest city of Islam and birthplace of Mohammed.

Medicine Hat
Town in south *Alberta, Canada*
Indian name is Saamis = 'hat of a medicine man'. Name perhaps refers to some incident involving Indian 'medicine man'—possibly inter-tribal battle in which he lost his hat—or to resemblance of nearby hill to a medicine man's hat. Name was given by W. Johnson in 1882.

Medina
City in *Saudi Arabia*, north of *Mecca*
Full formal Arabic name is Al-Madīnah Al-Mudawwarah = 'the most glorious city' or Madīnat Rasūl Allāh = 'city of the messenger of God' (ie of Mohammed). Medina is one of the two most sacred cities of Islam (other is *Mecca*), and Mohammed fled here (from *Mecca*) in 622, year from which Muslim calendar dates.

Mediterranean Sea
Large sea between *Europe, Africa* and South-West *Asia*.
From Latin Mare mediterraneum = 'sea in the middle of the earth'; Romans regarded it as central sea of Roman empire. Earlier, in 1st century AD, it was Mare nostrum = 'our sea'.

Mekong, River
In South-East *Asia*, on peninsula of Indochina
Perhaps = 'head of waters' or 'mother of rivers'; 2nd element, kong, probably derives from Sanskrit ganga = 'river' (compare *Ganges*).

Melanesia
Islands in *Pacific*, north-east of *Australia*
Name = 'black islands', ie 'islands inhabited by black people', and was modelled on name of *Polynesia*. See also *Micronesia* and *Indonesia*.

Melbourne
Capital of *Victoria, Australia*
Founded in 1835 with name Dutigala; in 1837 renamed Melbourne in honour of English prime minister Lord Melbourne.

Memphis
City in south-west *Tennessee*, USA
Named in 1826 after ancient Egyptian city of Memphis, partly because name suggested grandeur and wealth of the East, partly, perhaps, because American city had similar position on River *Mississippi* to that of Egyptian city on River *Nile*.

Menorca
Spanish name, also used in English, of *Minorca*

Menton
Town and resort in south-east *France* on *Mediterranean*
Perhaps from personal Roman name Mento or, more likely, from Celtic men = 'rock'. No connection with French menton = 'chin'.

Mesopotamia
Region of South-West *Asia* approximating to modern *Iraq*
From Greek mesos = 'middle' + potamos = 'river'; much of region is between River *Tigris* and River *Euphrates*.

Messina
City and seaport in east *Sicily*, south *Italy*, and strait between *Italy* and *Sicily*
Founded in 735 BC by Greek settlers with name of Zankle = 'sickle-shaped', perhaps with reference to curve of headland. In 4th century AD acquired name of Messina, after Greek region of Messenia in *Peloponnese*, from which many of emigrants had come. Strait is named after city.

Metz
City in *Lorraine*, east *France*, south of *Luxembourg*
Roman version of Gaulish name was Divodurum, from diu-dur = 'two rivers'. Later Latin name was Mediomatricum = 'middle of the Matricii' (Gaulish tribe), which was later simplified to Mettis and finally became Metz.

Meuse, River
Rises in north-east *France* and flows north through *Ardennes* into *Belgium* and *Netherlands*, then west to join River Waal
Name, as Dutch version Maas, derives from Celtic Mosa, ultimately connected with Indo-European root word mus = 'damp, moisture'.

Mexico
Republic in Central *America*

Possibly derived from name of lake which once stood where capital, Mexico City, now is, and which was called Metzlianan by Aztecs, from metz-tli = 'moon' (to which lake was dedicated) + atl = 'water'; in 1325 Aztecs founded city on island of this lake, which later came to be called Metz-xih-co = 'in the centre (literally 'navel') of the waters of the moon'. Town gave name to whole territory.

Miami
City and resort in *Florida*, USA

Original name of settlement here was Mayaimi, from Indian (Tequesta) = 'big water'. Reference may have been to Lake Okeechobee, largest lake in southern United States, or to marshy Everglades, both to north-west of Miami.

Michigan
State and lake in north USA

Lake gave name to state; derives from Indian (Chippewa) word, perhaps michaw = 'great' + sasigan = 'lake', or perhaps michigan = '(forest) clearing'.

Micronesia
Large group of islands in West *Pacific*, north of *Melanesia*

From Greek micros = 'small' + nesos = 'island', with ending -ia denoting territory. Most of islands in group are small (*Caroline, Marshall, Mariana, Kiribati* and others) compared to those of *Melanesia*.

Midway Islands
In North *Pacific*, west of *Hawaii*

Atoll here was first named Middlebrooks in 1859, after a Captain Brooks; name Midway dates from US annexation in 1867 and refers to location of islands midway between *America* and *Asia* in central *Pacific*.

Milan
2nd largest city in *Italy*, in north-west

In 222 BC was Mediolanum, from Gaulish medio = 'middle' + lan = 'meadow, plain'; town arose in middle of plain of River Olona.

Milwaukee
City in *Wisconsin* and port on Lake *Michigan*, USA
From name of Indian (Algonquian) tribe once living here, with meaning probably = 'meeting place by the river': city is where 3 rivers (one the Milwaukee) flow into Milwaukee Bay.

Minneapolis
City in *Minnesota*, north USA
From Minne-, 1st element of *Minnesota*, + Greek polis = 'town'. One of city's parks has Minnehaha Falls, from Indian (Sioux) minnehaha = 'waterfalls' (heroine of Longfellow's *Hiawatha* has this name, with false interpretation of 'laughing water').

Minnesota
State and river in north USA, bordering on *Canada*
State takes name from river, in turn from Indian (Sioux) minne = 'water' + sota = 'cloudy'.

Minorca
2nd largest of *Balearic Islands*, in west *Mediterranean*
Roman name was Minorica (insula), from Latin minor = 'lesser' (in relation to *Majorca*). Spanish name of island is Menorca.

Minsk
Capital of republic of *Byelorussia*, USSR
Probably named after some river, though in fact on River Svisloch. There exist Russian Rivers Men, Mena and Menka, whose names can be linked with German River *Main*. Or perhaps from Latvian main = 'marsh'.

Mississippi
State in south USA and longest river, with *Missouri* its longest tributary, in North America
From Indian (Algonquian) word = 'great river'; recorded in French text of 1666 as Messipi. River gave name to state when latter was established in 1817. Spanish name for river in 1542 was Soto Rio Grande = 'big river of Soto', after Spanish explorer Ferdinando de Soto who led expedition here in 1539. Familiar name of Mississippi is 'Old Man River'.

Missouri
State, and also longest tributary of *Mississippi*, in central USA
From Indian (probably Dakota) word = 'muddy' (river carries down much silt). Or perhaps from name of Indian tribe = 'big boat'. State took name from river. Nickname of 'Old Muddy' seems to reinforce first origin.

Moldavia
Republic in south-west USSR, bordering on *Romania*
Named after inhabitants, Moldavians, whose own name probably derives from molid = 'pine', or perhaps from Slavonic mol (Indo-European mel) = 'black' (ie earth).

Mombasa
Chief port of *Kenya*, on Indian Ocean
Probably named after Mombasa, *Oman*; Arab settlement at Mombasa, *Kenya*, dates from about 11th century.

Monaco
Principality and its capital in south-east *France*, on *Mediterranean*
From Greek monoikos = 'hermit, monk'; on rock on which city of Monaco stands there was once (7th–6th centuries BC) a Greek temple to god Hercules the Hermit (Heracles Monoecus).

Mongolia
Republic in east Central *Asia*, formerly called Outer Mongolia
From inhabitants, Mongols, whose name has basic meaning 'brave ones', and became established in 13th century as a result of their numerous conquests; earlier they had called themselves simply Bide = 'we'.

Monrovia
Capital of *Liberia*, West *Africa*
Named in honour of James Monroe (1758–1831), 5th president of the USA, in whose term of office it was founded (1822) as a settlement for liberated American slaves.

Montana
State in north-west USA, bordering on *Canada*
From Spanish = 'mountainous'; Rocky Mountains are in west of state. Name was originally that of small town of gold-seekers, then of surrounding territory, then in 1889 of whole state.

Mont Blanc
Highest mountain in *Alps*, in south-east *France*
French = 'white mountain', with reference to permanently snow-covered peaks.

Monte Carlo
Resort in *Monaco* on *Mediterranean*
Italian = 'Mount Charles'; town was founded in 1866 in reign of Monegasque prince Charles III.

Montenegro
Republic in south-west *Yugoslavia*, bordering on *Albania*
From Old Italian = 'black mountain', probably either because mountains are inaccessible and inhospitable or because of their dark colour. Serbo-Croat name, Crna Gora, has same meaning.

Monterrey
City in north-east *Mexico*, Central *America*
Originally founded as León in 1560, after Spanish town *León*; name changed to Monterrey in 1599 in honour of Gaspar de Zuñiga, Count of Monterrey, Viceroy of New Spain. (American town Monterey on coast of *California* derives from this, with one 'r' reflecting spelling of the time.)

Montevideo
Capital of *Uruguay*, South *America*
Name probably given by Magellan in 1520 to mountain here of which there was a good view, from Portuguese monte vidi eo = 'I saw the mountain' (perhaps a cry from one of the sailors who sighted it). Or possibly from Portuguese map-maker's note on mountain with words monte VI de O = 'sixth mountain from the west', Roman figure VI being read as syllable -vi- and 'O' the Portuguese abbreviation for oeste = 'west'.

Montgomery
State capital of *Alabama*, USA
Named in 1819 in honour of American general Richard Montgomery, hero of War of Independence.

Montpelier
State capital of *Vermont*, USA
From name of French city *Montpellier*, as tribute for French support in American War of Independence.

Montpellier
Chief city of *Languedoc*, south *France*, north-west of *Marseilles*
In 975 had Latin name Mons pestellarius = 'woad mountain', probably because was place where this dye was produced. Name eventually contracted to Montpellier.

Montreal
City in *Canada*, in south *Quebec*
Name originally given by French settlers in 1642 was Ville-Marie = 'Marytown' (ie protected by Virgin Mary); later named Montreal = 'royal mountain' (modern French Mont Royal) in honour of French king Francis I who had sent leader of expedition, Jacques Cartier, on colonising mission here. City stands on slope of extinct volcano Mount Royal, so named by Cartier in 1535.

Montreux
Town and resort at east end of Lake *Geneva*, *Switzerland*
From Latin monasterium = 'monastery'; town arose from monastery on island in Lake *Geneva* in 9th century and was then rebuilt on present site in 13th century.

Montserrat
One of *Leeward Islands*, *West Indies*, south of *Antigua*
Discovered by Columbus in 1493 and named by him probably after monastery of Montserrat (= 'jagged mountain') in *Catalonia*, *Spain*.

Moose Jaw
Town in *Saskatchewan, Canada*
First settled in 1882, when named after Moose Jaw Creek.
Probably of Indian origin, with meaning on lines of 'place
where the white man mended the cart wheel with the
jawbone of a moose'. However, could also refer to course of
creek, comparing it to jawbone of moose.

Moravia
Historic region in central *Czechoslovakia*
Named about 500 BC after River Morava, tributary of River
Danube. Name of river perhaps derives from Illyrian marus
= 'marsh', or Germanic word = 'marshy river'. Or could be
connected with Celtic maros = 'great'.

Morocco
Kingdom in North-West *Africa*
Name is Spanish corruption of traditional south capital of
Marrakesh.

Moscow
Capital of USSR
Named after River Moskva on which it stands. Name of
river has many possible origins, among which are: 1. from
Slavonic moskva = 'damp, marshy'; 2. from Slavonic most-
kva = 'bridge water'; 3. from Finno-Ugrian moska = 'calf'
+ va = 'river, water' (ie 'calf ford').

Moselle, River
Rises in *Vosges*, and flows north to join River *Rhine* at
Coblenz
From Gaulish name Mosella = 'little Mos (Maas)', ie 'a little
river like the river Maas (*Meuse*)'.

Mozambique
Republic in South-East *Africa*
Portuguese settled on coral island off coast here in 1508;
according to records of Vasco da Gama native word mo-
sambuco = 'gathering of boats'. Name then spread to
whole territory. But this may be only popular legend, and
name may actually originate in personal name of chieftain
here.

Mukden
Alternative name for *Shenyang, China*
From Manchurian = 'height'.

Munich
City in West *Germany*, in south
From Old High German munih = 'monk'; city was built on site of Benedictine monastery at Tegernsee.

Münster
City in west of West *Gemany*, north of *Dortmund*
From Old High German munistri, in turn from Latin monasterium = 'monastery'. City has been bishop's seat (see) since 803.

Murchison Falls
Former name of *Kabalega Falls, Uganda*, East *Africa*
Named, as are Murchison Rapids on River Shire, south *Malawi*, and River Murchison in Western *Australia*, after British geologist Sir Roderick Murchison (1792−1871). Murchison Falls were renamed in 1972.

Murcia
Region and historic kingdom in south-east *Spain*
Origin uncertain. Name of town here in 3rd century BC, and that of Roman town, unknown.

Murmansk
City and seaport in north-west USSR, on *Barents Sea*
Built in 1915 as terminus of railway leading to *Arctic Ocean*. Original name was Romanov-na-Murmane (= 'Romanov-on-Murman'), from ruling dynasty of tsars, Romanovs, + Murman, which is not name of river but of coastal region, perhaps deriving from same root as Norman (ie as inhabitants of region were northerners).

Murray, River
Chief river of *Australia*, for much of its course forming boundary between *New South Wales* and *Victoria*
Named in 1830 by English explorer Charles Sturt after Sir George Murray, English Colonial Secretary. Explanation of name as derived from Gaelic muireach = 'watery land' unlikely.

N

Nagasaki
City in south-west *Japan*
Japanese = 'long mountains'; city was founded in 1568.

Nairobi
Capital of *Kenya*, East *Africa*
Name probably derives from that of small stream here, known to Masai people as Enkare Nairobi = 'cold water'. Town developed from railway encampment here at close of 19th century.

Namur
Province and city in south-west *Belgium*
In 7th century was Namucum, probably from Celtic nam = 'to bend, to wind' + suffix -uco (perhaps = 'bend of a river'). But could also be from Celtic nan-to = 'valley, meadow', ie 'settlement in a valley', or from nemeto = 'holy wood'. Final letter 'r' is still unexplained.

Nanking/Nanjing
City in east *China*, on River *Yangtse*
Chinese = 'southern capital', in contrast to northern capital, *Peking/Beijing*.

Nantes
City in west *France*, on River *Loire*
From name of Gaulish tribe Namneti, whose capital it was.

Napier
Seaport and capital of *Hawke's Bay* province, North Island, *New Zealand*
Founded in 1856 by English commissioner of crown lands Alfred Domett, who named city after British field-marshal Baron Robert Napier (1810–90).

Naples
3rd largest city in *Italy*, seaport on *Tyrrhenian Sea*, south-east of *Rome*
Greek name was Neapolis = 'new town'; town was 'new' in relation to older town of Cumae.

Nashville
State capital of *Tennessee*, USA
Named in honour of American general Francis Nash (1742
—77), hero of War of Independence, + French ville =
'town'.

Nassau
Capital of *Bahamas*
Founded in 1729 with name Charlestown, in honour of
English king Charles II; later changed to Nassau when
William III, of house of Orange-Nassau, came to throne.
(Royal house derived name from former German duchy of
Nassau, in turn from Old High German naz = 'damp,
marshy' + augia = 'land'.)

Natal
East province of South *Africa*
Discovered by Portuguese expedition led by Vasco da
Gama on Christmas Day (Portuguese Natale) 1497. The 1st
English settlement here was called Port Natal, later re-
named *Durban*.

Navarra
Province in north-east *Spain*
Name dates back to before 8th century. Probably from
Basque nava = 'plain' + arra, word of unknown meaning.

Nazareth
Town in north *Israel*, south-east of *Haifa*
Probably from Old Hebrew natzar = 'to guard' (ie 'defence
post'). Not likely to be from Arabic natara = 'to be green'.
But town is not mentioned in Old Testament, so original
source may have been lost.

N'Djamena
Capital of *Chad*, Central *Africa*
African = 'repose'. Until 1973 was called *Fort Lamy*.

Nebraska
State in central USA
From Indian (Sioux) ni = 'water' + bthaska = 'flat', name
given to River Platte, in turn anglicised version of French
Rivière Plate, translation of Indian name. State adopted
Indian name of river.

Nepal

Kingdom in South *Asia*, bordering on north-east *India*
Possibly from Sanskrit nipalaya = 'abode at the foot' (ie of
the *Himalayas*), or from Tibetan niyampal = 'holy land'.
Both names imply sanctity of mountains.

Netherlands

Kingdom in north-west *Europe*
Name is literal, ie 'nether (low-lying) lands'. Also known as
Holland, strictly the name of 2 provinces, North and South,
in the country.

Nevada

State in west USA
Named after *Sierra Nevada*, range of mountains which are
in fact not in Nevada, but in neighbouring state of *California*.

Nevis

With *St Kitts* independent state and one of *Leeward
Islands, West Indies*
From original Spanish name Nuestra Señora de las Nieves
= 'Our Lady of the snows' (referring to white cloud on
peak of mountain giving appearance of snow). Last word
was corrupted to Nevis, also used for highest mountain
on island. Name probably not given by Columbus, though
island was discovered by him in 1493. No connection with
mountain of Ben Nevis, *Scotland*, in naming, though this
mountain has similar origin and meaning (from Gaelic
beinn-nimh-bhatais = 'mountain with its peak in the
clouds').

Newark

City in *New Jersey* and town in *Ohio*, USA
Ohio town takes name from one in *New Jersey*, which was
given to it in 1666 by English settler and missionary Abraham Pierson (1608–78), from English town of Newark
(present Newark-on-Trent). Not likely, in spite of religious
background, that name derives from 'new ark'.

New Brunswick

Province in east *Canada*, on Gulf of *St Lawrence*
Separated from *Nova Scotia* in 1784, with name as compliment to English king George III, of house of *Hanover* or
Brunswick.

New Caledonia
Island in South-West *Pacific*, east of *Queensland, Australia*

Name given by Cook, who discovered it in 1774, after Roman name for *Scotland*, with which, however, neither it nor he has any connection.

New England
Name of 6 states in north-east USA: *Maine, New Hampshire, Vermont, Massachusetts, Rhode Island, Connecticut*

Name was given to territory by English captain John Smith in 1614—appropriately, since 1st English settlement was established 6 years later at Plymouth, *Massachusetts*, by Puritans who had sailed from English town Plymouth in the *Mayflower* (although Smith gave name in general way, on lines of New France and New Spain).

Newfoundland
Province in extreme east of *Canada*, consisting of island and *Labrador*

Discovered by Italian-born English explorer John Cabot in 1497. Territory acquired this obvious name almost immediately (an English text of 1498 refers to 'the new-found land').

New Hampshire
State in *New England*, north-east USA, bordering on *Canada*

Name given in 1629 by English settler Captain John Mason (1586–1635), to whom King Charles I had granted the territory, after his home county of Hampshire.

New Hebrides
Former name of republic of *Vanuatu*, group of islands in South-West *Pacific*, west of *Fiji*

Discovered by Portuguese navigator Pedro Fernandes de Queirós in 1606; in 1774 named New Hebrides by Cook after Scottish islands, with which, however, neither he nor they are connected.

New Jersey

State in east USA, on *Atlantic* coast

Name given in 1664 by one of proprietors of territory, Sir George Carteret (1610−80), after his native island of *Jersey*, Channel Islands.

New Mexico

State in south-west USA bordering on *Texas* and *Mexico*

Name first given, as Nuevo México, by Spanish explorer Francesco de Ibarra in 1562, in hope that territory would become as rich as original *Mexico*, lying to the south. In 1848 name was anglicised as New Mexico.

New Orleans

Largest city in *Louisiana*, USA

Founded by French settlers in 1718 and named, as Nouvelle Orléans, in honour of French regent Philippe, Duc d'Orléans (during minority of Louis XV). Name anglicised as New Orleans in 1803.

New South Wales

State in south-east *Australia*

Discovered by Cook in 1770 and so named by him because of apparent resemblance of coastline to that of south *Wales*. Originally Cook considered name New Wales but rejected it in favour of New South Wales. Name originally applied to whole east coast of *Australia*, and present territory of state is much smaller than original lands claimed by Cook.

New York

State and its capital—New York City, largest city in USA—in north-east USA

Settled by Dutch in 1624 who named it New Amsterdam; captured by English in 1664 and named New York in honour of Duke of York, to whom colony had been entrusted by his brother, King Charles II.

New Zealand
Independent state in South-West *Pacific*, consisting of two islands, North Island and South Island
Sighted by Dutch explorer Abel Tasman in 1642 and named by him Staaten Landt = 'land of the States' (ie of the *Netherlands*), but name was changed following year by Dutch authorities to Nieuw Zeeland= 'new sea-land' (with reference also, doubtless, to Dutch province of Zeeland, which consists largely of islands). Name was later anglicised to New Zealand.

Niagara
River and falls on frontier of *Canada* and USA between Lake *Erie* and Lake *Ontario*
Probably from Indian (Huron) word = 'thundering water', but could also be from Iroquois word = 'point of land cut in two' (referring to point where river flows into Lake *Ontario*).

Nicaragua
Republic in Central *America*
Discovered in 1522 by Spanish explorer Gil Gonzalez, who named territory after Indian chief Nicarao who owned it. Chief's name is of uncertain meaning. Name is also that of Lake Nicaragua here, on whose shores chief's tribe lived. Spanish called lake Mar Dulce = 'freshwater sea'.

Nice
Seaport and resort in south *France*, on *Mediterranean*
Was Greek colony of Nikaea (Latin Nicaea); city was dedicated to Nike, Greek goddess of victory, and so named to mark victory of Greek settlers from Massilia (modern *Marseilles*) over Ligurians in 3rd century BC.

Nicosia
Capital of *Cyprus*
Name is apparently a mediaeval distortion of Greek name of city, Lefkosia, perhaps influenced by Greek nike = 'victory' (compare *Nice*).

Niger

Republic in North-West *Africa* and long river flowing south through it and *Nigeria* into Gulf of *Guinea*

River name derives from African (Tamashek) gher ngheren = 'river among rivers', and country is named after river, as is *Nigeria*. Therefore no connection with Latin niger = 'black'.

Nigeria

Republic in West *Africa*

Named after River *Niger*, in whose basin it is situated.

Nijmegen

City in east *Netherlands*, south of *Arnhem*

In Roman times was Noviomagus = 'new field', ie new settlement of the Batavi (Batavians).

Nikolayev

Port on *Black Sea* in republic of *Ukraine*, USSR

Named not after one of Russian tsars Nicholas but after ship *St Nicholas* which was the first to be launched from the ship-building yard here in 1784.

Nile, River

Longest river in *Africa*, rising near Lake *Victoria* and flowing north into *Mediterranean*

One of oldest geographical names in the world; probably from Semitic-Hamitic nagal = 'river'. Ancient Egyptians called river Ar or Aur = 'black', referring to colour of sediment when it is in flood.

Nîmes

City in south *France*, north-west of *Marseilles*

Roman name was Nemausus, from Gaulish nem = 'sanctuary' + Latin suffix -ausum, said to denote a spring and the genie who lived in its waters.

Nome

Port in west *Alaska*, USA, on *Bering* Strait

A 'mistake' name: written note '? name' made on chart of coastal region here by English map-maker was misread as name of cape (ie Cape Name); this was later corrupted to Cape Nome, which gave name to port.

Norfolk Island
In South *Pacific*, north-east of *Sydney, Australia*
Discovered by Cook in 1774 and named by him probably
not after English county of Norfolk but after 9th Duke of
Norfolk.

Normandy
Region and historic province in north-west *France*
Named after Norsemen ('north men') who invaded it in 9th
century and settled here as Normans.

North Sea
Between *Great Britain* and continent of *Europe*
So named by Dutch, as Noord Zee, in contrast to *Zuider Zee*
(= 'south sea'). Roman name was Oceanus Germanicus =
'German sea'.

Norway
Kingdom in north-west *Europe*
Original name was Norreweg; Norsemen had 3 chief sea-
routes to and from *Scandinavia*: Austurweg (= 'eastern
way') through the *Baltic*, Vesturweg (= 'western way')
across *North Sea*, and Norreweg (= 'northern way') to and
from the north along the Scandinavian coast. Last of these
came to denote the coast and later, in 9th century, the
territory approximating to Norway.

Nouakchott
Capital of *Mauritania*, North-West *Africa*
African = either 'one who has no ears' or 'one whose ears
are very small', presumably relating to chief here.

Nova Scotia
Province in east *Canada*, on *Atlantic* coast
Latin = 'new Scotland'. French were 1st settlers here, and
called territory Acadia. In 1621 English and Scottish king
James I granted territory to Scot Sir William Alexander,
who named it, in classical style, after his native land.

Novaya Zemlya
Group of islands in *Arctic*, in north USSR
Russian = 'new land'. English explorer Sir Hugh Willough-
by, who discovered islands in 1553, reported them under
this name, which was possibly given by north coastal
dwellers as long ago as 12th century.

Novgorod

City in north-west USSR, south-west of *Leningrad*

Russian = 'new town'. Novgorod is one of most ancient of all Russian cities (founded in 9th century). Name is common for a number of Russian towns, eg Nizhny Novgorod (now *Gorky*), Novgorod-Seversky in *Ukraine*, and many more. Varangians (Scandinavian Vikings who settled in *Russia* in 9th century) called it Holmgard = 'island town'.

Nyasaland

Former name of *Malawi*

Named after Lake Nyasa, in turn with native name = 'lake'. Renamed *Malawi* in 1964.

O

Ob, River
Long river in west *Siberia*, USSR, flowing north into *Arctic* Ocean
Possibly from Iranian ab = 'water, river' or, less likely, from local (Komi) word = 'aunt'.

Oberammergau
Small town and resort in *Bavaria*, West *Germany*, south-west of *Munich*
From German ober = 'upper' + Ammer (name of river, from Old High German am = 'to flow') + Gau = 'district'.

Oceania
Loose term for islands of Central and South-West *Pacific*
Name was invented by Danish-French geographer Conrad Malte-Brun (1775–1826) about 1812, and generally refers to islands of *Polynesia, Melanesia, Micronesia* and, usually, Australasia.

Odense
City and port in south-east *Denmark*
Derived from name of Odin, great god of Scandinavian mythology (same as Woden), who was worshipped here.

Oder, River
Rises in *Moravia, Czechoslovakia*, and flows generally north through *Poland* into *Baltic Sea*
Probably from Indo-European adu = 'current', or possibly from Slavonic dr = 'wearing through, eroding'. Not likely to be from Old High German atar = 'rapid' since this would have given name as Ader.

Odessa

City and port on *Black Sea* in republic of *Ukraine*, USSR

When town was built in 1795, by order of Catherine II, it was given, according to current fashion, name of Greek origin: in this case Odessos, as it was thought to be on site of former Greek colony of this name on north coast of *Black Sea* (actually west of present city). Name is often falsely linked with Greek mythical hero Odysseus. (For similar 'Greek' Russian names see *Sebastopol, Simferopol*.)

Ohio

River and state in north USA

From Indian (Iroquois) word = 'beautiful' (referring to river); when French settlers explored river about 1680 they translated Indian word and named river La Belle Rivière (= 'the beautiful river'). River gave name to state.

Oise, River

Rises in *Belgium* in *Ardennes* Mountains and flows south-west into *France* to join River *Seine* just below *Pontoise*

From Indo-European eiso, oiso = 'rapid'.

Okhotsk, Sea of

In North-West *Pacific*, south-east USSR, between *Sakhalin* and *Kamchatka*)

Named by Russian Cossacks after River Okata (with its own name derived from Evenki word = 'river') which flows into it. Same river is also called Okhota, a more popular name as it is (falsely) associated with Russian okhota = 'hunting'.

Oklahoma

State in south USA

From Indian (Choctaw) okla = 'people' + homa = 'red', ie 'red-skinned people'. Name came into use as late as 1866 when it was proposed by Choctaw chief as official name for territory.

Olympia
State capital of *Washington*, USA
City was laid out in 1851 as Smithfield, but was soon renamed after nearby Olympic Mountains, whose highest peak, Olympus, was so named in 1788 by English voyager John Meares as it suggested suitable 'home of the gods', like Greek *Olympus*.

Olympus
Mountain range in north *Greece*
Traditional home of Greek gods in mythology; not likely to derive from Greek olympos = 'glittering' as name was known in pre-Greek times. Perhaps from Caucasian word = 'mountain'.

Omaha
Largest city in *Nebraska*, USA, on River *Missouri*
From Indian (Sioux) tribal name, perhaps = 'dwellers on the upper reaches of the river'.

Oman
Sultanate in east *Arabia*
From name of ancient city, now no longer in existence. City derived name from Arabic word, perhaps = 'stopped here' (referring to nomads who settled here), or from name of founder Oman-ben-Ibrahim.

Omdurman
City in *Sudan*, north-west of *Khartoum*
Named after local Moslem saint Um-Marium (1646−1730)

Ontario
Province in central *Canada* and lake on its south-eastern border
From Indian (Iroquois) oniatar-io = 'beautiful' (referring to lake). Lake gave name to province. (Compare *Ohio*: ending -io is common to both.)

Oporto
City and seaport in north-west *Portugal*
From Portuguese o porto = 'the port'. Roman name was Portus cale = 'warm harbour' (ie not freezing over), which gave name of whole country *Portugal*.

Oran

City and seaport on *Mediterranean* in north-west *Algeria*

Either from Arabic Wahran or from Warahan, name of mediaeval Berber ruler. Roman name was Portus divinus = 'port of the gods'.

Orange Free State

Province in South *Africa* between River Orange and River *Vaal*

State is named after river, in turn named by Dutch settlers in 1777 in honour of Dutch royal house of Orange (who had owned principality of Orange in south *France* from 8th century to 1713).

Oregon

State in north-west USA, on *Pacific* coast

Name has had derivation ascribed to numerous languages, including Spanish, French, Iranian and Indian, with meanings varying from 'hurricane' to 'piece of dried apple'. More likely (and interesting) theory is that name results from mistake of French map-engraver who in 1715 rendered River *Wisconsin* as 'Ouariconsint' with last 4 letters ('sint') on line below, thus inventing a mythical River Ouaricon, anglicised as Oregon and eventually becoming name of state.

Orinoco, River

In *Venezuela*, South *America*

Name is believed to derive from indigenous (Guarauno) words meaning 'a place to paddle', ie river that is navigable in small boats.

Orkney Islands

North of *Scotland, Great Britain*

Of uncertain origin. Pliny wrote of them in 1st century as Orcades, which Angles 'translated' as orku = 'dolphin' + ey = 'island', but this was merely attempt to explain unknown meaning.

Orléans
City on River *Loire*, south-west of *Paris*, *France*
Gaulish name was Cenabium, from Celtic cenna = 'hill'.
Original city was destroyed by Caesar and rebuilt in 3rd
century as Roman fortified town with name Aurelianum, in
honour of Emperor Aurelius. From this comes modern
name Orléans.

Osaka
2nd largest city in *Japan*, south-west of *Tokyo*
Name known since 14th century, when city became capital.
From Japanese oo-saka = 'big hill'.

Oslo
Capital of *Norway*
Probably from Indo-European os = 'mouth' + name of
River Lo, though could perhaps be from Norwegian ass og
lo = 'forest clearing'. From 1624 to 1925 was Christiania
(spelt Kristiania from 1877), after King Christian IV, in
whose reign it was rebuilt when earlier city had been
destroyed by fire. City was first founded in 1048 by Viking
Harald Hardraade.

Ostend
Seaport and resort in west *Belgium*, on *North Sea*
In Flemish Oostende = 'east end', ie either of bay or
because at east end of sandbank (at west end of which is
resort Westende).

Otranto, Strait of
Between south-east *Italy* and *Albania*
Strait is named after town Otranto, formerly Roman Hyd-
runtum, formerly Greek settlement of Hydrus, in turn from
Greek hydor = 'water'.

Ottawa
Capital of *Canada*, in south-east *Ontario*
Named after Indian tribe, the Outaouacs or Outaouais,
who had moved here from region of Lake Huron, with
their own name perhaps = 'traders'. Town was founded in
1827 with name Bytown, after English colonel John By of
Royal Engineers whose men built Rideau Canal here;
named Ottawa in 1854 when it became capital.

Ouagadougou
Capital of *Burkina Faso*, West *Africa*
Difficult name, with no certain etymology.

P

Pacific Ocean

Between *Asia* and Western *Australia* and North and South *America*

Spanish explorer Vasco Núñez de Balboa first sighted Pacific in 1513 from Panama isthmus and called it South Sea (as opposed to North Sea, ie *Atlantic*). When Magellan crossed the ocean from *Tierra del Fuego* to *Philippines* in 1520–21 he encountered no storms and so named it Mar Pacifico = 'calm sea'.

Padua

City in north-east *Italy*, west of *Venice*

Possibly from Latin padus = 'pine-tree' (compare *Po*), or from name of River Adda, in turn derived perhaps from padvos = 'rapid'. Roman name was Patavium.

Pago Pago

Chief port of American *Samoa*, South *Pacific*

From native (Polynesian) name Pango Pango. (According to story, missionaries printing news-sheet here in 19th century were short of letter 'n' so printed name without this letter.)

Pakistan

Republic of South *Asia*, bordering in east with *India*

Name was first proposed in 1931, and established with partition of *India* in 1947; possibly from Urdu or Iranian pak = 'clean' (ie in spirit) + stan = 'country', but alternative explanation says that name was devised in 1933 by group of Moslem students at Cambridge University from initial letters of Moslem states *Punjab, Afghanistan, Kashmir, Iran*, Sind and final element of *Baluchistan*.

Palermo

City and seaport in north-west *Sicily*, south *Italy*

From Greek name Panormos, from pan = 'all, every' + hormos = 'harbour'. Seventeen ports with this name were known to have existed on *Mediterranean* in time of Greek empire.

Palestine

Former name of *Israel*

From ancient people, Philistines, enemies of Israelites, who inhabited south-west Palestine from the 12th century BC. Their name is from Hebrew palash = 'to travel' and so = 'wanderers'.

Palma

Capital of *Majorca* and *Balearic Islands*

Name is Roman (= 'palm') and is translation of name of Phoenician colony here, Tamar.

Pamirs

Range of mountains in Central *Asia*, mainly in *Tadzhikistan*, south USSR

Noted by Chinese travellers of 7th century as Po-mi-lo. Many explanations suggested, among which are: 1. from name Upa-Meru = 'under Meru' (mountain of Meru in Hindu mythology is centre of the world); 2. from Sanskrit mir = 'lake' (of which there are many in Pamir mountains); 3. from Po-i-mur = 'foot of death' or Po-i-murg = 'bird's foot'; 4. (more possibly) from Pa-i-mihr = 'foot of the sun', ie at the foot of Mithras, god of the sun.

Pamplona

Capital of province of *Navarra*, north *Spain*

According to tradition, founded in 75 BC by Pompey, Caesar's rival, and was known as Pompeiopolis = 'Pompey's town'.

Panama

Republic in Central *America*

From one of a number of like-sounding Indian words, perhaps = 'many fish' (Spanish explorers found many fishermen's huts here in 16th century). Country named after its capital, now Panama City, founded in 1519. Panama Canal is named after country.

Papua

Former territory on island of New Guinea, north of *Australia*

From name of inhabitants, Papuans, who are native to many islands of *Melanesia* and *Polynesia*. Their name is of Malay origin, probably from papuvah = 'curly-headed', or perhaps from pua-pua = 'dark brown'.

Papua New Guinea
Nation formed from two former areas of Papua and
New Guinea, comprising eastern half of island of New
Guinea
Island of New Guinea discovered by Portuguese explorer
Jorge de Menezes in 1526; given present name in 1545 by
Portuguese navigator Ortez de Rez because of resemblance
of natives to those of *Guinea*, West *Africa*. Papua New
Guinea became independent nation in 1975.

Paraguay
Republic in central South *America*
Named after River Paraguay, in turn after native Indian
tribe, Paragua, with name derived from Indian para =
'water'.

Paramaribo
Capital and chief seaport of Surinam, north-east South
America
From Indian para = 'water, sea' + maribo = 'dwellers,
inhabitants'.

Paraná
River and state in south *Brazil*, South *America*
State—and city of Paraná, formerly Bajada de Santa Fé (=
'hill of the Holy Faith')—named after river, in turn derived
from Indian para = 'water'.

Paris
Capital of *France*
Full Roman name was Lutetia Parisiorum = 'Lutetia of the
Parisii'. Lutetia probably derives from Latin lutum = 'clay,
sludge'. Parisii were Gaulish tribe with name perhaps
deriving from Celtic par = 'ship' (ie 'shipmen, sailors',
dwelling on banks of River *Seine*), or from word = 'border
town'.

Parma
City in central north *Italy*
Name is of Etruscan (pre-Roman) origin, of uncertain
meaning. May be connected with Semitic (Arabic) barma =
'circle, turn', ie 'curve in the river'. Name persisted in spite
of Roman renaming as Colonia Julia Augusta (= 'colony of
Julius Augustus') and Greek renaming as Chrysopolis (=
'gold-town').

Parry Islands
In *Arctic,* north of *Canada*
Named by John Ross after English polar explorer Sir William Parry (1790—1855) who discovered them in expedition of 1818—20.

Pasadena
City in *California,* USA, north-east of *Los Angeles*
Founded in 1874 as Indiana Colony, being renamed Pasadena following year from Indian (Chippewa) word = 'crown of the valley'.

Patagonia
Part of *Argentina* and *Chile*
Name comes from native inhabitants, called Patagones by Spanish explorers in 16th century. Story goes that Magellan, first European to explore coast here, coined name after Patagon, dog-headed monster of Spanish 16th century romance 'Amadis de Gaula', since natives wore thick furs and had bushy hair and painted faces.

Paterson
City in north-east *New Jersey,* USA
Named in 1791 in honour of Governor William Paterson (1745—1806).

Peking/Beijing
Capital of *China*
From Chinese bei = 'north' + kin(tsing) = 'capital'; ie 'northern capital' (as distinct from *Nanking*). Alternative name of Peiping has same meaning, as does modern spelling (in Pinyin) Beijing.

Peloponnese
South peninsula of *Greece*
From Greek = 'island of Pelops': Greek nesos = 'island' + Pelops, in Greek mythology the son of Tantalus, who in a chariot race beat King Oenomaus and won the hand of his daughter and this territory. Name is good example of a myth evolving from a place-name whose true meaning is unknown.

Pemba

Island in Indian Ocean, north-east of *Zanzibar*, off east coast of *Tanzania*

Name is from a Bantu language, as yet unexplained. Arabic name is al-Hathera, from khaḍrā = 'green' (compare *Algeciras*); implication is that Pemba is more fertile than Zanzibar.

Pennsylvania

State in north-east USA, bordering on Lake *Erie*

Territory to west of River *Delaware* was granted in 1681 by English king Charles II to Quaker William Penn after whom, + element derived from Latin silva = 'wood', it was named, ie 'Penn's woodland'. (Penn himself claimed that 1st element derived not from his own name but from Celtic pen = 'headland'.)

Périgueux

Town in central south-west *France*, south-west of *Limoges*

Name is derived from that of Gaulish tribe Petrocorii, whose own name was mentioned by Livy as Tricori (= 'three armies'), from Gaulish corio = 'army' which became final element (-gueux) of modern name.

Pernambuco

State in north-east *Brazil*, South *America*

Named after former capital, now *Recife*, from Indian parana = 'big river' (compare *Paraná*) + mbucu = 'arm'; town was built on delta of two rivers. Less likely derivation is from Indian peranabuco = 'stone with a hole bored through it'.

Persia

Former name, still sometimes used, of *Iran*

From name of one of peoples, Farsi (after whom also is named province Fars in south of country), whose own name is of uncertain origin, though has been linked with Pharisees and with Sanskrit parasah = 'steed' (ie 'horsemen'). Name was regarded as unsuitable and officially changed to *Iran* in 1935.

Perth

Capital of Western *Australia*, near coast of Indian Ocean

Site here was selected for town by Scottish captain James Stirling in 1827. Two years later it was named after Perthshire, *Scotland*, native county of Sir George Murray, then secretary of state for colonies.

Peru

Republic in west of South *America*

Name was given in 16th century by Spanish settlers, after River Biru, where they landed after sailing here from *Panama* isthmus. Name of river probably derives either from Indian word = 'river' or from name of Indian chief. Incas, encountered here by Spanish explorers, called their country Tahuantin-suyn = 'four provinces'.

Peshawar

City in north-west *Pakistan*, north-west of *Lahore*

From Sanskrit purasha-pura = 'frontier town'.

Petrograd

Former name of *Leningrad*, USSR

Name *St Petersburg* came to be regarded in 1914 as too 'Germanic', so was changed to Slavonic variant Petrograd, with same basic meaning ('Peter's town'). Renamed *Leningrad* in 1924.

Philadelphia

Largest city in *Pennsylvania*, USA

Founded by English Quaker William Penn in 1682 with name, expressing his religious ideals, derived from Greek = 'brotherly love'. No doubt Penn also had biblical city of Philadelphia in mind.

Philippines

Group of islands in South-West *Pacific*, and republic which they form

Discovered by Magellan in 1521, who named them St Lazarus Islands after saint's day, 17 December, on which he sighted them. Twenty-two years later, when settled by Spanish, they were renamed after heir to Spanish throne, future king Philip II.

Phnom Penh
Capital of Kampuchea, former *Cambodia*
Khmer words = 'mountain of abundance'.

Phoenix
State capital of *Arizona*, USA
Name not connected with Greek Phoenicia (although in-habitants are known as Phoenicians). Connection with phoenix, mythological bird, seems inappropriate, as city has never risen from the ashes (ie been rebuilt after a fire). But perhaps it was built on site of a burned-down Indian village.

Picardy
Historic province in north-east *France*
From Old French pic = 'pike, lance', name given to in-habitants who in 13th century were armed with pikes.

Piedmont
Region in north *Italy*, bordering on *Switzerland* and *France*
From Old Italian pie di monte = 'foot of the mountain' (ie *Alps*).

Pierre
State capital of South *Dakota*, USA
Originally named Mahto, Indian (Sioux) = 'bear'. Soon renamed Pierre (locally pronounced 'peer') after Pierre Choteau, French fur trader.

Pietermaritzburg
Capital of province of *Natal*, South *Africa*, west of *Durban*
Town was founded in 1838 by Boers after victory over Zulus, and was named in honour of their killed Voortrek-ker leaders, Piet Retief and Gerrit Maritz.

Pisa
City in *Tuscany*, north *Italy*, south-west of *Florence*
One of 12 Etruscan towns of this name, as yet not satisfac-torily explained (perhaps = 'river mouth').

Pitcairn Island
In South *Pacific*, midway between *Australia* and South *America*

Discovered by English explorer Philip Carteret in 1767 who named it after midshipman who first sighted it.

Pittsburgh
City in south-west *Pennsylvania*, USA

Founded by French settlers in 1754 with name Fort Duquesne, after governor of French *Canada*. Captured by English in 1758 and renamed Pittsburgh in honour of English statesman William Pitt (1708−78) as compliment for his support against French forces.

Plate, River
Estuary of River *Paraná* and River *Uruguay*, South *America*, flowing south-east between *Uruguay* and *Argentina* into *Atlantic*

Spanish name, Rio de la Plata = 'river of silver', was given by Sebastian Cabot in 1526 when he discovered it and bartered here with natives for silver. (See *Argentina*.) Earlier, the Spanish navigator Juan Díaz de Solís had named the estuary Mar Dulce = 'freshwater sea', and for a while, after his death, it was also called Río de Solís in his honour.

Plenty, Bay of
On north-east coast of North Island, *New Zealand*

So named by Cook in 1770 on account of numerous flourishing villages observed by him along coast here, with whose inhabitants he had had profitable dealings.

Plovdiv
2nd largest city in *Bulgaria*, south-east of *Sofia*

Founded (or rebuilt) in 359 BC by Macedonian king Philip II, after whom it was originally named, as Philippopolis (= 'Philip's town'), or, in local language of Daco-Moesian, Pulpudava, with same meaning (Pulp = 'Philip' + dava = 'town'). Latter name persisted and became modern Plovdiv, although Romans renamed town as Trimontium (= 'with three hills').

Po, River
In north *Italy* flowing east into *Adriatic Sea*
From Latin name Padus, of uncertain origin; perhaps from
Ligurian bodincus, bodeghos = 'bottomless' or from
Gaulish padi = 'pine', which is probably origin of city of
Padua.

Poitiers
Town in central west *France*, south-east of *Nantes*
Before Roman occupation was (in Latin version) Lemonum,
probably from Gaulish leima = 'lime-tree'. It was territory
of Gaulish tribe Pictavi (Pictones), from whose name
modern Poitiers evolved.

Poitou
Historic province in west *France*, part of *Aquitaine*
From Latin Pictavum, of same origin as that of its capital,
Poitiers.

Poland
Republic in east central *Europe*
From inhabitants, Poles, with name derived from Slavonic
= 'plain dwellers'. Country is largely low-lying.

Polynesia
Large group of islands in Central and South-East
Pacific, including *Hawaii, Samoa* and *Tonga*
From Greek polys = 'many' + nesos = 'island'; name was
first used by Portuguese explorer Barros in 16th century but
applied only to large islands between *Asia* and *Australia*.
Name served as 'model'—as did *Oceania*—for *Micronesia,
Melanesia* and *Indonesia*.

Pomerania
Region in north central *Europe* bordering on *Baltic Sea*,
mainly in *Poland*.
From Slavonic po = 'by' + morze = 'sea', ie = 'region by
the sea'. Polish name of region is Pomorze.

Pondicherry
Territory and its capital in south-east *India*
Originally Poducheri = 'new town', from Tamil putu =
'new' + cheri = 'town'. Name refers to town's origins in
1674 as a French colony.

Pontoise
Town in north *France* on River *Oise*, north of *Paris*
From Latin pontus (French pont) = 'bridge' + name of River *Oise*.

Popocatapetl
Volcano in *Mexico*, south-east of Mexico City
From Nahuatl popocani = 'to smoke' + tepetl = 'mountain', ie 'smoking mountain'.

Port Arthur
Former name of Chinese port *Lüshun*
Named after English Lieutenant Arthur who surveyed coast here in 1860. Together with *Talien/Dalian* (formerly *Dairen* or *Dalny*) now forms part of large port of *Lü-ta/Lüda*.

Port-au-Prince
Capital of *Haiti, West Indies*
French = 'port of the Prince'; story is that ship named *Prince*, probably French but possibly English, had taken shelter in bay on which town is now situated. Bay was called Le Port du Prince and in 1743 French authorities decided to make town that had arisen here the capital of Saint-Domingue (present *Haiti*). Name, which had already become Port-au-Prince, was formalised by French royal decree in 1749.

Port Elizabeth
Seaport in *Cape Province*, South *Africa*, east of *Cape Town*
Founded by English settlers in 1820 and planned by Sir Rufane Donkin who named it after his late wife.

Port Harcourt
Seaport in south-east *Nigeria*, West *Africa*
Founded in 1912 and named after then British Colonial Secretary Lewis Harcourt.

Port Moresby
Chief seaport of *Papua New Guinea*, in south-east of the island
Harbour here was explored in 1873 by British Captain (later Admiral) John Moresby (1830–1922), who named it after his father, Admiral Sir Fairfax Moresby.

Porto Novo
Capital and seaport of *Benin*, West *Africa*
Portuguese = 'new harbour'; so named by Portuguese slave-traders who landed here in 16th century.

Port Phillip Bay
Inlet of *Bass Strait*, south *Victoria, Australia*
Originally named Port King by Lieutenant John Murray, of Royal Navy, who discovered it in 1801, after the then governor, but later changed name to Port Phillip in honour of Captain Arthur Phillip (1738–1814), British founder and 1st governor of *New South Wales*.

Port Said
City and seaport on *Mediterranean* at entrance to *Suez* Canal, *Egypt*
Founded in 1859 when *Suez* Canal was begun by French diplomat Ferdinand de Lesseps and named by him after Muhammad Said, then Viceroy (Khedive) of *Egypt*.

Portugal
Republic in south-west *Europe*
Name derives from port of Portus Cale (modern *Oporto*), with its own name from Latin = 'warm harbour' (ie ice-free). Town was captured by Moors in 11th century and gave its name first to surrounding territory, then to whole country.

Potomac, River
In east USA, flowing into *Chesapeake Bay*
Name is of Indian origin, but of uncertain meaning. Perhaps a tribal name. Recorded by English explorer John Smith in 1608 as Patawomeck.

Potsdam
City in north *East Germany*, south-west of *Berlin*
In 993 was Poztupimi. Possibly from Slavonic pod dubimi = 'under the oak-trees', but more likely from personal name Postamp.

Poznan
City in west *Poland*
Perhaps from some personal name, although could be based on Slavonic pan = 'lord', denoting territory owned by him.

Prague
Capital of *Czechoslovakia*

Many theories as to origin; perhaps connected with Czech praziti = 'place where wood has been burned', or with Slavonic prati = 'to work' (referring to fish-dykes constructed in river).

Pretoria
Capital of South *Africa*, and of *Transvaal*

Founded and named, in 1855, in honour of Andries Pretorius (1799–1853), Boer leader, by his son, the 1st president of *Transvaal*.

Prince Albert
Town in central *Saskatchewan, Canada*

Founded in 1866 as mission station and named after English prince consort Albert, husband of Queen Victoria (compare Lake *Albert, Africa*).

Prince Edward Island
Province of east *Canada*, in Gulf of *St Lawrence*

Discovered by French explorer Jacques Cartier in 1534, who named it Île St Jean, anglicised as St John's Island when ceded to *Britain* in 1763. In 1798 renamed Prince Edward Island in honour of English prince Edward (1767–1820), 4th son of King George III and father of Queen Victoria.

Prince of Wales Island
North of Cape *York, Queensland, Australia*

Discovered by Cook in 1770 and named by him in honour of Prince of Wales, future English king George IV.

Provence
Historic province in south-east *France*

From Latin provincia = 'province'. South Gaul, as part of Roman empire, was called Provincia Narboniensis (after town of Narbonne) and was originally much larger territory than modern Provence, extending from *Alps* to *Pyrenees*.

Providence
State capital of *Rhode Island*, USA

So named by English settler Roger Williams in 1636, to express 'God's merciful providence' in delivering him from hostile Indian tribesmen.

Prussia
Former principal state of *Germany*
Named after inhabitants, Prussians, who dwelt on south-east coast of *Baltic Sea*. Their name derives from Lithuanian prud, prut = 'pond, lake'.

Puebla
State and its capital in central *Mexico*, Central *America*
From Spanish pueblo = 'village, settlement'. Town was founded in 1531 by Franciscan friar T. Motolineo with name Puebla de los Angeles = 'town of the angels', from belief that angels helped in construction of church here. City gave name to state.

Puerto Rico
Island in *West Indies*
Spanish = 'rich port'; originally name of bay on north coast discovered and named by Columbus in 1493 (though island itself he named San Juan = 'Saint John', as he landed here on St John's Day, 24 June). Name of bay became that of town founded in 1508 by Ponce de León, its 1st governor, then spread to whole island. From 1898 to 1932 was known as Porto Rico.

Punjab
State, former province, in north-west *India*
From Persian panj = 'five' + ab = 'water', ie 'five rivers' (Jhelum, Chenab, Ravi, Beas and Sutlej, all tributaries of River *Indus*). Name is now really a misnomer, since only 2 rivers (Beas and Sutlej) flow through state.

Pusan
City and chief seaport of South *Korea*, on south-east coast
From Japanese = 'pot-mountain', probably with reference to pot-shaped mountain at foot of which city is situated.

Pushkin

Town in north-west USSR, south of *Leningrad*

Named (since 1937) after Russian national poet Alexander Pushkin, who spent childhood years here. From 1918 to 1937 was Detskoye Selo = 'children's village': town was planned to be holiday centre for children. Before 1918 was Tsarskoye Selo; from 18th century was country residence of Russian royal family, although name was not derived from word tsar but from Estonian saari = 'island, hill', and in 1708 was recorded as Sarskoye Selo.

Pyongyang

Capital of North *Korea*, north-west of *Seoul*

From Korean p'yŏng = 'large flat' + yang = 'field', referring to plain on which city was established. Name appears on some maps as Heijo, which is Japanese pronunciation of Chinese characters for name.

Pyrenees

Range of mountains in south-west *Europe* dividing *France* from *Spain*

Name is of uncertain origin, but may derive from some Celtic root such as ber or per = 'point, summit'.

Q

Quebec
Province and its capital in east *Canada*
Probably from Indian (Algonquian) quilibek = 'place where the river narrows' (ie River *St Lawrence*), but perhaps from word = 'place of shooting'. City was founded in 1608 by French coloniser Samuel de Champlain.

Queen Charlotte Islands
Off coast of British *Columbia, Canada*
Named by English Captain George Dixon in 1787 after his ship, the *Queen Charlotte*, in turn named after Queen Charlotte, wife of King George III.

Queen Maud Land
Norwegian territory in *Antarctic*
Discovered by Norwegian expedition of Rieser and Larsen in 1930 and named after Queen Maud, wife of Norwegian king Haakon VII.

Queensland
State in north-east *Australia*
Formed part of colony of *New South Wales* until 1859 when became separate colony named in honour of Queen Victoria. (Originally, name of Cooksland had been proposed, but was rejected in favour of Queensland.)

Quetta
City in central west *Pakistan*
Name is respelling of Pashto word kwatkot = 'fort'.

Quimper
Town in *Brittany*, north-west *France*, south-east of *Brest*
From Breton cenbera = 'confluence'; town is at point where River Odet joins River Steir.

Quito
Capital of *Ecuador*, South *America*

Was name of whole country until 1830; city was named Quito by Spanish explorers in 1533 after Indian Quitu tribe who inhabited territory (but who were extinct by end of Spanish rule in 1822).

R

Rabat
Capital of *Morocco*, North-West *Africa*
Name is Arabic word ribat = 'fort'. City was founded as fortress in 12th century.

Raleigh
State capital of North *Carolina*, USA
Named in 1792 in honour of Sir Walter Raleigh who more than 200 years earlier had made several unsuccessful attempts to colonise *'Virginia'* (present North *Carolina*).

Rangoon
Capital of *Burma*
Original name of city was Dagon, after Shwe Dagon pagoda here, centre of Burmese religious life, its own name meaning 'grain', as god Dagon was believed to have invented the plough. In 18th century city was renamed Rangoon by king Alaungpaya, with this = 'the end of strife', marking his victory over Lower Burma in 1755.

Ravenna
City in north-east *Italy*, south-east of *Bologna*
Name existed BC and is probably of Etruscan origin, but of unknown meaning. Ending -enna is common to many names of Asia Minor and suggests language group common to *Mediterranean* countries.

Recife
Capital of *Pernambuco*, north-east *Brazil*, South *America*
First settled by Portuguese about 1535 who named it Ciudad de Recife = 'reef town'. City's harbour and beaches are sheltered from force of sea by an offshore chain of rocks. Earlier (Indian) name was *Pernambuco*.

Red Sea
Between North-East *Africa* and *Arabia*
Several possible explanations: 1. because of reddish colour of water caused by brightly-coloured shells or algae that have died; 2. from reddish colour of banks; 3. from name of ancient tribe of Himyarites (= 'red'); 4. with meaning 'southern', as many Asian and African peoples denoted countries by colours, with red = south, black = north, etc (compare *Black Sea*).

Reggio di Calabria
City in *Calabria*, south *Italy*, on Strait of *Messina*
From Latin regium = 'royal town, royal castle' + name of region *Calabria*. Town was founded about 700 BC as Greek colony.

Regina
Capital of province of *Saskatchewan, Canada*
Latin = 'queen'. Name was suggested in 1882 by Princess Louise, wife of Governor General Lord Lorne (see also *Alberta*) as compliment to Queen Victoria (whose own name was already widespread as a place-name). No doubt this new name was felt to be much more acceptable, too, than original name of site here, Pile of Bones.

Réunion
Island in Indian Ocean, south-west of *Mauritius*
French = 'reunion'. Discovered by Magellan in early 16th century and originally named after him. Annexed by French in 1639, who in 1649 named it Bourbon, after French royal house. In 1793, year of French Revolution, was renamed Réunion to mark union of revolutionaries from *Marseilles* with National Guard in *Paris* on 10 August previous year. (With restoration of monarchy, name reverted to Bourbon, but with revolution of 1848 was re-established as Réunion.)

Reykjavik
Capital of *Iceland*
From Icelandic reyka = 'to smoke' (referring to steam of geysers) + Old Norse vik = 'inlet'.

Rheims

City in north-east *France*, north-east of *Paris*
Named after Gaulish tribe Remi, mentioned by Caesar in 51 BC, whose capital it was. (Tribal name may = 'rulers'.) Earlier Roman name of 1st century BC was Durocortorum, from Gaulish durum = 'fortress'.

Rhine, River

In central and west *Europe*, flowing north-west from *Alps* into *North Sea*
From Old High German ri = 'to go, to flow' + Gaulish element (r)enos = 'water'.

Rhode Island

State in *New England*, north-east USA, bordering on *Atlantic*
Discovered in 1524 by Italian explorer Giovanni da Verrazano who noted that island was 'about the size of the island of Rhodes' (ie Greek island in *Mediterranean*). But in 1635 Dutch settlers were calling island rode = 'red', probably referring to colour of earth. So name seems to have two origins, with 1st probably influencing 2nd.

Rhodes

Largest island in *Dodecanese*, off south-west coast of *Turkey*.
Probably from Greek rhodon = 'rose', as this flower once grew in abundance here, though this could be attempt to explain earlier pre-Greek name of unknown meaning. Some claim that name is development from Phoenician erod = 'snake', since snakes were once common here.

Rhodesia

Former name of *Zimbabwe* (Southern Rhodesia), in south-east Central *Africa*
Named in 1884 after Cecil Rhodes (1853−1902), British founder of South Africa Company, who administered it.

Rhône, River

River in west *Europe* rising in *Switzerland* and flowing through Lake *Geneva* into *France* and then south into *Mediterranean*

Latin name was Rhodanus, possibly from Indo-European erer = 'to flow' or perhaps from Celtic rho = 'to flow quickly' (in contrast to slower flowing *Saône*, its chief tributary). Name could also be of pre-Indo-European (Ligurian) origin.

Rialto

Commercial region in *Venice, Italy,* consisting of an island with surrounding district

From Italian ripa alta = 'high bank'. Rialto Bridge over Grand Canal is named after island.

Richmond

State capital of *Virginia*, USA

So named in 1737 by English settler William Byrd, probably because of similarity between situation of American town on River James to that of English town Richmond in Surrey on River *Thames*.

Riga

Capital of republic of *Latvia*, north-west USSR

Founded at end of 12th century on River Dvina. Name probably derives from Slavonic reka = 'river', referring not to River Dvina, but to another river, the Reka, which has silted up and no longer exists.

Rio de Janeiro

Chief seaport and former capital of *Brazil*, South *America*, on South *Atlantic*

Portuguese members of expedition of Italian navigator Amerigo Vespucci sighted bay on which town is now situated on 1 January 1502 and took it for the estuary of a large river. They therefore named it Rio de Janeiro = 'January river'. Town was founded in 1566 and took this name. Name is commonly shortened to Rio.

Rio de Oro
Coastal territory in south Spanish *Sahara*, West *Africa*
Portuguese expedition of 1436 discovered here a long
stretch of water in the desert which they took for a river,
therefore naming it Rio de Oro = 'river of gold' (either
because local inhabitants traded gold dust here, or simply
referring to colour of sand).

Rio Grande
River rising in *Colorado*, USA, and flowing south-east
through *Mexico* into Gulf of *Mexico*
Spanish = 'great river'. Many South American rivers have
this name. Mexican name is Rio Bravo = 'stormy river'.

Rio Tinto
River in south-west *Spain* and town on it
Spanish = 'coloured river'; river is yellowish from copper
mined here.

Riviera, the
Name of south coastal strip with popular resorts in
many countries, but notably in *France*, where it ex-
tends along *Mediterranean* coast from *Marseilles* to La
Spezia, *Italy*
Italian = 'coast'. See also *Côte d'Azur*.

Riyadh
Capital of *Saudi Arabia*
Name is corruption of Arabic Ar-Riyad = 'the grassland'.
Since city was built by an oasis in middle of desert, this
appears to be a sarcastic name.

Rochester
City in *New York* state, USA, on Lake *Ontario*
Originally Rochesterville when named in 1811 after Colonel
Nathaniel Rochester, one of owners of territory here. Name
became Rochester in 1822. (Most other American towns
Rochester are named after this one, but not Rochester,
Massachusetts, which was named in 1686 by settlers from
English town Rochester, Kent.)

Romania
More correct spelling of *Rumania*

Rome
Capital of *Italy*
Named after River Ruma, ancient name of River *Tiber*, with name probably of Etruscan origin, or possibly from root word = 'to flow'. According to tradition, Rome was founded by Romulus, twin brother of Remus (whose name resembles his), and was named after him, but he was mythical figure.

Ross Dependency
Sector of *Antarctic*, south of *New Zealand*, to whom it belongs
Ross Sea was discovered in 1841 by English polar explorer James Ross (1800–62) after whom it, Ross Island and Ross Dependency are named.

Rotterdam
Chief seaport of *Netherlands*
Named after River Rotte, which joins River Maas (*Meuse*) at point where city stands, + dam (compare *Amsterdam*). Name of river is probably derived from Indo-European roth = 'hurrying'.

Rouen
City in north *France*, north-west of *Paris*
Roman name was Rotomagus, probably from name of Gaulish tribe or person.

Ruhr
River in north-west of West *Germany*, and industrial region mainly in its valley
River gave name to region, with name derived from Indo-European reu = 'to dig up, excavate'.

Rumania
Republic in south-east *Europe*
Was an outpost of Roman empire early AD; native population, Dacians (Roman province was called Dacia), mingled with Roman settlers, began to speak a form of Latin, and called themselves Romani, ie 'people from Rome'. From their name comes modern name Rumania (more correctly Romania).

Russia

Alternative name in many contexts for USSR, and country's official name before 1922

Name has been in use since 15th century for whole country, from earlier name Rus, after inhabitants of same name. Origin of name is still uncertain; possible explanations are: 1. name given by Slavs to Varangians (Swedish Vikings) whose leaders were first princes of Kievan Russia in 9th century, with meaning = 'foreigners'; 2. from Swedish tribe Ruotsi (= 'rowers'), oarsmen of Viking ships. The 1st of these theories seems more likely as Varangians came from coastal district of Roslagen (present south-east *Sweden*), and may have derived their name from 1st element of this.

Ruwenzori Range

Mountain massif on *Zaïre-Uganda* frontier, Central *Africa*

Perhaps from African words = 'lord of the clouds', from element ru (see *Rwanda*).

Rwanda

Republic in Central *Africa*

From name of inhabitants, of uncertain meaning. Element ru appears in many names of Rwanda, *Uganda, Tanzania, Zimbabwe* and *Zaïre* (eg *Ruwenzori* Mountains, River Ruiru, River Rufiji, Mount Rungwe).

S

Saar, River

In west *Europe* rising in *Vosges* and flowing through *France* into West *Germany* to become tributary of River *Moselle*

Probably from Indo-European ser = 'to flow'. River has given its name to Saarland, coalmining region (Land) in west of West *Germany*, as well as to its capital city, Saarbrücken (Saar bridge).

Sacramento

State capital of *California*, USA

Spanish = 'sacrament'. Name was originally given to River Sacramento in 1808 with some kind of religious association (probably with Holy Sacrament). River gave name to city, which was originally a trading post called Fort Sutter, after John Augustus Sutter, who established trading community of Swiss immigrants here in 1839.

Sahara

Largest desert in world, in North *Africa*

From Arabic ṣaḥrā' (plural ṣaḥārā') = 'desert' (with basic meaning 'brownish'). Name said to have been given to this particular desert by Ibn-al-Hakam in 9th century.

Saigon

Former name of *Ho Chi Minh City*, in *Vietnam*

Named after River Saigon, on whose estuary it is situated. Name of river probably = 'sandy shore' or 'shore dam', but 2nd element also = 'river', in which case meaning is perhaps 'west river'.

St Bernard Pass

1. Great St Bernard: through *Alps* on Swiss-Italian frontier; 2. Little St Bernard: through *Alps* on French-Italian frontier south of *Mont Blanc*

Both passes named after hospices founded about 960 by St Bernard of Menthon (923–1008).

St Cloud
Suburb of west *Paris, France*
Named after St Clodvald who built a monastery here in 6th century.

St Denis
Large suburb of north *Paris, France*, on River *Seine*
Named after St Denis (Greek Dionysius), 1st bishop of Paris and patron saint of *France*, who was martyred at place now called Montmartre (= 'martyr's mount') by the Romans about 258.

St Étienne
City in central south *France*, south-west of *Lyons*
French = 'St Stephen', to whom town was dedicated when founded in 11th century.

St Gotthard Pass
Through *Alps* in south-east *Switzerland*
Named after nearby chapel and hospice built in 11th century and dedicated to Bishop of Hildesheim, St Gotthard (Godehard) (died 1038).

St Helena
Island in South *Atlantic*, west of *Angola*
Discovered by Portuguese navigator João da Nova Castella on St Helena's Day (21 May) 1502.

St John, River
On frontier of *Canada* and USA flowing south-east through *New Brunswick* into *Atlantic*
Discovered by French explorers the Sieur de Monts and Samuel de Champlain on St John's Day (24 June) 1604. Named after river is city of St John, *New Brunswick*, founded in 1783 as Parr Town, after governor, Colonel Parr, but in 1785 renamed St John.

St Kitts
With *Nevis* independent state and one of *Leeward Islands, West Indies*
Originally named St Christopher by Columbus, after his patron saint, in 1493; in 1623 name was shortened to St Kitts by English settlers. (Kit is familiar form of name Christopher in English.)

St Lawrence
River, gulf and seaway in north-east *Canada*
River and gulf were explored by French navigator Jacques Cartier in 1534 and named after St Lawrence, on whose feast-day (10 August) he first sailed into a small bay on the north shore of the gulf. Present seaway constructed along upper section of river in 1955—59.

St Louis
Largest city in *Missouri*, USA
Founded by French fur trading company in 1764 and named in honour of French king Louis IX ('Saint Louis') and as patriotic tribute to reigning king Louis XV (1710—74).

St Lucia
Independent state and one of *Windward Islands, West Indies*, south of *Martinique*
Discovered by Columbus in 1502 and named after St Lucy (Spanish Santa Lucia), Sicilian virgin martyr, on whose feast-day (13 December), he landed here.

St Malo
Seaport on English Channel in north *Brittany, France*
Named after Maclou or Malo (Maclovius), Welsh bishop of nearby Aleth (present St Servan) in 6th century.

St Moritz
Resort in *Switzerland*
Named after river, in turn named after abbey, founded in 515 but no longer in existence, dedicated to St Maurice (German St Moritz).

St Nazaire
Seaport at mouth of River *Loire*, west *France*
Named after St Nazarius, early Italian martyr, to whom church built here in 11th century was dedicated.

St Paul
State capital of *Minnesota*, USA
Named after mission church built here in 1841 by French priest Lucien Galtier and dedicated to St Paul.

St Petersburg
1 Former name of *Leningrad*, USSR

Founded by Tsar Peter the Great in 1703 with German-style name (Russian Sankt-Peterburg) = 'St Peter's town', after church of St Peter and St Paul in fortress here built to defend mouth of River Neva (and doubtless also to act as fitting reminder of its founder). Was capital of *Russia* (1712 −28 and 1732−1918), having been renamed *Petrograd* in 1914. (See also *Leningrad*.)

St Petersburg
2 City in west *Florida*, USA, on Gulf of *Mexico*

So named in 1875 by Peter A. Demens, president of local rail company, after his former home city of *St Petersburg* in *Russia*.

St Pierre and Miquelon
Group of islands off south *Newfoundland*, North *Atlantic*

Portuguese explorer Joãs Alvarez Faguendez landed on St Pierre on 21 October 1520 and named islands Eleven Thousand Virgins after feast-day, that of St Ursula and the (11,000) virgin martyrs, on which landing was made. Reason for change to St Pierre not clear; perhaps one of Portuguese navigators was named San Pedro. Name was recorded by French explorer Jacques Cartier who landed here in 1536 as 'ysles Sainct Pierre'. Name of Miquelon is similarly obscure: perhaps is diminutive of Miguel (or Miquel), name of earlier Portuguese navigator.

St Quentin
Town in north-east *France* on River *Somme*

Named after St Quintin, martyred here in 3rd century by Roman emperor Diocletian.

St Tropez
Resort in south *France* on *Mediterranean*, south-west of *Cannes*

Named after Roman martyr Torpes of Pisa (died 1st century). Church dedicated to him was built here in 1055.

St Vincent

Independent state (St Vincent and the Grenadines) and one of *Windward Islands, West Indies*

Name probably given by Columbus who landed here on St Vincent's Day (22 January) 1498.

Sakhalin

Island off east coast of *Siberia*, USSR, in Sea of *Okhotsk*

Probably from Sahalyanula = 'black river', Manchurian name of River Amur, opposite whose estuary island lies.

Salem

State capital of *Oregon*, USA

Named after Salem, *Massachusetts*, in 1840s, which in turn was named by English Puritan settlers in 1629 knowing that this Hebrew word = 'peace' and that it was short variant of *Jerusalem*. At same time name was translation of Indian name for settlement, Chemeketa = 'place of rest'.

Salisbury

Former name of *Harare*, capital of *Zimbabwe*, Central *Africa*

Not named, as are 4 towns called Salisbury in USA, after English city, but after Lord Salisbury, English prime minister when city was founded in 1890 (with original name of Fort Salisbury).

Salonika

City and seaport in north-east *Greece*, capital of *Macedonia*

May derive from name of beautiful Thessalonica, sister of Alexander the Great, who was married by Cassander, the son of one of his generals and later king of *Macedonia*. Or from victory (Greek nike = 'victory') over the Thessalonians. The 1st version is more likely as King Cassander founded the city in 315 BC. Greek name of city is Thessaloniki.

Salt Lake City

State capital of *Utah*, USA

Founded in 1847 by Brigham Young and a band of Mormons as a 'new Jerusalem', or place of refuge from religious persecution. Was known as Great Salt Lake City, after lake near which it was established, until 1868, when name was shortened to present form.

Salzburg
City in *Austria*, south-west of *Vienna*
City is named after river Salzach, on which it stands, with river itself named after German Salz = 'salt'. Region has long been centre of salt mining and trading.

Samoa
Group of islands (Western Samoa and American Samoa) in South *Pacific*, north-east of *Fiji*
Name possibly given by Maoris who came from *New Zealand* to settle here and were impressed by large numbers of moas (gigantic birds of ostrich family, now extinct). More likely, moa became the totemic bird of the natives who named islands Samoa = 'place of Moa'.

San Antonio
City in *Texas*, USA, west of *Houston*
Named after river discovered by Spanish explorers on St Anthony's Day (19 May) 1691.

Sandwich Islands
Former name of *Hawaii*
So named by Cook in 1778 in honour of First Lord of British Admiralty Earl of Sandwich (1718–92). Name fell out of use after Cook was killed here in 1779 and earlier native name of *Hawaii* was readopted.

San Francisco
Seaport in *California*, USA, north-west of *Los Angeles*
Name (Spanish = 'St Francis') is connected with Francis in two ways: 1. Spanish Franciscan monks set up missionary station here in 1776, but also 2. Sir Francis Drake had landed here earlier, in 1578, when bay was named Port Sir Francis. Name San Francisco was officially adopted by city in 1847.

San José
Capital of *Costa Rica*, Central *America*
Spanish = 'St Joseph'. City was founded by Spanish in 1736, originally with name Villa Nueva = 'new town'; name was later changed to San José.

San Juan
Capital of *Puerto Rico, West Indies*
Named after founder of original settlement, to west of present city in 1508, Spanish explorer Juan Ponce de León, who is buried here.

San Marino
Republic within *Italy*, south-west of Rimini, near *Adriatic* coast
Said to have been founded about AD 300 as a religious community on Monte Titano by St Marinus (Italian San Marino), a stone-cutter.

San Remo
Port and resort in north-west *Italy*, south-west of Genoa
Originally known as San Romulo (Italian = 'St Romulus'), bishop who founded it in 6th century. In 15th century became San Remo (= 'St Remus'), possibly by confusion with French St Rémi (Remigius), or perhaps through contraction of Latin Sancti Romuli in Eremo = '(church) of the hermitage of St Romulus'.

San Salvador
Capital of *Salvador*, Central *America*
Spanish = 'holy saviour' (ie Christ). Name was given by Spanish settlers who founded city in 1525 on Feast of Transfiguration (6 August).

Santa Cruz
City in central *Bolivia*, South *America*
Spanish = 'holy cross'. City was founded by Spanish missionaries on Holy Cross Day (14 September) 1560.

Santa Fé
State capital of *New Mexico*, USA
Spanish = 'holy faith'. Founded by Spanish missionaries in 1610 and given, like *Sacramento* and other towns named Santa Fé in USA and *Argentina*, a name of religious significance. Original full name of settlement was Villa Real de la Santa Fé de San Francisco de Asis = 'royal city of the holy faith of St Francis of Assisi'.

Santiago
Capital of *Chile*, South *America*
City was founded in 1541 by Spanish conqueror Pedro de Valdivia and named in honour of St James (Spanish San Jago), saint of special significance to the Spanish people as, according to tradition, it is said that he visited *Spain* and preached the gospel there, and that after his martyrdom his body was brought to *Spain* from *Jerusalem*. It is still venerated in the shrine of Santiago de Compostela, *Galicia*, once one of the chief places, with *Jerusalem* and *Rome*, of European Christian pilgrimage. Official full name was originally Santiago del Nuevo Extremo = 'Santiago of the new frontier'.

Santo Domingo
Capital of *Dominican Republic, West Indies*
City was founded in 1496 and has name that could be interpreted as either 'St Dominic' or 'holy Sunday'. If former, reference could be to either Domenico (Domingo) Columbus, father of Christopher Columbus, or Spanish saint Dominic (Domingo de Guzmán). If latter, name could indicate city was founded on a Sunday. From 1936 to 1961 was known as Ciudad Trujillo, after president and dictator Trujillo Molina (assassinated 1961).

Saône, River
In *France* rising in the *Vosges* and joining River *Rhône* at *Lyons*
Oldest known name of river is Brigoulos; Roman name was Arar, from Indo-European ar = 'to flow'. From 4th century became Sauconne, from Gaulish soghan = 'calm' (in contrast to *Rhône*).

São Paulo
State and its capital in south-east *Brazil*, South *America*
Portuguese = 'St Paul'. City was founded by Jesuit monks in 1554 who celebrated first mass here on St Paul's Day (25 January).

Saragossa
City in north-east *Spain*, on River *Ebro*, west of *Barcelona*

Before Roman occupation was Salduba. In 27 BC was renamed, as were many towns throughout Roman empire about this time, in honour of Emperor Augustus, with full name Caesarea Augusta. This name, over the centuries, and corrupted by Goths, Arabs and Spanish, resulted in modern name of Saragossa. Spanish name of city is Zaragoza.

Sardinia
2nd largest island in *Mediterranean*, south of *Corsica*

Name probably derives from Sardi, Iberian tribe who inhabited north *Egypt* in 14th century BC. Link is also possible with Carthaginian sarado = 'foot' (referring to outline of island), and other ancient names of island are close to this in meaning, eg Ichnusa = 'footprint', Sandaliotis = 'sandal-shaped'.

Sargasso Sea
Region of North *Atlantic* extending east off coast of *Florida*, USA

Named after its floating seaweed (*Sargassum bacciferum*), with its own name derived from Portuguese sargaço, from resemblance of air bladders on the seaweed to the 'sarga' grape. Sea was named after Columbus's expedition of 1492.

Saskatchewan
Central southern province of *Canada*

Named after River Saskatchewan, in turn with name derived from Indian word; possibly from susquehanna = 'winding river', kisiskachewan = 'fast-flowing river' or siskachiwan = 'great rapids'.

Saskatoon
2nd largest city in *Saskatchewan, Canada*

From Indian (Cree) missaskatoomina = 'fruit of the tree of much wood'. Name of city is used for the serviceberry (kind of shadbush) and its fruit, which grows abundantly in region.

Saudi Arabia
Kingdom in South-West *Asia*
From name of King Ibn-Saud, who in 1932 founded kingdom from two former states of Nejd and Hejaz.

Savoy
Former duchy, now two departments, in south-east *France*
From Swiss dialect word zaù, dsaù = 'uplands, mountains' (ie *Alps*).

Saxony
Former 'Land' of *Germany*, in south of East *Germany*
Named after Saxons, Germanic people who once inhabited it, having come south from north-west *Germany* in 3rd century BC; their name derives from Old High German sahs = 'stone sword' (weapon with which they fought). Name of Saxons is also preserved in English counties of Essex, Sussex and Middlesex, as well as former kingdom of Wessex.

Scandinavia
Peninsula of north-west *Europe* comprising *Norway* and *Sweden*
Pliny wrote of 'an island of unknown size named Scatinavia'. Ending is Latin suffix -ia denoting territory; middle element -av- is from Old Norse ey = 'island'; 1st element scan(din) is unexplained (meaning 'good' has been suggested). In Scandinavia itself, root name is preserved in province of Skåne (Scania), southern *Sweden*.

Scapa Flow
Stretch of sea in *Orkney Islands*, north of *Scotland, Great Britain*
From English scape = 'channel' + Flow in sense of 'current'. Not likely to be from Germanic skapa = 'cliff, rock'.

Scheldt, River
Rising in north-east *France* and flowing north-east through *Belgium* into south *Netherlands* and *North Sea*
All versions of name—English Scheldt; Dutch, Flemish, German Schelde; French Escaut—probably derive from mediaeval Latin form of name Scaldis = 'shallow'.

Schleswig-Holstein

'Land' in north of West *Germany*, south of *Denmark*

Name is formed from two historic territories, independent up to 1386 as duchies of Schleswig and Holstein. Former is named after town of Schleswig, known in 804 as Sliesthorp, after bay of Schlei (from Old Scandinavian sle = 'reed' or perhaps 'channel, canal') on which it is situated + Old German wik = 'village'; latter was known in 840 as Holsatia, possibly from German holt = 'wood' + perhaps Old High German sittan = 'to sit' (later taken to be derived from Stein = 'rock').

Scilly, Isles of

Group of islands in North *Atlantic*, south-west of *England*

Perhaps derived from one rock of group named Scilly, from Irish sceilig = 'rock', scillic = 'stone splinter' or sceillic = 'rocky islands, sea cliffs'. In 475 BC were known as Tin Islands (Cassiterides); tin was not mined here but islands were trading centre for it.

Scotland

North country of *Great Britain*

Roman name was Caledonia. In 4th–5th centuries Irish Celts called Scots settled here and gave their name to country, with their own name perhaps derived from Celtic scuit = 'to rove, to wander'.

Sebastopol

City and seaport in republic of *Ukraine*, USSR, on south-west coast of *Crimea*

More correctly, Sevastopol, but derived, when founded in 1783, from Greek sebastos = 'majestic, royal' + polis = 'town'. To west of modern city lies ancient Greek colony of Chersonesus, founded in 5th century BC. (For fashion for 'Greek' names in this region at this time see *Odessa*.)

Seine, River

In north *France*, flowing north-west through *Paris* and *Rouen* into English Channel

Roman name was Sequana, based on Celtic name which was itself formed from some pre-Celtic word probably = 'calm, quiet' (compare *Saône*). Name gradually changed (Siguna, Signe, Seinne) to present form Seine.

Senegal
Republic in West *Africa*
Named after River Senegal, in turn Portuguese version of name of local tribe (perhaps Berber Zenaga). Has also been explained as deriving from African word = 'navigable'.

Seoul
Capital of South *Korea*
Name is Korean = 'capital city'. Official name during Yi dynasty (1392–1910) (see *Korea*) was Hansong, and under Japanese rule (1910–45) was Kyongsong, both having sense 'city on the (river) Han'.

Serbia
Province of south-east *Yugoslavia*
From inhabitants, Serbs, whose own name probably derives from Indo-European serv = 'servant, slave' or perhaps = 'neighbour, ally'.

Severnaya Zemlya
Group of islands in *Arctic* Ocean, north of *Siberia*, USSR
Russian = 'northern land'. Discovered in 1913 by Russian expedition of Vilkitsky and named Nicholas II Islands, after ruling tsar. Named changed to Severnaya Zemlya in 1926.

Seville
Province and its capital in south *Spain*
Probably from Carthaginian sephalas = 'lower', either in sense of 'lowland' or perhaps because situated lower down River *Guadalquivir* than some other town.

Seychelles
Group of islands in Indian Ocean, north-east of *Madagascar*
Discovered by Portuguese in 1504 who named them 'Seven Sisters'. In 1743 islands were captured by French who named them La Bourdonnais, after French governor of *Mauritius*. In 1756 renamed Seychelles after French finance minister, Vicomte de Séchelles. Became independent republic in 1976.

Shanghai
Largest city in *China* and seaport on east coast
From Chinese = 'on the sea' (Chinese hai = 'sea').

Shannon, River
Chief river of *Ireland*, flowing south and west into *Atlantic*

Ptolemy, writing in 2nd century, referred to it as Senos. Name probably derives from Celtic sen = 'big' + amhan = 'water'. Not likely to be from Old Irish sinda = 'river'.

Shantung/Shandong
Province in east *China* bordering on *Yellow Sea*

From Chinese shan = 'mountain' + tung/dong = 'east'; ie 'east of the mountain', referring to holy Mount Taishan.

Shenyang
City in *Manchuria*, north-east *China*

From Chinese yang = 'opposite the sun' (ie northern, as opposed to ing = 'southern'), + name of River Shen, on which it is situated. Better known by former Manchurian name of *Mukden* = 'height'.

Shetland Islands
North-east of *Orkney Islands*, north of *Scotland*, *Great Britain*

Most recent theory derives name from Old Norse hjalt = 'hilt' + land = 'land', referring to sword-shaped outline of islands or of chief of them (Mainland). Alternative spelling of name is Zetland, with same origin.

Siam
Former name of *Thailand*

From Sanskrit sian = 'brown' (referring to colour of skin of natives). Unlikely to be connected with siamang (type of large gibbon). Name changed to *Thailand* in 1939.

Siberia
Region in east USSR, extending from *Urals* to *Pacific*

Name in 13th century applied to much smaller territory than now. Several possible origins, among which are: 1. related to Russian sever = 'north'; 2. from Mongolian subr = 'mountain wolf'; 3. after Siber, legendary dog who appeared from depths of Lake *Baikal*; 4. from Mongolian shibir = 'marsh'. Last explanation seems most plausible.

Sicily
Island south of *Italy*, in *Mediterranean*
From Siculi (Sekeloi), tribe who inhabited island in 1st century BC, with name probably = 'reapers'.

Sierra Leone
Republic in West *Africa*
Portuguese explorer Pedro de Cintra sighted coast here in 1460 and named it Serra da Leão = 'lion ridge', referring to outline of mountains. Spanish version of name, Sierra Leone, appeared on maps from 1500 with meaning 'lion mountains', perhaps because lions were heard roaring in mountains or referring to roaring sound of wind or sea breaking.

Sierra Madre
Mountain system in *Mexico*
Spanish = 'mother mountains', ie chief mountains of country.

Sierra Nevada
Mountain range in east *California*, USA
Spanish = 'snowy range'. Name was given by Spanish expedition in 1518 to snow-capped mountains, after native Spanish mountains, also named Sierra Nevada. (See also *Nevada*.)

Silesia
Region in central east *Europe*, mainly in south-west *Poland*
Perhaps derived from name of Mount Slenz (present Zobtenberg), religious centre for Vandal tribe of Silingi. Or possibly from Slavonic name of River Slenza, with basic meaning = 'damp'.

Simferopol
City in *Crimea*, south-west USSR, north-east of *Sebastopol*
So named in 1784, according to prevailing fashion for 'Greek' names (see *Odessa*), from Greek symphero = 'to gather together' or 'to be profitable' + polis = 'town'. Earlier name, when city was under Turkish rule, was Akmechet = 'white mosque'. Town arose close to ancient site of Neapol (= 'new town'), occupied by Scythians from 3rd century BC to 4th century AD.

Simonstown
Town and seaport in South *Africa*, south of *Cape Town*
Named after Dutch Governor of Cape from 1679 to 1699
Simon van der Stel (compare *Stellenbosch*).

Simplon Pass
Through *Alps* in south *Switzerland*
Named after small village of Simpelen, at south foot of
pass, whose own name derives from Old German words =
'soft height'.

Sinai
Peninsula in north-east *Egypt*
Named after Mount Sinai, itself perhaps from Hebrew
word = 'dirt, mud' or derived from name of Sumerian
moon god Sin.

Singapore
Republic, island and city at south extremity of *Malaya*
peninsula, South-East *Asia*
From Sanskrit singa = 'lion' + pura = 'town'. Name of
uncertain origin, as lions are not native to this region.
Perhaps given with sense of 'strong', or from some personal name. One story tells how Indian prince, arriving
here in 7th century, took the first animal he saw to be a
lion.

Skagerrak
Strait between *Norway* and *Denmark*, north of *Kattegat*
In Scandinavian sagas was called Norgeshavet = 'north
harbour'. In 16th century Dutch called it Nordzee = 'north
sea', and present *Kattegat*—Skagerrak, from Dutch skagi =
'cape' + rak = 'flowing through a channel'.

Slovakia
Eastern part of *Czechoslovakia*, former province
From name of Slovaks, Slavonic people who inhabited this
region. (For meaning of their name see *Yugoslavia*.)

Slovenia
Republic in north-west *Yugoslavia*
From name of Slovenes, Slavonic people who inhabited
this region. (For meaning of their name see *Yugoslavia*.)

Society Islands
In South *Pacific*, east of *Tonga*, French *Polynesia*
Named by Cook in 1769 with a scientific expedition from the Royal Society in *London* who were chief instigators of his voyage. Not named after 'society-loving' natives.

Socotra
Island in Indian Ocean, north-east of *Somalia*, East *Africa*
From Sanskrit dvipa sakhadara = 'island of portent of success': island was centrally situated on ancient trade routes from *India* to *Arabia* and *Africa*.

Sofia
Capital of *Bulgaria*
Town of Serdica was built here in 8th−7th centuries BC on site of mineral springs, with name derived from Thracian tribe Serds. Slavs who settled here in 6th century AD took name to mean 'centre' (from Slavonic sered) and called it Sredets. In 11th century after capture by Byzantium re-named Triaditsa, in honour of Holy Trinity. Present name is from Greek = 'wisdom' (used by Byzantium in religious sense) and appeared in 14th century.

Solomon Islands
Independent state in South-West *Pacific*, south-east of *Bismarck Archipelago*
Discovered in 1567 by Spanish explorer Álvaro de Mendaña de Neyra, who seeing gold ornaments worn by natives took islands to be legendary land of Ophir from which, in Bible story (1 Kings 9:28), gold was brought to King Solomon.

Somalia
Republic in North-East *Africa*
Probably from Cushite word = 'dark, black' (referring to colour of skin of natives).

Somme, River
In north *France* flowing west into English Channel
In Caesar's time was Samara, possibly from Indo-European sai = 'to flow' + ar = 'water'; could also be connected with Celtic soghar = 'quiet' (compare *Seine*, *Saône*).

Soviet Union
Official name of *Russia*
Name first officially used in 1922 when, after 1917 Revolution, new constitution of socialist republics was set up with soviet (Russian = 'council') as basic unit of local and national government.

Spain
Kingdom in south-west *Europe* on Iberian Peninsula
Carthaginians, who set up colonies on shores here, are said to have named country Span = 'rabbit' (because animal was abundant here). But this may have been attempt to explain Basque ezpaña = 'shore', or to give meaning to the name of some Iberian tribe. Roman name was Hispania, from which derives modern Spain.

Spencer Gulf
Inlet of Indian Ocean in coast of South *Australia*
Discovered by Matthew Flinders in 1802 and named after English Earl Spencer, First Lord of Admiralty at time voyage of Flinders was commissioned.

Spitsbergen
Group of islands in *Arctic* Ocean, north of *Norway*
Russian coastal dwellers of 15th century knew islands as Grumant, from Swedish Grönland = 'green land'. Name Spitsbergen derives from Dutch spits = 'point' + bergen = 'mountains' and was given by Dutch explorer Barents who landed on islands in 1596. Scandinavian name is Svalbard = 'cold country'.

Split
Town and seaport on *Adriatic*, west *Yugoslavia*
Original Palatium = 'palace' (compare modern Italian name Spalato). In 7th century inhabitants built their houses on walls of restored palace of Diocletian, which remains as fine example of Roman palatial architecture.

Springfield
State capital of *Illinois*, USA
Common name in USA, usually denoting place grown up around a spring or some water-source. The 1st name of Springfield was given in 1641 to town in *Massachusetts* by English settler William Pynchon after village of Springfield in Essex; other towns, including capital of *Illinois*, derived from this (with exception of Springfield, South *Carolina*, which is named after man called Spring).

Sri Lanka
Island republic off south-east coast of *India*
From native (Sinhalese) = 'blessed island'. Tibetan name of island is Langka (Sanskrit lanka = 'island'). Until 1972 name was *Ceylon*.

Stanley Falls
Former name of Boyoma Falls, on River *Congo* (now *Zaïre*), *Zaïre*, Central *Africa*
Named after English explorer H. M. Stanley (real name John Rowlands), who discovered them in 1877.

Stellenbosch
Town in *Cape Province*, South *Africa*, east of *Cape Town*
Founded in 1679 by Dutch coloniser Simon van der Stel (compare *Simonstown*) + bosch = 'wood'. Town is oldest in South Africa after *Cape Town*.

Stockholm
Capital of *Sweden*
Second element is from Swedish holm = 'island'; 1st element is of doubtful origin: perhaps from stäk = 'bay' or stock = 'post, pole' (referring to landmark or remains of some building).

Strasbourg
City in *Alsace*, north-east *France*
Frankish name in 5th century was Strateburgum, corresponding to modern German words Strasse = 'street' + Burg = 'town'. Sense is thus 'town by the road', referring to way leading from River *Rhine* to the west, crossing the *Vosges*.

Stromboli

Volcanic island north of *Sicily*, in *Tyrrhenian Sea*
From Greek strongylos = 'round' (referring to shape of volcano).

Stuttgart

City in south-west of West *Germany*
Recorded in 1229 as Stutengarten, literally = 'mare's garden' (from German Stute = 'mare' + Garten = 'garden'), from horse-breeding carried on here.

Sudan

Republic in North-East *Africa*
From Arabic bilādas-sūdān = 'country of the blacks' (ie referring to black skins of inhabitants).

Suez

Gulf forming north-west arm of *Red Sea*, linked with *Mediterranean* by Suez Canal
Possibly connected with Egyptian suan = 'beginning' (ie situated at 'beginning' of *Red Sea*).

Sumatra

Island in *Indonesia*, south-west of *Malaya*
Name known in this form since 1390; perhaps from Sanskrit samudra = 'ocean', but origin not really certain.

Superior, Lake

Largest of Great Lakes between *Canada* and USA
In sense of 'upper, higher' (upstream from other Great Lakes); flows into Lake *Huron* and Lake *Michigan*. Name is French in origin.

Swaziland

Kingdom in South-East *Africa*, bordered on three sides by *Transvaal*
Name is corruption of tribal name, itself deriving from tribe's warrior king Mswati III, who ruled here in mid-19th century.

Sweden
Kingdom in north *Europe*
From Swedish Svea-rike = 'kingdom of the Svea (Suiones)', Germanic people who with the Goths once inhabited south *Sweden*. Their name comes from Old High German geswion = 'kinsman'.

Switzerland
Republic in west *Europe*
Named after canton Schwyz, with its own name perhaps connected with Old High German suedan = 'to burn' (ie territory where forest was cleared by burning).

Sydney
Largest city in *Australia*, capital of *New South Wales*
Founded as 1st English colony in Australia by English explorer Captain Arthur Phillip in 1788 and named by him after English Secretary of State Lord Sydney.

Syracuse
City on south-east coast of *Sicily*, south *Italy*
First Greek colony on the island. Name is of pre-Greek origin, of uncertain meaning, but perhaps from Phoenician serach = 'to stink' (town was built by swamp). Name was transferred to American town of Syracuse in *New York* state in 1825.

Syria
Republic in South-West *Asia*, south of *Turkey*
Of uncertain origin, though country called Suri in Asia Minor is mentioned in Babylonian cuneiform script of about 4000 BC. Not likely to be Greek abbreviation of *Assyria*.

T

Table Mountain
In *Cape Province*, South *Africa*
So named in 1503 by Portuguese navigator Antonio de Saldanha, who was struck by appearance of flat top of mountain with white cloud hanging over it like a cloth.

Tadjikistan
Republic in south central USSR, north of *Afghanistan*
Named after inhabitants, Tadzhiks (+ Iranian stan = 'country'), whose name may derive from word = 'wreathed' (referring to national headdress), or from Old Persian tachik = 'Arab' (because of Moslem faith).

Tagus, River
Rising in east *Spain* and flowing west through *Portugal* into *Atlantic*
Name is of Iberian origin, of unknown meaning; not likely to be from name of some early Spanish king Tago, as sometimes stated.

Tahiti
Largest island in French *Polynesia*, South *Pacific*, one of *Society Islands*
Earlier name was Hiti-nui, from Polynesian nui = 'island', perhaps with 1st element derived from iti = 'small island'. Name changed later to Hitiiti, then to Tahiti.

Taiwan
Island 'republic' off south-east coast of *China*
From Chinese = 'terraced shore' (referring to appearance of highlands, foothills and sandy beaches descending as a 'terrace'). Earlier (Portuguese) name was *Formosa*.

Talien/Dalian
Part of Chinese port of *Lü-ta/Lüda*
Chinese variant of Russian name *Dairen*, in turn a variant of *Dalny*.

Tallahassee
State capital of *Florida*, USA
From Indian (Muskogean) word = 'old town'.

Tallinn
Capital of republic of *Estonia*, north-west USSR
From Estonian taani = 'Danes' + linna = 'town'; territory
was ruled by Danes from 1227 to 1346. Name before 1917
was Revel, of uncertain meaning: perhaps connected with
Danish revele = 'sandbank'.

Tananarive
Former name of *Antananarivo*, capital of *Madagascar*
Probably from Malagasy word = 'thousand villages' (from
tanana = 'village'). Element -riv occurs many times on
island, probably indicating passage of Malayan settlers
from east coast.

Tanganyika
Former name of chief part of present *Tanzania*, East
Africa, and lake here
English explorer Burton, who discovered lake in 1858,
explained name as deriving from kou tanganyika = 'to
join, to meet' (ie 'place where waters meet'). Stanley, on the
other hand, explained it as coming from tonga = 'island' +
hika = 'plain'. In many Bantu languages -nyika = 'plain'.
Lake gave name to country.

Tangier
Seaport on north coast of *Morocco*, North-West *Africa*
Perhaps connected with Berber andji = 'river', but Car-
thaginian name was Tingis, from Semitic tigisis = 'har-
bour', and this could have evolved into modern name
Tangier.

Tanzania
Republic in central East *Africa*
From 1st elements of *Tanganyika* and *Zanzibar* + Latin-type
ending -ia denoting territory. Two countries united to form
Tanzania in 1964.

Taranto
City and seaport in *Apulia*, south-east *Italy*
Founded in 8th century BC by emigrants from *Greece*.
Name may derive from Illyrian darandos = 'oak'.

Tashkent
Capital of republic of *Uzbekistan*, USSR
Probably from Turkish tash = 'stone' + Iranian kent = 'town'.

Tasmania
Island state of *Australia*, south of mainland
Named in 1853 after Dutch navigator Abel Tasman (1603–59) who was the first European to sight it, in 1642. He named it Van Diemen's Land, after Dutch admiral Anthony van Diemen, governor general of Dutch settlements in East Indies.

Tbilisi
Capital of republic of *Georgia*, USSR
From Georgian tbili = 'warm' (referring to mineral springs here). Before 1935 was known as Tiflis, corruption of Tbilisi.

Tehran
Capital of *Iran*
Name is from Old Persian teh = 'warm' + ran = 'place', referring to great heat here in summer.

Tel Aviv
Largest city in *Israel*, on *Mediterranean* north-west of *Jerusalem*
Hebrew = 'hill of spring' (from tel = 'hill' + aviv = 'spring'). This is Hebrew title of Theodor Herzl's novel of 1902, *Altneuland*, after which city is named: in this, founder of modern Zionism set forth principles of new Jewish state. At same time, name is biblical (Ezek. 3:15), and is mentioned as settlement of exiled Jews in Babylon. City was founded in 1909 near *Jaffa*, with which it amalgamated in 1949.

Tenerife
Largest of *Canary Islands*, off north-west coast of *Africa*
Roman name was Nivaria, from Latin nix, nivis = 'snow'. Name of Tenerife was recorded in 16th century with meaning 'white mountain'.

Tennessee
State in central south USA
Named after River Tennessee, tributary of River *Ohio*, from Indian (Cherokee) Tenn-assee, perhaps name of tribe = 'crooked ears', or with simple meaning 'river'.

Texas
State in south-west USA
True origin unknown. Story is that Spanish monk Damian, landing on coast here in 1690, asked Indians to which tribe they belonged, receiving reply 'texia' (= 'good friend'— their form of greeting). But this could have been tribal name.

Thailand
Kingdom in South-East *Asia*, north of *Malaya*
From native name Prathet Thai = 'country of the free'. Name before 1939 was *Siam*.

Thames, River
Chief river of *England* flowing east through *London* into *North Sea*
Julius Caesar wrote of it in 51 BC as Tamesis (last element of which is said to give name of river at and above Oxford— Isis). Perhaps derives from Celtic tam = 'widening' + isis = 'water', or from Indo-European root word ta = 'to flow'.

Tiber, River
In *Italy* rising in *Apennines* and flowing south through *Rome* into *Tyrrhenian Sea*
From Roman name Tiberis, perhaps derived from Celtic dubr = 'water'.

Tibet
Autonomous region in south-west *China*
Of uncertain origin. Perhaps connected with Tibetan thub = 'strong, powerful'. Original name was Tu-pho, possibly corrupted by Arabs into Tibat.

Tientsin/Tianjin
3rd largest city in *China*, south-east of *Peking/Beijing*
Of uncertain meaning. Has been explained as deriving from Chinese tyang/tian = 'heaven' + tsin/jin = 'entrance, gates', but 1st word means both 'heaven' and 'day' so that meaning could be 'day ford'.

Tierra del Fuego
Group of islands at south extremity of South *America*, divided between *Chile* and *Argentina*

Spanish = 'land of fire'. On his 1st journey round the world in 1520 Magellan sighted fires here, either bonfires or on moving boats, and so named islands thus. Or, more prosaically, name refers to many volcanoes here.

Tigris, River
In South-West *Asia*, rising in east *Turkey* and flowing south-east through *Iraq* to join *Euphrates* and enter Persian Gulf

In cuneiform was named as Indigna, and later as Dignat. Sumerian name was Tig-ru-shu, from tig = 'spear' + ru = 'to overthrow' + shu = 'to capture', ie 'running with an overthrowing (conquering) spear'. Sanskrit name Tigris was connected with Old Persian tigra = 'arrow', perhaps in sense of 'fast-flowing' (in contrast to River *Euphrates*).

Timor
Island in Malay Archipelago, belonging to *Indonesia*

From Indonesian word = 'east'. Island is most easterly of Lesser Sunda Islands.

Tirana
Capital of *Albania*

Origin has been explained as name given by Turkish general, Barkinzade Süleyman Pasha, who when founding city about 1600 called it Tigran after his native Teheran (*Tehran*). But a Venetian document of 1572 mentions settlement here as 'il borgo di Tirana' (= 'the village of Tirana'). Tirania was ancient name of *Tuscany*, and so connected with the Tuscans, an Albanian people (south *Albania* was known as Toscenia). (See also *Tyrrhenian Sea*.)

Titicaca, Lake
Largest lake in South *America*, divided between *Peru* and *Bolivia*

Name derives from island on lake, whose name has been variously explained as 'sunny island', 'crag of lead' or 'rock of the puma'.

Titograd
Capital of *Montenegro, Yugoslavia*
Named in 1946 in honour of Marshal Tito, President of
Yugoslavia from 1953 to 1980, + Slavonic grad = 'town'.
Earlier name was Podgorica = 'under the mountain'.

Tobago
Island in *West Indies*, north-east of *Trinidad*
Discovered by Columbus in 1498, who named it Tobago
from Haitian tambaku = 'pipe' (used by natives for smoking tobacco, which word also derives from it). Became
republic with *Trinidad* in 1976.

Tobruk
Seaport in *Libya*, east of *Benghazi*
Greek name was Antipirgos = 'opposite the tower' (bay
was protected from the wind by an island opposite which,
on the beach, was a tower). Present name is probably
Arabic corruption of Greek name.

Togo
Republic in West *Africa*, on Gulf of *Guinea*
Named after Lake Togo, with name of unknown origin.

Tokyo
Capital of *Japan*
From Japanese to = 'east' + kio = 'capital' (as distinct from
Kyoto, = western capital', which it replaced as capital in
1868). Before this, its name was Edo = 'estuary', as it stood
at point where River Sumida entered Tokyo Bay.

Toledo
Province and its capital in central *Spain*, south of
Madrid
From Celtic tol = 'mountain' (town stands on hill of granite).
(Compare *Toulon, Toulouse*.)

Tonga
Kingdom and group of islands in South *Pacific*, south-
east of *Fiji*
Native name for main island is Tonga, or Tongatabu, =
'holy'. Name was spread by Dutch explorers, who discovered it in 1616, to whole group. Cook named group
Friendly Islands.

Tonkin

Former French protectorate in north Indochina, present north *Vietnam*

From Chinese tong = 'eastern' + kin = 'capital'; name originally applied to *Hanoi*, but later spread to whole country. Tonkin was under Chinese rule until 1802, and from 1950 became part of *Vietnam*.

Topeka

State capital of *Kansas*, USA

From Indian (Sioux) word = 'potato good place' (ie where wild tuber, which English called potato, was dug up by natives).

Toronto

Capital of *Ontario*, largest city in *Canada*

Founded in 1794 with name of York, in honour of Duke of York, son of English king George III, on site of Indian settlement named Toronto, perhaps derived from Iroquois Toron-to-hen = 'timber in the water', or from similar Indian words = 'place of assembly' or 'place of plenty'. Toronto became official name of city from 1834.

Torrens, Lake

In state of South *Australia*

Named after English economist and soldier, Colonel Robert Torrens (1780–1864), one of founders of colony of South *Australia* in 1834.

Torres Strait

Between *Papua New Guinea* and Cape *York*, *Queensland*, north *Australia*

Named in 1769 in memory of Spanish navigator Luis Vaez de Torres, who discovered the strait in 1606 when sailing west from *Pacific* towards *Indonesia*.

Tortuga

Island north of *Haiti, West Indies*

Spanish = 'turtle'. Name given by Columbus in 1492, with reference to many turtles found here.

Toulon

City and seaport in south *France*, south-east of *Marseilles*

Greek name was Telonion. Name is pre-Gaulish and very ancient. May be of Ligurian origin with lost meaning, from unknown Phoenician word, or from pre-Indo-European word based on t-l = 'mountain', passed down to Celts in form tul or tol (compare *Toledo*).

Toulouse

City in south-west *France*, on River *Garonne*

Possibly from Celtic tul = 'mountain', or Iberian (pre-Latin) word of unknown meaning.

Touraine

Historic province in west central *France*

From name of its inhabitants, Turoni, Gaulish tribe with name probably derived from Celtic tur = 'water'. (See also *Tours*, its capital.)

Tours

City in west central *France*, south-west of *Paris*

Former capital of *Touraine*; Roman name was Civitas Turonum = 'town of the Turoni'. Official name—Caesarodunum = 'Caesar's city' (from Gaulish dun = 'town')—did not last and by 3rd century had fallen out of use.

Trabzon

Town and port on *Black Sea*, north-east *Turkey*

Dispute about origin of name, also rendered *Trebizond*, has lasted over 2000 years. Could derive from Greek trapeza = 'table', referring to shape of nearby mountain. (Many mountains on *Black Sea* coast are called 'Table' from their flat top.) Or could be connected with geometrical figure trapezium. The 3rd theory is that immigrants from town of Trapezos in Arcadia (ancient Greek province) colonised Trabzon and named it after their native town (in turn probably derived from a personal name).

Trafalgar, Cape

In south *Spain* between *Cadiz* and *Gibraltar*

From Arabic Tarf-el-garb = 'western point' (Arabic tarf = 'point, sand, earth' + el garb = 'the west'). Or possibly from Arabic taraf-al-aghar = 'pillar-cave', referring to one of pillars of Hercules in Greek mythology.

Transvaal
Province in north-east of South *Africa*
From Latin trans = 'across' + name of River *Vaal*. Name arose in 1830s when Boers from Cape Colony retreated north-east from English troops to other side of River *Vaal*.

Transylvania
Former province in north-west *Romania*
From Latin trans = 'across' + silva = 'forest', ie 'land beyond the forest'.

Trebizond
Alternative name of *Trabzon*

Trenton
State capital of *New Jersey*, USA
Original name of Quaker settlement here (from 1679) was The Falls, after location on River Delaware. In 1721 re-named Trenton after William Trent, merchant who had laid out present town in 1714.

Trieste
Seaport in north-east *Italy*, on *Adriatic Sea*
Recorded by Caesar in 1st century as Tergeste. May derive from Illyrian terga = 'trade', or terst = 'reed'.

Trinidad
Island in *West Indies*, off north-west coast of *Venezuela*
Discovered by Columbus in 1498, perhaps on Trinity Sunday, after which day he named it (Spanish trinidad = 'trinity'), but more likely because of 3 peaks he saw as he approached. Became republic with *Tobago* in 1976.

Tripoli
Capital of *Libya*, North *Africa*
From Greek tripolis = 'three towns', ie ancient cities of Oea (present Tripoli), Sabratha and Leptis Magna. (Tripoli in *Lebanon* has same origin, referring to Tyre, Sidon and Aradus.)

Tristan da Cunha
Group of islands in South *Atlantic*, south-west of South *Africa*
Named after Portuguese admiral who discovered them in 1506.

Trucial States
Former name of *United Arab Emirates*
So named from agreement made with *Britain* in 1820 to ensure condition of truce in territory, once known as the Pirate Coast. Became *United Arab Emirates* in 1971 (for names of states see this).

Tuamotu
Group of islands in French *Polynesia* (*Oceania*), South *Pacific*, east of *Society Islands*
From native name Puamotu = 'distant islands', probably given by inhabitants of *Tahiti*. Also known as Low Islands, Pearl Islands, Dangerous Islands, all self-explanatory names.

Tunisia
Republic in North-West *Africa*, with capital Tunis
Country named after its capital, with name falsely connected with Phoenician goddess Tanith. City was known in pre-Phoenician times, and was mentioned by Greek historians Polybius and Diodorus, writing in 1st century BC. Exact origin still uncertain.

Turin
4th largest city in *Italy*, in north-west on River *Po*
Region was inhabited by Ligurian tribe Taurini, with name perhaps connected with Celtic tur = 'water'. Roman name of city was Augusta Taurinorum, after Emperor Augustus.

Turkestan
Region in Central *Asia*, partly in USSR, partly in *China*
Name is of Iranian origin = 'country of the Turks' (Iranian stan = 'country').

Turkey
Republic in South-West *Asia*, with small area in south-east *Europe*
Named after inhabitants, Turks, + ending -ey = Latin suffix -ia denoting territory. Name of people is probably derived from tora = 'to be born', or perhaps connected with English 'turban', their headdress.

Turkmenistan

Republic in south USSR bordering on *Iran*

Named after Turkmens, who form bulk of population, + Iranian stan = 'country'. Name of people is of doubtful origin, possibly from turkmend = 'Turk-like'—though 'men' in Turkish languages has many meanings and native name has been variously interpreted as 'pure Turks', 'good Turks', 'great Turks', etc.

Turks Islands

In *West Indies*, north of *Hispaniola*, east of Caicos Islands

Said to derive from local cactus known as Turk's head or fez, from its shape.

Turku

2nd largest city in *Finland*, on Gulf of *Bothnia*, north-west of *Helsinki*

From Finnish turku = 'trading place, market square', word borrowed from Old Russian torg = 'trade'. For long time official name of town was Åbo, from Swedish, deriving from Indo-European word = 'water'.

Tuscany

Region in central *Italy* bordering on Ligurian and *Tyrrhenian* Seas

Named after Etruscans (Tuscans), who inhabited region here 1000 BC. Their name is of unknown origin. (See also *Tyrrhenian Sea*.)

Tuvalu

Island state, South *Pacific*

Name is native word = 'eight standing together', referring to coral atolls here (officially 9 in number). Until 1975 was called *Ellice Islands*, and separated from *Gilbert Islands* following year.

Tyrol

Province in west *Austria*

Mediaeval Latin name was Castrum Terolis = 'fort of Terol', in turn from ancient fortress of Teriolis, recorded about 400 BC, whose name has been preserved in small town of Zirl near *Innsbruck*.

Tyrrhenian Sea
Part of *Mediterranean* between south *Italy* and *Sardinia*
and *Sicily*

From Greek name for Etruscans—Tyrrhenoi—who inhabited BC region that is now *Tuscany*.

U

Uganda
Republic in East *Africa*
Name derives from province of *Buganda*; Uganda is Swahili form, used along east coast.

Ukraine
Republic in south-west USSR, bordering on *Black Sea*
Name = 'border territory', from Slavonic root krai = 'boundary, frontier'. After Tatar invasion of 13th century and that of Poles and Lithuanians in 14th century many peasants fled to unpopulated area along River *Dnieper* and set up a 'border territory'.

Ulan Bator
Capital of *Mongolia*
Until 1924 was Urga, Mongolian = 'abode' or 'palace'. Renamed Ulan Bator, from Mongolian ulan = 'red' + bator = 'warrior', in honour of Dandimy Sühbaatar (1893–1923) who founded modern republic of *Mongolia* in 1911 and who was born near Urga.

Ulm
Town in south of West *Germany*, south-east of *Stuttgart*
Probably of Celtic origin, with basic meaning = 'marshy', or possibly from Germanic word of similar meaning (Low German ulm = 'decay', Norwegian dialect word ulma = 'mould').

Ulster
Alternative name for Northern *Ireland*
From ancient tribal name Ulaid + Old Norse genitive 's' and Irish tir = 'district'.

Umbria
Region in central *Italy*, in *Apennines*
From Umbrians, Roman people who inhabited this region BC, with their own name derived from Indo-European root word = 'water-dwellers'.

United Arab Emirates
Union of 7 states on south coast of Persian Gulf, bordering on *Saudi Arabia*, and one on Gulf of *Oman*
Until 1971 was *Trucial States*, when formed independent state of 7 emirates of Abu Dhabi, Ajman, Dubai, Fujairah (which joined state in 1972), Ras al Khaimah, Sharjah and Umm al Qaiwain.

Urals
Mountains running from north to south in USSR and forming natural frontier between *Europe* and *Asia*
Perhaps from Tatar ural = 'girdle', in sense of 'belt' between East and West, or connected with name of *Aral Sea* (from whose depths, according to legend, mountains came) with meaning 'island', in sense of mountains rising like islands from surrounding flat country.

Uruguay
Republic in South *America*
Named after River Uruguay (tributary of River *Plate*) with origin perhaps in Indian guay = 'tail' + uru = 'bird', referring to species of bird with remarkable tail living in forests here. Or perhaps connected with guay = 'river', common element in South *American* names.

Ushant
Island off west coast of *Brittany, France*
French name is Ouessant, falsely connected with French ouest = 'west'. Name is in fact derived from Roman Axantos or Uxantis Insula, from Gaulish ux = 'high' + ending denoting superlative.

Utah
State in west USA
From name of Indian tribe Ute = 'tall' (either literally, or in sense of living in mountains).

Utrecht
City in central *Netherlands*, south-east of *Amsterdam*
In 723 was Roman Trajectum castrum = 'camp crossing' (ie 'camp by the crossing over the *Rhine*'). In 10th century name had been shortened to Trecht, but in 11th–12th centuries appeared in modern form Utrecht (with Dutch prefix ut = 'lower'), first applying to (lower) suburbs, then to whole town.

Uttar Pradesh

State in north *India*

Sanskrit = 'northern province'. Present name was adopted in 1950; before this (from 1902) name was United Provinces of Agra and Oudh.

Uzbekistan

Republic in south USSR, bordering in south on *Afghanistan*

Named after inhabitants, Uzbeks, + Iranian stan = 'country'. Name of people said to derive from Khan Uzbek, chief of Golden Horde in 14th century, though Uzbek language and race existed before this.

V

Vaal, River
In South *Africa*, rising in *Transvaal* and flowing south-west into *Cape Province* to join River Orange
Name was given by Boers (Dutch colonisers), from Dutch vaal = 'grey, murky', possibly translation of Hottentot ki-garep = 'yellow'.

Valencia
Region and historic province in east *Spain*
Founded by Romans in 137 BC with name Valentia Edetanorum = 'stronghold of the Edenti'; 1st word has survived to give modern name of city of Valencia.

Valenciennes
Town in north-east *France* on River *Scheldt*, south-east of *Lille*
Name arose during period of Roman occupation, from Latin Valentinianae, later Valentiana, after Roman emperor Valentinian I (ruled AD 364−75). Name is thus related to English words 'valiant' and 'valour'.

Valladolid
City in *Spain*, north-west of *Madrid*
From Spanish valle = 'valley' + Olid, possibly personal name of founder or ruler.

Valletta
Capital of *Malta*
Named after Jean Parisot de La Vallette, Grand Master of the Knights of St John of Jerusalem, who founded city in 1565 after victory over Turks.

Valparaiso
City and seaport in *Chile*, South *America*, north-west of *Santiago*
Founded by Spanish explorer Juan de Saavedra in 1536 with name = 'valley of paradise' (Spanish valle paraiso), because of beauty and fertility of region.

Vancouver
City, seaport and island on *Pacific* in west *Canada*
City originated as sawmill settlement in 1870s with name Granville. In 1886 was renamed Vancouver after English navigator George Vancouver (1757–98) who had accompanied Cook on his 2nd and 3rd voyages as midshipman in Royal Navy and who surveyed Vancouver Island in 1792.

Vanuatu
Island republic in South-West *Pacific*
Name = 'our land'. Island was known as the *New Hebrides* until 1980.

Varanasi
Official name of *Benares, India*

Varna
City, seaport and resort on *Black Sea, Bulgaria*, southeast of *Sofia*
Possibly from Slavonic voron = 'raven' (perhaps in sense of 'black' as situated on *Black Sea*), or perhaps from Indo-European var = 'water'.

Vatican
Papal state in *Rome, Italy*
From Latin name of hill on which it stands, Mons Vaticanus, in turn perhaps from vaticinia = 'place of divination' (ie a pagan shrine).

Venezuela
Republic in South *America*, on *Caribbean Sea*
Spanish explorers discovered here in 1499, on shores of Lake *Maracaibo*, an Indian village built on piles. This reminded them of *Venice*, so they named it Venezuela = 'little Venice'. Name subsequently spread to surrounding territory and in 1830 became official name of country.

Venice
City and seaport on *Adriatic Sea*, north-east *Italy*
In 5th century BC territory here was inhabited by Illyrian tribe Veneti, whose own name may derive from an Indo-European or even pre-Indo-European root meaning either 'friend' (ie 'our people') or simply 'water'. Romans named territory after tribe, and name then passed to town which arose here in AD 451 out of an 'amalgamation' of fishing villages on the various islands.

Veracruz
State and seaport in *Mexico*, on Gulf of *Mexico*
Spanish soldier Hernán Cortés founded town here in Holy Week, 1519, and named it Villa rica de la Vera Cruz = 'rich town of the true cross', in commemoration of Crucifixion.

Verdun
Town in east *France* on River *Meuse*, west of *Metz*
From Celtic dun = 'mountain' or 'fort', with doubtful 1st element. Name perhaps meant something like 'defensive dam on the river (*Meuse*)'.

Vereeniging
Town in *Transvaal*, South *Africa*, on River *Vaal*
Dutch = 'association'. Town was founded in 1892 and named after original owners, De Zuid Afrikaansche en Oranje Vrijstaatsche Kolen- en Mineralen- Mijn Vereeniging = 'South African and Orange Free State Coal and Mineral Mining Association'. Name does not refer to attempts at political union between South African Republic and *Orange Free State*.

Vermont
State in *New England*, north-east USA
From French vert mont (correctly, mont vert) = 'green mountain', a rendering by Dr Thomas Young of earlier English name Green Mountain. Reference is to coniferous forests that kept mountains green throughout the year here.

Verona
City in north *Italy*, north of *Venice*
Name is of uncertain origin, but may derive from root word = 'water' (as Sanskrit var that lies behind name of *Benares*). Verona is half surrounded by River Adige.

Versailles
Town with famous palace of Versailles, south-west of *Paris, France*
From Latin versus = 'slope' + ending -alia.

Vesuvius
Volcano in *Campania*, south *Italy*, south-east of *Naples*
From Oscan fesf = 'smoke' (compare *Etna*).

Vichy
Resort and spa in central *France*
From Roman name Vicus calidus = 'warm place', referring to warm springs for which town is famous.

Victoria
1. State in south-east *Australia*; 2. capital of British *Columbia*; 3. lake, otherwise Nyanza, in East *Africa*; 4. falls on River *Zambezi* on *Zambia-Zimbabwe* frontier; 5. island in *Arctic* Ocean, north *Canada*; 6. land in *Ross Dependency, Antarctic*
All named after English queen Victoria (reigned 1837–1901); all once part of British empire; all either discovered or founded and named during her reign.

Vienna
Capital of *Austria*
Named after River Vienna, which at this point flows into River *Danube*. Name of river probably derives from Celtic vedunia = 'tree', or perhaps from Celtic vindo = 'white', 'building'. From 50 AD was Roman settlement of Vindobona, last part of name being of uncertain meaning.

Vientiane
Capital of *Laos*
Name = 'town of sandalwood', and is corruption of local form, Viengchan.

Vietnam
Republic in South-East *Asia*, south of *China*
From Annamese = 'land of the south'. Before 1945 was Annam, *Tonkin* and part of *Cochin-China*.

Vilnius
Capital of republic of *Lithuania*, north-west USSR
From River Viliya (or Nyaris) on which it stands. Name of river probably derives from Baltic-Slavonic word = 'winding'.

Virginia
State in central east USA, bordering on *Atlantic*
Founded by English settlers in 1607 and named in honour of Elizabeth I (reigned 1558–1603), the 'Virgin Queen'. In American Civil War of 1861–65 state was divided into North and South, as a result of which state of West *Virginia* was formed. Name may originally have also had suggestion of 'virgin land', ripe for settlement.

Virgin Islands
In *West Indies*, east of *Puerto Rico*
Islands were discovered by Columbus in 1493 and he named them Santa Ursula y las Once Mil Virgines = 'St Ursula and the Eleven Thousand Virgins', on whose feast-day (21 October) he may have landed. See also *Virginia*.

Vistula, River
Rising in *Carpathians* and flowing west and north-west through *Poland* into *Baltic Sea*
Of uncertain origin. Possibly from Slavonic word derived from Indo-European veis = 'to flow', which explanation is supported by west Slavonic dialect word visla = 'river, stream' (Polish name of river is Wisla). But even Celtic origin has been suggested, with connection with Irish uisge = 'water'.

Vladimir
City in west USSR, east of *Moscow*
Founded as a fortress at beginning of 12th century, and named after prince who founded it, Vladimir Monomakh.

Vladivostok
City and seaport in east USSR on Sea of *Japan*
Founded in 1860 with name modelled on that of Vladikav-
kaz (founded 1784), with meaning 'eastern possession'
(Russian vladenie = 'possession' + vostok = 'east'). (Vladi-
kavkaz = 'possession of the *Caucasus*'.)

Volga, River
Longest river in *Europe*, in west USSR, flowing east
and south into *Caspian Sea*
Many possible meanings, none of them certain. More likely
derivations are: 1. from Slavonic vlaga = 'damp, moisture';
2. from Estonian valge, Finnish valkea = 'white, bright'; 3.
from Old Slavonic volkoi, Russian veliki = 'great'.

Volgograd
City in south-west USSR on River *Volga*
Slavonic = 'Volga town'. Until 1961 was Stalingrad (=
'Stalin's town'). Until 1925, from foundation in about 1589,
was Tsaritsyn, not from Russian tsaritsa (tsar's wife) but
from Turkish sarygshin = 'yellowish' (referring to colour of
water of River *Volga*).

Volta, River
In central West *Africa* flowing south-east through
Burkina Faso and *Ghana* into Gulf of *Guinea*
Name was given by Portuguese explorers and first appeared on map of 1741 as Rio de volta = 'river of return' or
'river of turning', ie either river by which original expedition returned or for winding course.

Vosges
Mountains and department in east *France*
Perhaps from Celtic root = 'peak' or for name of some
deity.

W

Walachia
Region in south *Romania*
From inhabitants, Walachians or Vlachs, non-Slavonic people with name = 'foreigner' and corresponding to Welsh of *Wales* and Walloons of south *Belgium* and north-east *France*.

Walcheren
Island in estuary of River *Scheldt, Netherlands*
Name in 7th century was Walacria; main element is Germanic walh = 'foreigner', referring to inhabitants who were of non-Germanic origin. (See *Walachia, Wales.*)

Wales
Principality in south-west *Great Britain*
Latin name was Cambria, from native inhabitants, Cymry (= Celts). Name Wales was probably given by Anglo-Saxons, who invaded *Britain* in 5th–6th centuries, from Old English walh (plural walas) = 'foreigner' (in sense of people who were of different stock to themselves and who would not assimilate with them). (See also *Walachia, Walcheren.*)

Warsaw
Capital of *Poland*
Many (unlikely) stories regarding origin, eg named after twins War and Sawa, found by king out hunting; from cry of raftsmen on River *Vistula* to their cook, 'Warz, Eva!' (Polish = 'Broth, Eve!'). Possibly derived from rich Czech family named Warsew who founded city in 11th century or perhaps from Hungarian varos = 'fortified town'. Most likely to be derived from name of founder Warsz, + ending -ev = 'belonging to'. Polish name of city is Warszawa.

Washington
1. Capital of USA in District of *Columbia*; 2. state in extreme north-west USA

Capital was founded in 1791 and named after George Washington (1732–99), 1st president of the USA. State was founded in 1853 and was nearly named Columbia, but at last moment one of members of Congress proposed name Washington, also in honour of president. Objections that state and capital might be confused were overruled. Name has been given to hundreds of places in all parts of USA.

Waterloo
Small town in province of *Brabant, Belgium*, south of *Brussels*

Flemish = 'watery marsh'; but there is no marsh nearby so 2nd element may derive not from Flemish loo = 'marsh' but from Old High German loh = 'wood', or, more likely, from Old High German losi = 'ditch', element often combined with word water.

Weddell Sea
In *Antarctic*, in British Antarctic Territory

Discovered by English explorer and seal-hunter James Weddell in 1823. He himself named sea George IV Sea, after reigning king, but it was renamed in his honour in 1900.

Weimar
Town in south-west of East *Germany*, south-west of *Leipzig*

From Old High German win = 'meadow, pasture', or wih = 'holy', + mari = 'standing water, lake'.

Wellington
Capital of *New Zealand* and its province, at south end of North Island

City founded in 1840 and named in honour of English soldier and statesman Duke of Wellington (1769–1852). Province named after city. (Capital before 1865 was *Auckland*.)

Weser, River
In north of West *Germany* flowing north into *North Sea*

Old German name was Wisuraha, possibly connected with Indo-European wis-ko-s = 'running water' (or with German Wasser = 'water').

West Indies
Large group of islands off Central *America*, separating *Àtlantic* from *Caribbean Sea*
Discovered by Columbus in 1492–1504 and so named by him in error, in the belief that he had reached *India* by a western route.

Westphalia
Former province in north-west of West *Germany*, originally west part of *Saxony*
Now part of 'Land' of North Rhine-Westphalia. Named after Westphalians (= 'western Phalians'), as distinct from Ostphalians ('eastern Phalians'), Germanic tribe inhabiting territory in time of Charlemagne. The 2nd element of name derives from Old High German falaho = 'field-dweller'.

White Russia
English name for *Byelorussia*
Translation of name, from Russian byely = 'white' + Russia.

White Sea
Inlet of *Barents Sea*, north-west USSR
Probably so named from colour of water reflecting snowy *Arctic* sky, or from snow-covered ice of sea in winter, but could also = 'north' according to ancient system of naming parts of world by colour (compare *Black Sea*).

Wiesbaden
City in central West *Germany*, west of *Frankfurt*
In 1st–2nd centuries had Latin name Aquae Mattiacae = 'waters of Mattiacus'. In 830 was Uisibada, with element bad also = 'waters' (ie mineral waters), but with 1st element uisi of doubtful origin—perhaps connected with German Wies = 'meadow'.

Wight, Isle of
In south *England*, in English Channel
Latin name was Vectis, corrupted to modern Wight. Meaning 'white' (referring to chalk cliffs) is attempt to 'translate' Latin name, which itself is of uncertain origin, though could = 'lever', in sense of 'land that has been pushed up out of the sea'. Alternatively, name could be understood as = 'turning point', ie at location in channel where ships have to alter course.

Wilhelmshaven
City and seaport in north-east of West *Germany*, north-west of *Bremen*
Naval base was established here in 1853 and named Wilhelmshaven (= 'Wilhelm's harbour') in 1869 in honour of German emperor Wilhelm I.

Wilkes Land
Territory in Australian Antarctic Territory
First sighted by American explorer Charles Wilkes in 1839.

Windhoek
Capital of South-West *Africa*
Dutch = 'windy cape', so named from prevailing south-east winds. Original native names for site here translated as 'fire water' (referring to steam from local hot springs) and 'place of smoke' (similarly). Original European name, given in 1837, was Queen Adelaide's Bath, likewise referring to springs.

Windward Islands
In *West Indies*, south of *Leeward Islands*
Located in path of north-east Trade Winds (unlike *Leeward Islands*, which are sheltered from them).

Winnipeg
Capital and largest city of *Manitoba, Canada*, and lake in this province
City is named after lake, in turn from Indian (Cree) vinipi = 'muddy water'. Original name of city when founded in 1738 was Fort Rouge (French = 'red fort'), as it stood on Red River. Name was then changed twice: to Fort Douglas, after family name of Lord Selkirk, who established Scottish colony here, and to Fort Garry, after one of officers of Hudson Bay Company. Eventually became Winnipeg in 1873.

Wisconsin
State in north USA, bordering on Lake *Superior* and Lake *Michigan*
Named after River Wisconsin, in turn probably French variant of Indian (Algonquian) name of uncertain meaning, perhaps = 'big long river', 'grassy plain' or simply 'our homeland'. State officially adopted name in 1783.

Witwatersrand
Range of mountains in south *Transvaal,* South *Africa*
Afrikaans = 'white waters ridge'. Contains largest gold-
field in the world, so that familiar name of mountains,
Rand, became word used as basic unit of country's decimal
currency in 1961.

Woomera
Town in South *Australia*
From aboriginal word = 'throwing stick' (not = English
word 'boomerang').

Worms
Town in West *Germany* on River *Rhine*, north-west of
Mannheim
Ancient name was Borbetomagus, from personal name +
Gaulish magos = 'field'. Name gradually shortened and
changed (in 2nd century was Wormatia) to present form
Worms.

Wrangel Island
In *Arctic* Ocean, off north-east coast of *Siberia,* USSR
Named in 1867 in honour of Russian admiral and polar
explorer Ferdinand von Wrangel (1796−1870) who led expedition in this region in 1820−24.

Wuppertal
City in west of West *Germany,* east of *Düsseldorf*
From name of River Wupper, tributary of River *Rhine* (with
name derived from wippeln = 'to hop along'), + German
Tal = 'valley'. Name was given in 1930 to amalgamation of
Barmen and Elberfeld with some smaller towns.

Württemberg
Former kingdom in south-west of West *Germany*
Now part of 'Land' of *Baden-Württemberg.* Originally was
name of town, with 2nd element German Berg = 'mountain', and 1st element of uncertain origin—perhaps personal name or from Old High German root word = 'turn'
(as in English 'vortex').

Wyoming

State in central west USA

From Indian (Algonquian) meche-weami-ing = 'big-flats-at', originally applied to valley in east *Pennsylvania*. Name became popular through poem 'Gertrudc of Wyoming' (1809) by Thomas Campbell and was officially adopted when state was formed in 1868.

Y

Yangtse-Kiang/Chang Jiang, River
Longest river in *Asia*, rising in central *China* and flowing mainly east into east China Sea near *Shanghai*
Name derives from ancient city of Yangchow + Chinese kiang = 'river'. Chinese apply name only to lower reaches of river. Alternative European name has been Blue River, effectively a misnomer since water for much of course is brownish-yellow.

Yarra, River
In south *Victoria, Australia*, flowing west through *Melbourne* into *Port Phillip Bay*
From aboriginal word = 'running water, river'.

Yellow River
2nd longest river in *China*, flowing mainly east and north into *Yellow Sea* south-west of *Peking/Beijing*
Name is English translation of Chinese name *Hwang Ho* (*Huanghe*) = 'yellow river', referring to large quantities of silt (loess) it carries down.

Yellow Sea
Inlet of *Pacific* between *Korea* and *China*
Name is English translation of Chinese name Hwanghai/ Huanghai = 'yellow sea', referring to dullish yellow colour of water caused by silt (loess) carried into it by *Yellow River*.

Yellowstone River
In *Wyoming* and *Montana*, USA
Name is translation of earlier French name Roche Jaune = 'yellow rock', in turn probably translation of Indian nissi-a-dazi = 'river of yellow rocks'. River, tributary of *Missouri*, gave name to famous Yellowstone National Park.

Yemen

Yemen Arab Republic and People's Democratic Republic of Yemen, in south-west of Arabian peninsula, south of *Saudi Arabia*

Popularly believed to derive from Arabic yamin = 'on the right hand', ie country lying on one's right hand as one faces *Mecca* (as opposed to Sham, territory in modern *Syria*, whose name = 'left').

Yenisei, River

In *Siberia*, USSR, flowing north into *Arctic* Ocean

Name is Turkish variant, adopted by Russian population in 16th century, of native (Khanty, Selkup or Evenki) word iondessi = 'big river'.

Yerevan

Capital of republic of *Armenia*, USSR

Very old name, of uncertain meaning; perhaps = 'abode of the god Aru'. Not likely to be derived from name of founder (Khan Revan) or from Armenian yerevan = 'to appear' (in semi-jocular sense of 'first town to appear after the Flood').

Yokohama

City in *Japan*, seaport on *Honshu*, south of *Tokyo*

From Japanese yoko = 'side' + hama = 'shore', ie 'cross shore'. Original fishing village here was located on a lateral beach of Tokyo Bay.

York, Cape

Peninsula in north *Queensland, Australia*

Name given in 1770 by Cook 'in honour of his late Royal Highness the Duke of York'.

Ypres

Town in province of west *Flanders, Belgium*, south-west of *Ghent*

From name of River Ypres (Flemish Ieper), with original form Ivara, of Celtic derivation with basic meaning = 'yew-tree'.

Yucatan

Peninsula in Central *America* separating Gulf of *Mexico* from *Caribbean Sea*

According to story, Spanish explorer Hernán Cortés, landing here in 1517, asked Indian tribesmen what place was called and received reply 'tektetan' or 'yukatan' = 'I don't understand', which he took to be name of region. Or could be from Indian ki-u-tan = 'he speaks', tribal name, in sense of 'he who speaks our language'.

Yugoslavia

Republic in south-east *Europe*

From Slavonic yug = 'south' + Slavs, name of inhabitants, ie 'land of the southern Slavs'. Name of Slavs, as well as of Slovaks and Slovenes, derives possibly from Slavonic slava = 'fame' (ie 'famous people'), or from Slavonic slovo = 'word' (ie 'people who use the same words').

Yukon

Territory in north-west *Canada*, bordering on *Alaska*

Named after River Yukon, in turn with name from Indian word = 'big river'.

Z

Zagreb

Capital of *Croatia, Yugoslavia*, north-east of *Trieste*
Recorded in 11th century but founded much earlier than
this. Not likely to be from German Graben = 'trench,
ditch', but from some Slavonic origin, perhaps = 'beyond
the ditch (dam)'.

Zaïre

Republic in Central *Africa*
From native name of River *Congo*, with African root za =
'river' (as in *Zambezi*). Until 1971 was Democratic Republic
of *Congo*. Change of name was designed to emphasise
country's true African identity, since River *Congo* was
named (albeit with indigenous name) in colonial period.

Zambezi, River

In *Africa*, rising in *Zambia* and flowing south-east into
Mozambique Channel north-east of *Beira*
From African word = 'big river' (African za = 'river').
Vasco da Gama, Portuguese explorer who first sighted its
estuary in 1498 on his voyage to *India* named it Rio dos
Bons Sinães = 'river of good signs' (in sense that it showed
him he was on correct course for *Asia*).

Zambia

Republic in Central *Africa*
From River *Zambezi*, which rises in north-west of republic.
Until 1964 was Northern *Rhodesia*.

Zanzibar

Island and its capital in Indian Ocean off coast of
Tanzania, Africa
From Arabic zang = 'black' + Iranian bar = 'coast, country',
ie 'country of black-skinned people'. (Territory was under
Arab rule in 8th–9th centuries.) Before 15th century name
applied to east African coast here, not to island. In 1964
united with *Tanganyika* to form *Tanzania*.

Zeebrugge
Seaport in *Belgium*, north of *Bruges*
Town is port for *Bruges* (Flemish Brugge), so name = 'sea Bruges'. Two towns are linked by canal.

Zermatt
Village and resort in *Switzerland* at foot of *Matterhorn*
Name = 'on the meadow' (German zur Matte), and is related to *Matterhorn*.

Zimbabwe
Republic, south-east Central *Africa*
Before 1980, country was Southern *Rhodesia*. Present name is that of ancient complex of ruins south of Masvingo = 'great stone building'. Ruins are of fortified settlement which at its height in 15th century may have been capital of extensive empire in South-East Africa.

Zuider Zee
Former gulf of *North Sea*, north *Netherlands*
Dutch = 'southern sea' (as opposed to *North Sea*). Today consists, after reclamation work begun 1920, of polders Waddenzee and Ijsselmeer.

Zürich
Largest city in *Switzerland*
Roman name was Turicum, from Celtic dur = 'water' + Latin suffix -icum; town is on shore of large lake which bears its name. Name changed to Zürich under influence of Germanic tribe Alemanni.

Select Bibliography

There are obviously hundreds of books that deal with the subject of place-names and their origins, ranging from works such as the present one that deal with names worldwide, to detailed publications tracing the origins of names over a much more restricted area and much more comprehensively, too, such as the many volumes issued by the English Place-Name Society. These give the history and origins of place-names within a single county, from major towns and natural features to street-names in a particular town or even field-names in a given parish.

Any bibliographical guide here, therefore, must necessarily be a selective one, and I have chosen in the main to concentrate on works that deal with place-names on the broadest scale, ie worldwide, and with the names of English-speaking countries (since this book is written in English and will presumably have mainly English-speaking readers). Those who wish for more detailed information on place-name works dealing with particular countries, areas or historical periods should consult sources such as Emil Meynen's bibliographical study, *Gazetteers and Glossaries of Geographical Names of the Member-Countries of the United Nations* (Wiesbaden, 1984), or, say, the bibliographical pages in one of the works listed below, depending on the area of interest. For general and specific works, the reader is recommended to consult pp 7–30 of Serge Losique's dictionary (see particulars below).

Most of the works listed are dictionaries, like the present book. Others, however, are discursive, and deal with place-names on a thematic basis of some kind. The best of such books will have an index, giving all names treated. The least satisfactory will have no index. Generally speaking, too, it holds true that the earlier the work, the less reliable it will be, and conversely, the more recent it is, the more accuracy the reader is entitled to find in it. Despite this general principle, some of the 'pioneering' place-name studies of the nineteenth century are still valuable, if used with caution. One work that stands out in this respect is the book by Canon Isaac Taylor, *Names and their Histories*. For its time, and despite its author lacking the sophisticated linguistic and scholarly resources of today, it is a work that is in many respects sound and accurate, although obviously it has long been superseded by more recent publications, and could not deal with some of the newer place-names of the twentieth century (although sometimes such apparently new names are really revivals or 'come-backs', so are not as new as they may appear).

At the end of the main lists, I have added some titles that can be regarded as useful, even though they may not deal specifically with the origins of place-names, as most of the other works do.

I have not translated the titles of non-English books, since I assume that many readers will have a basic knowledge of one or more foreign languages and will in any case be resourceful enough to handle non-English material satisfactorily, should they need to consult any of these particular works.

1 *Place-names worldwide*

Adams, Edwin, *The geographical word expositor, or, Names and terms occurring in the science of geography, etymologically and otherwise explained*, London, 1856.

Blackie, Christina, *Dictionary of Place-Names*, London, 1887.

Bodnarsky, M.S., *Slovar' geograficheskikh nazvaniy*, Moscow, 1958.

Burgess, James, *Geographical Place-Names in Europe and the East*, London, 1896.

Egli, J.J. *Nomina Geographica*, Leipzig, 1893.

Encyclopaedia Britannica, 15th ed., Chicago, London etc., 1976.

Ganzenmüller, Konrad, *Definitions of Geographical Names*, New York, 1894.

Ladvocat, Jean-Baptiste, *Dictionnaire géographique*, Lyon, 1811.

Losique, Serge, *Dictionnaire étymologique des noms de pays et de peuples*, Paris, 1971.

Matthews, C.M., *Place-Names of the English-speaking World*, London, 1972.

Mel'kheev, M.N., *Geograficheskiya imena*, Moscow, 1961.

Nikonov, V.A., *Kratkiy toponimicheskiy slovar'*. Moscow, 1966.

Perkins, A., *A manual of the origin and meaning of geographical names*, New York, 1852.

Stewart, George R., *Names on the Globe*, New York, 1975.

Sturmfels, W. and Bischof, H., *Unsere Ortsnamen*, Bonn, 1961.

Taylor, Isaac, *Words and Places*, 2nd ed., London, 1865.

Taylor, Isaac, *Names and their Histories*, London, 1896.

2 *Place-names of the British Isles*
(some dealing with an individual country)

Cameron, Kenneth, *English Place Names*, London, 1961.

Copley, G.J., *Names and Places*, London, 1963.

Copley, G.J., *English Place Names and their Origins*, Newton Abbot, 1968.

Davies, C. Stella and Levitt, John, *What's in a Name?*, London, 1970.

Dorward, David, *Scotland's Place-names*, Edinburgh, 1979.

Ekwall, Eilert, *The Oxford Dictionary of English Place-Names*, Oxford, 1960.

Field, John, *Place-Names of Great Britain and Ireland*, Totowa, NJ, and Newton Abbot, 1980.

Johnston, James B., *Place-Names of Scotland*, London, 1892 [reissued 1970].

Joyce, P.W., *The Origin and History of Irish Names of Places*, Dublin, 1875 [reissued 1972].

Joyce, P.W., *Irish Local Names Explained*, Dublin, 1870 [reissued 1984].

Nicolaisen, W.F.H., *Scottish Place-names*, London, 1976.

Nicolaisen, W.F.H., Gelling, Margaret, and Richards, Melville, *The Names of Towns and Cities in Britain*, London, 1970.

Reaney, P.H., *The Origin of English Place Names*, London, 1960.

Room, Adrian, *A Concise Dictionary of Modern Place-names in Great Britain and Ireland*, Oxford, 1983.

Room, Adrian, *Guide to British Place Names*, Harlow, 1985.

Room, Adrian, *A Dictionary of Irish Place-Names*, Belfast, 1986.

3 *Place-names of the USA and Canada*

Armstrong, G.H., *The Origin and Meaning of Place Names in Canada*, Toronto, 1930.

Charnock, R.H., *Local Etymology: A Derivative Dictionary of Geographical Names*, London, 1859.

Gannett, Henry, *American Names: A guide to the origin of place names in the U.S.A.*, Washington, 1947.

Hamilton, William B., *The Macmillan Book of Canadian Place Names*, Toronto, 1978.
Harder, Kelsie B. (ed.), *Illustrated Dictionary of Place Names: United States and Canada*, New York, 1976.
Stewart, George R., *Names on the Land*, New York, 1945.
Stewart, George R., *American Place-Names*, New York, 1970.
Wolk, Allan, *The Naming of America*, Nashville, 1977.

4 Place-names of Australia and New Zealand

Australian Encyclopedia (ed. A.H. Chisholm), Sydney, 1965.
Martin, A., *Twelve Hundred and More Place Names*, Sydney, 1943.
Reed, A.W., *The Story of New Zealand Place-Names*, Wellington, 1952.
Reed, A.W., *A Dictionary of Maori Place-names*, Wellington, 1961.
Tyrrell, James R., *Australian aboriginal place-names and their meanings*, Sydney, 1933.

5 Place-names of Southern Africa

Nienaber, P.J., *Suid-Afrikaanse Pleknaamwoordeboek*, Cape Town, 1972.
Pettman, C., *South African Place Names, Past and Present*, Queenstown, 1931.
Room, Adrian and Wilcocks, Julie, *A Dictionary of the Place-Names of Southern Africa*, Johannesburg, 1987.
Rosenthal, Eric, *Encyclopaedia of Southern Africa*, 7th ed., Cape Town, 1978.

6 New and renamed places worldwide

Geographical Digest, London, 1962– [annually, except 1985].
Room, Adrian, *Place-Name Changes since 1900: A World Gazetteer*, Metuchen, NJ, and London, 1979.
Spaull, Hebe, *New Place-Names of the World*, London, 1970.
Wilcocks, Julie, *Countries and Islands of the World*, 2nd ed., London, 1985.

7 Other books on place-names worldwide

Graesse, J.G.T. and Benedict, F., *Orbis latinus*, Berlin, 1909 [reissued 1980].
Where's Where: A Descriptive Gazetteer, London, 1974.